FASHION FABULOUS LONDON
By Tracy Rose and Russell Rose

FASHION FABULOUS LONDON
Written by Tracy Rose and Russell Rose

Published in 2009 by
Monjune Publications
PO Box 6928
London W1A 2EU
Tel: 07913 443088
Email: tracyroselondon@btinternet.com

Worldwide Distribution by
Kuperard Publishers
59 Hutton Grove, London, N12 8DS, UK
Tel: +44(0) 20 8446 2440
Fax: +44 (0) 20 8446 2441
Email: sales@kuperard.co.uk
Web: www.kuperard.co.uk

Designed by MAA Designs
Web: www.maadesigns.co.uk
Tel 0208 500 6029
gops@maadesigns.co.uk

Printed and Bound in China by 1010 Printing International Ltd.

A catalogue record for this book is available at the British Library.

ISBN 978-0-9561163-0-7

Dedicated to the memory of
Lily and Harry Misell

ACKNOWLEDGEMENTS

Special thanks to Joshua Kuperard, Martin Kaye and Matthew Willey at Kuperard Publishers for their help, advice and support. We must also thank Gops Kumar at MAA Designs for making the book look so good.

ABOUT THE AUTHORS:

TRACY ROSE

Fashion industry insider, hat designer, Tracy Rose is a renowned world famous personality at Royal Ascot Her designs are amongst the most photographed hats in the world. She is a fashion contributor and writer for several magazines and TV. Tracy Rose with Russell Rose has also co-written and co-presented a specialist exercise and diet video, Curvenetics.

RUSSELL ROSE

Russell Rose has written for Now Magazine, Daily Mail, Daily Express, Daily Telegraph, Total Style, and Hair and Style. He has also worked in collaboration with Tracy on a variety of features on fashion, make-up, skincare, and bridal fashion. Since 1998, Russell Rose has also been a restaurant reviewer and was a contributor for Metro Crushguide 2002, Sainsbury's Carlton Taste Reviews 2003 and author of the first and second editions of Veggie and Organic London.

CONTENTS

INTRODUCTION

London is the creative fashion capital of the world. It's a city of ideas, a city with a tradition for breaking the rules of fashion and a city whose designers are headhunted globally. Leading designers such as Alexander McQueen, Vivienne Westwood and Matthew Williamson are just a few of the great names that have stores in London that are known worldwide. London is also a city with fashion heritage producing clothes that are amongst the finest in the world. For men's bespoke suits there are none better than those made by the talented tailors in Savile Row.

In the current economic climate the key rule is there are no rules. Collaborations that would have been thought unimaginable years ago are happening all over the Capital. Leading designers are collaborating with charity shops. Charity shops are re-branding themselves as vintage boutiques. Vintage boutiques are becoming a fashion stylists paradise. The stylists don't just come to buy – they own them. Amongst the success stories are Palette, One of A Kind, and Rellik. Vintage boutiques such as Palette are fusing with contemporary designers as are a number of ethical fashion specialists. Eco-conscious shops such as From Somewhere In Notting Hill are designing their own collections and platforming designs at London Fashion Week where there is a complete exhibition, Estethica, devoted to ethical designs. At the top end of the spectrum Bamford and Sons have combined ethics with pure luxury and Stella McCartney continues to pave the way in combining world class alluring designs with an ethical and vegetarian ethos.

One of the most important trends emerging and a positive antidote to the credit crunch for shoppers is the Designer-Run Boutique. Where they score is that they offer good quality, straight from the designer, non-mass market creations at a high street price. Designer-Run Boutiques such as Nico D, Weardowney and Junky Styling are just a few examples that offer great value for money and you'll be getting something original. London has always been a breeding ground for world class design talent and finding these rising stars is really exciting. Because the designer is so involved, service is usually excellent and often they will make to size and colour according to customers requirements.

Several of London's street markets, notably Camden, Portobello and Spitalfields have been the springboards for new designers and have often been the forerunners for Vintage specialists prior to opening their boutiques. Low overheads and savvy sourcing, street markets continue to be a terrific place for fashion bargains.

Whilst the low overheads of running fashion internet sites are potentially posing a major threat to retail shops, London is experiencing a fascinating trend towards shopping as entertainment. Guest appearances of Kate Moss at Topshop, live rock bands playing at Beyond Retro, special customer evenings with champagne and even whole streets are putting on special events. The high streets chains have revamped their décor with New Look and Reiss trailblazing in shop eye-candy. Department stores notably Selfridges run sensational themed extravaganzas whilst the Westfield shopping mall has a custom built an atrium specifically for live music entertainment and catwalk shows. At an even higher level of fascination and entertainment are the shop designs that emulate gallery installations such as at Balenciaga in Mount Street , Swarovski Crystallized in Argyll Street that are quite breathtaking. Other venues of artistic interest are The Shop at Bluebird, Matthew Williamson in Bruton Street and JC de Castelbajac nearby. London designers also now showcase at special exhibitions such as the Victoria and Albert Museum in South Kensington and The Fashion and Textile Museum in Bermondsey.

The biggest fashion showcase of all is London Fashion Week that takes place twice yearly and is a focal point for fantastic designs. London's restaurants, cafes, clubs and bars fill with fashionistas, celebrities, international fashion buyers and the world's fashion media. Whilst London Fashion Week is essentially a trade-only event, anyone can now really experience some of the excitement by attending London Fashion Week-end that showcases catwalk shows, events and is a tremendous opportunity to buy runway items at vastly reduced prices.

GUIDE TO FASHION FABULOUS LONDON

When the world of a fashion-conscious restaurant reviewer collides with the world of a flamboyant fashionista hat designer, a great opportunity arises to make a fashion guide book on shops. Fashion Fabulous London is based on our personal experiences of visiting stores, shops and boutiques, unannounced as customers looking to buy clothes, shoes and accessories. Whilst both of us have written on fashion for maga-zines, have close ties with the fashion media, have inside knowledge of working within the fashion industry itself and have been part of the London Fashion Week scene for many years, we are totally independent from the retail trade so that the reviews remain unbiased.

In writing this book we visited thousands of retail outlets and from them picked our Top 200. We searched high and low to get the best of everything in the fashion spec-trum. During the course of our visits, 23 zips got stuck, there were umpteen pairs of misfitting trousers that we tried on and dozens of ill-fitting shoes. We were smiled at, sneered at, ignored, schmoozed and even hugged.

In an attempt to give an assessment we've included a rating system to supplement our comments. The Wow factor is the visual impact of the place in terms of décor, clothes and it's entertainment value. In addition, there are over 60 Must Visit venues. These are not exceptional enough to be in the Top 200 but very worthwhile to visit . At the end of the book the Fashion Fabulous London Hot List gives you a rapid guide to help you find the fashions you want by category.

Eating, drinking and shopping are always a great combination and we've included a selection of the wonderful cafés, restaurants, bars and clubs where the fashion crowd goes. If you've shopped to you've dropped and still have energy left, we have further details of fashion events, courses and fashion museums !

Wow factor   (the visual impact of décor, clothes and it's entertainment value)
⌂⌂⌂⌂⌂ Spectacular
⌂⌂⌂⌂ Very Good
⌂⌂⌂ Good
⌂⌂ Okay
⌂ Charisma bypass

Choice   (Style, colour, sizes and availability)
⌂⌂⌂⌂⌂ Excellent
⌂⌂⌂⌂ Very Good
⌂⌂⌂ Good
⌂⌂ Okay
⌂ Poor

Service
⌂⌂⌂⌂⌂ Excellent - they will move mountains for you
⌂⌂⌂⌂ Very Good – faultless service
⌂⌂⌂ Good – highly satisfactory
⌂⌂ Okay - passable
⌂ No service - you may as well have been invisible!

Price
£   Inexpensive – most clothes are under £100
££   Top end high street – most clothes under £300
£££   Mid-range, - most clothes under £500
££££   Expensive – most clothes under £1000
£££££ Very Expensive – credit card buster

Page Explanation

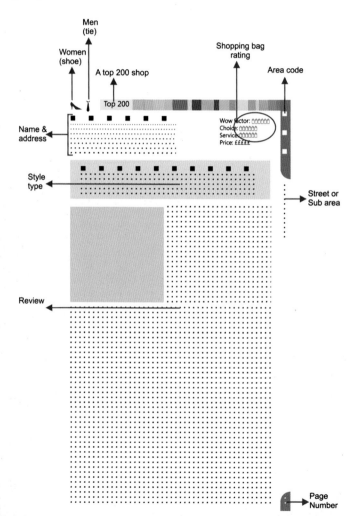

CENTRAL LONDON

BondStreet

The Bond Street area houses many of the most prestigious British design genius-es and luxury global brands in London including Alexander McQueen, Vivienne Westwood and Stella McCartney. Branching off of Bond Street is Conduit Street with JC de Castelbajac and John Richmond whilst on Bruton Street is the ever colourful Matthew Williamson. Near Bond Street too is the pedestranised South Molton Street where Browns, Poste and Wolfords reside.

Alexander McQueen

4-5 Old Bond Street,
London W1
tel: 020 7355 0080
www. alexandermcqueen.com

Wow factor: 🏠🏠🏠🏠🏠
Choice: 🏠🏠🏠🏠🏠
Service: 🏠🏠🏠🏠🏠
Price: £££££

Glam, cool
Green Park LU, 5 min walk
Mon-Sat, 10am-6pm, Thurs, 10am-7pm
Own label
Sizes: Women 6-14; Men: 34-48

One of the coolest, ultramodern settings in London offering genius fashion designs by world famous Alexander McQueen. Inside, it's a voluminous white curvaceous cavern, decked out with Oscar-grade evening dresses through to upscale edgy jeans and trainers, snazzy sunglasses, swanky bags, jewellery and a grand

circular display of sensational, if not over the top shoes. The luxurious atmosphere, relaxing trance music, collection lookbooks, plasma screen catwalk shows create a satisfying ambience. The temptingly magnificent broad spiral staircase leads down to further women's' and an incredible array of menswear. Even on rainy days, when other Bond Street shops are empty, the McQueen magnet continues to attract. VIP's can expect to be served by six staff, such as when Princess Beatrice rolled in to buy an outfit. At such times, random customers don't get served until the staff have returned from the street after waving them goodbye.

On Women's: Signature sculptured dresses, pencil-skirts and jackets (£1500) for extra special occasions. Brilliantly tailored stiff materials that look beguilingly more chiseled than sown. Silks, taffetas and wools are in abundance with impeccable cut, intriguing colour details and structural originality. Floaty chiffon blouses and floral long dresses in contrast are creations from McQueen's softer dreamier side. Changing rooms are well lit, spacious, great mirrors for viewing yourself at different angles.

On Men's: Imaginative tuxedos (£1850); sharp immaculate distinctive suits with unique detailing and great long coats. Also interesting shirts, T-shirts, jumpers, very good leather clutch bags, ties, belts, shoes (£260) and jewellery. Check the "rib-cage torso" suitcases the macho fashionistas latest travelling accessory.

Service is schmooze-on demand, otherwise just the right level of sales contact without becoming imposing. Lots of staff on hand, knowledgeable and we can vouch for the prompt and efficient alterations service.

Central London

BondStreet

Aquaint
18 Conduit Street
London W1S 2XN
tel: 020 499 9658
www.aquaint.org

Wow factor: 🏠🏠🏠🏠
Choice: 🏠🏠🏠🏠
Service: 🏠🏠🏠🏠🏠
Price: £££££

Glam
Oxford Circus LU, 5 min walk
Mon-Sat, 10am-6pm
Designer mix
Sizes: Women: varies

Oscar red carpet fashions, slinky, sexy and sensationally draped that'll make you feel a Hollywood star . Gorgeous all-length dresses in bright colours, monochromes and metallics, this is the kingdom of designer Ashley Isham and displayed too are fashion pieces from an array of designers amongst whom are Almost Famous and Marchesa who share the same vision as him.

High glam in concept there's always eye-catching windows to enjoy, sometimes with a glitzy panache of fashion show theme. Inside, ornate crystal chandeliers, grey-tiled floor, well displayed rails and an inviting selection of handbags and shoes draw customers through the narrowness at the front into the larger area towards the back.

On trying on outfits, you may be forgiven for thinking you are going to be on display in their fish tank of a changing room and the subject of a new Damien Hirst art installation. But mercifully a satin curtain is drawn around this large space before you enter. In fact it is well equipped with large mirrors and a Philip Starcke, Louis style perspex chair.

Whether a regular customer or just window shopping you'll always be made welcome. Service is right on the button. With an A- list clientele of Kylie Minogue, Sharon Osbourne, Kelly Osbourne, Katherine Jenkins, Rosie Murphy and Camilla Rutherford, when shopping here you'll definitely be in good company. Aquaint offers a personal shopping service and holds loyalty customer events in store.

Armani Collezioni
115 New Bond Street,
London W1S 1DP
tel: 020 7493 8321
www.armani.com

Classic
Bond Street LU, 4 min walk
Mon-Sat, 10am-6pm, Thurs, 10am-7pm, Sun 12-6pm
Own label
Sizes: Women XS-XL; Men: XS-XXL

Feast your eyes on the rails and rails of elegant classics with a touch of nonchalance. Just when you think you've seen it all ...more rails! The restrained, suave, chic décor and atmosphere reflects perfectly the iconic clothes. The outside has imposing double fronted windows and you get a congenial welcome from doorman and staff.. As you walk in there's a small display of bags and shoes and the Collezioni collections that conceptually sit between the Georgio Armani and Emporio Armani ranges. Service is attentively and graciously formal although you might not always find an assistant when you need one. Once found quite attentive.

On Women's: Suits trousers and skirt, dresses for special occasions, also some great coats. A Matte Jersey dress in black is about £1000.

On Men's: Smart, conservative and oozing with classiness.

Also, Emporio Armani at 51 New Bond St, Emporio Armani at 191 Brompton Road SW3 see Page (130) , Boutique Georgio Armani at 37 Sloane St SW1, Armani Exchange, 244 Regent Street W1 see page (119)

 Top 200

Brown's (Women's)

24-27 South Molton Street
London W1K 5RD
tel: 020 7514 0016
www.brownsfashion.com

Wow factor:🛍🛍🛍
Choice:🛍🛍🛍🛍
Service:🛍
Price: £££££

Glam
Bond St LU, 2 min walk
Mon-Sat, 10am-6.30pm, Thurs, 10am-7pm
Designer mix
Sizes: Women: varies

Renowned for being at the cutting edge of buying emerging new designers' collections, the atmosphere in contrast is old fashioned. The selection of rising shoe designer supremo, Nicolas Kirkwood, Roksanda Ilincic, Pam Hogg, Roland Mouret's RM label, Lara Bohinc makes it a well worth visit. The four shop set-up has minimal but an attractive window display. The inside is divided into lots of small rooms with each rail having a designer capsule collection.

On levels of service, this is the most variable in London. On the one hand I was very well greeted on entry and on the other totally ignored intentionally when I wanted to try on a very tempting £425 pair shoes. This is the only shop in the Capital that I know that follows the antiquated tradition by certain sales assistants of scowling at customers who they don't resonate with. It's quite surprisingly as Joan Burstein, the owner, who we have met on a few occasions has always been entirely charming.

Check out their special evening events showcasing new design collections.

Also check out Browns Focus opposite at 38-39 South Molton St, that is less expensive but with more attitude from upcoming and original designers including Josh Goot. Service here is also better. A further Browns is at 6c Sloane Street that includes Marios Schwab.

Browns Labels for Less at 50 South Molton St is previous season's for both men and women and discounts.

Brown's (Men's)
23 South Molton Street
London W1K 5RD
tel: 020 7514 0038
www.brownsfashion.com

Wow factor: 🏠🏠🏠
Choice: 🏠🏠🏠🏠
Service: 🏠🏠🏠🏠
Price: £££££

Glam
Bond St LU, 2 min walk
Mon-Sat, 10am-6.30pm, Thurs, 10am-7pm
Designer mix and own label
Sizes: Men: varies

Whilst the small ground floor is shirts and accessories head straight upstairs for the remarkable top line list of designer collections. This is a place to take your time and savour the delights set before you. The mood is relaxed, suave and expect the high level of empathy and congenial service that you would get in the top boutiques in Hollywood. The changing rooms are good and the whole shopping experience a pleasure.

Amongst the great finds are the terrific Martin Margiela pieces of which the trousers have a great feel. Impressive too is the Baleciaga tuxedo suit at £1920 and , Lurex tweed coat. Brit art lover's can have their choice amongst Damien Hirst for Levi's limited editions jeans (£150), Butterfly T-shirts (£55), printed skull hoodies and jackets. Also worth a check are the Golden Goose sneakers and Dries Van Noten double breasted coat at £715. Browns own Mainline Label whilst strong on shirts also has so well priced great quality suits to choose from Also has Alexander McQueen, Lanvin, Dior...and so it goes on.

Burberry
21-23 New Bond Street,
London W1
tel: 0207 968 0000
www.uk.burberry.com

Wow factor: 🏠🏠🏠🏠🏠
Choice: 🏠🏠🏠🏠🏠
Service: 🏠🏠🏠
Price: £££££

Classic
Green Park Tube, 5 min walk
Mon-Fri, 10am-7pm, Sundays, 12am-6pm
Own label
Sizes: Women XS-XL, 4-18; Prorsum 36-48 Italian; Men: 46-56

Trenchcoat heaven, legendary Burberry checks and the sumptuous Prorsum range are just a few of the multitude of reasons to visit this most revered and charmingly elegant store. Established in 1856, think suitably classic, with a delicious range called Prorsum (Latin for forwards), think classy contemporary top drawer too. Prorsum is by far their most exclusive collection with a superior cut, smaller fit and more luxurious fabric.

The store's configuration is a maze of rooms with gorgeous accessories on ground floor, womenswear on 1st floor, men's' in basement. Store and changing rooms follow the Burberry famous beige and white. The famous check are on some lines whilst others are completely in check. Now more discrete as some regard it as a cliché.

On Women's: On top end, evening coats with matching shift dresses, heavily beaded in self-colour. Drawstring Tote bags from about £795, Pleat bags with famous Burberry Check £650. Their legendary trenchcoats start at £300. There's' a wide selection of classic check designed bags and new variants of the check also. Small check shoulder bag £295. The Alligator Cartridge Ribbon Lowry is £12,000 ! The store has the full range of accessories: belts, hats, scarves, sunglasses, gloves and purses.

On Men's: Signature trenches are from £350- £850. For guys who like their wares with a touch of history, Burberry developed the Tielocken coat in 1895 and sub-sequently the trenchcoat itself in 1914. In addition there's an excellent selection of all classic styles of coats, often with logo buttons and amongst some of the highlights are packaway sports jackets at £225, fitted suits around £900, shirts £95, Down- filled gilet £295, Crossbody Bag £295, all great quality but also on the expensive side. For those with cash to splash check out the Burberry Prorsum Dappled Feather Jumper with merino wool at £3995 and the Dappled Trenchcoat £6395. Excellent.

Service can be a bit snooty and not always forthcoming. It's the kind of place where you may find one sales assistant say "We'll still waiting for the Countess to decide." However, there's good attention afterwards once you get served!

Butler and Wilson
20 South Molton Street
London W1K 5QY
tel: 020 7409 2955
www.butlerandwilson.co.uk

(!) Must Visit

Glam
Bond Street Tube, 3 min walk
Mon-Sat, 10am-6pm, Thurs, 10am-7pm, Sun 12-6pm
Own label

Put on your sunglasses before entering as everything sparkles in this glitzerama. Began in 1970, this is super-bling central with fantastic marcasite, Swarovski crystal brooches at £28 and £38. Indeed, the choice is massive and a lot of the pieces very affordable.

Butler and Wilson's signature is large pieces with abundant colour and wit that includes spider brooches, and flowers and skulls motifs, but there's also small and pretty. Always fascinating are the necklaces and earings and there's an inventive and fierce selection of jewellery and cufflinks for the guys.

Also at 189 Fulham Road, London SW3, Tel 0207 352 3045. Here they have a huge collection of vintage dresses too.

DKNY
27 Old Bond Street,
London W1S 4QE
tel: 020 7499 6238
www.dkny.com

Wow factor: 🏠🏠🏠🏠🏠
Choice: 🏠🏠🏠🏠🏠
Service: 🏠🏠🏠🏠🏠
Price: £££

Glam, cool
Green Park Tube, 5 min walk
Mon-Sat, 10am-7pm, Sun 12noon-6pm
Own label
Sizes: Women XS-XL, shoes 37-41; Men: S-XL, shoes 7½-12

Donna Karan is legendary for clothes that truly flatter every kind of woman's figure. The DKNY brand is effectively a diffusion range that carries this approach forward with a more casual accent and are more affordable. There's no better place to experience Karan's ideas than in this impressive triple level store. The Café on the right with a long table and stools is a well known shopaholics chillout zone with good Bond Street views, whilst the glass lift and escalators motioning through the floors also has aesthetic appeal. Ground and first floors are women's and second is men's and at the store's back is a sweeping white staircase.

On Women's: Zoom in on the heavy knits and jumpers, there's lots to choose from. It's also particularly strong on on-trend jeans and tie-up tops that you can use your imagination to create different styles with and there are shelves and shelves of heavily logoed handbags from an attractive £100 upwards. Expect schmooze-on demand, friendly but not OTT with very good service .

On Men's, DKNY are strong on coats, with good biker jackets, graphic T's, cool crisp shirts and of course jeans. Changing rooms are good and service patient and friendly. Also their sunglasses watches are always popular as is the New York vibe here.

Dolce & Gabbana
6-8 Old Bond Street,
London W1S 4PH
tel: 020 7659 9001
www.dolcegabbana.com

Wow factor: 🏠🏠🏠🏠🏠
Choice: 🏠🏠🏠🏠🏠
Service: 🏠🏠🏠🏠
Price: £££££

Glam
Green Park Tube, 5 min walk
Mon-Sat, 10am-6pm, Thurs, 10am-7pm
Own label
Sizes: Women: 38-46

Temple of fashion glitz decked out with gigantic black crystal chandeliers, a plethora of narcissus mirrors and a glistening black décor that forms a sensual backdrop to some of the hottest full-on glamour and animal print designs in the Capital. For the less extroverted, more toned down options have surfaced.
Expect a good greet but hold onto your server as they do tend to disappear. But

once you've got their full attention they are pretty good. Tried on trouser suit in their room of mirrors changing room consisting of three walls and a ceiling all-mirrored, closed off with a black curtain. Whist the signature themes is corset dresses with slinky or voluminous skirts the trousers at £550 also waistcoats at £550 are also delectable. Oodles of shoes, bags, sunglasses to choose from.

Menswear is available here but the dedicated menswear collections are at their store at 6 Sloane Street, London SW1 see page (117) for review.

 Top 200

D&G
53-55 New Bond Street,
London W1S 1DG
tel: 020 7495 9250
www.dolcegabbana.com

Wow factor: 🏠🏠🏠🏠
Choice: 🏠🏠🏠
Service: 🏠🏠🏠🏠
Price: ££££

> Glam
> Bond St LU, 5 min walk
> Mon-Sat, 10m-6pm, Thurs, 10am-7pm
> Own label
> Sizes: Women 6-14; : Men: 34-48

D&G is the economy diffusion range of celebrated Dolce & Gabbana range although a jacket will still set you back £450. The outside all-window display is highly attractive. Inside, the décor palette is white, grey and chrome with the Ground Floor focusing on shoe and bag collections with other accessories. The main women's collection is on the first floor and men's on lower ground. Stairs and lift are available and changing rooms are well equipped, of a good size with grey carpet, mirror, rail, seat, wall of mirror outside..

On Women's: Fun glamour signature lace-up corset style dresses of the main collection but less so. Shorts, accessories, handbags, jewellery, sunglasses, shoes, scarves, lingerie, hats and belts are all worth a serious look. Staff have the patience of angels. Can drive them mad on trying different pairs of shoes for an hour and when you say thank you, expect your server to reply wholeheartedly "No, I thank you!" Staff are stock-knowledgeable, hard working and will work their cotton socks off to find shoes you will really be happy with.

On Men's: Can get extremely busy and on trying on a suit that just didn't quite fit, the sales assistant serving me became very disappointed not to get the sale. Service is very good and the five star welcome and goodbyes make you feel you would really want to visit again.

Diane von Furstenberg
25 Bruton Street,
London W1J 6QR
tel: 020 7499 0866
www.dvf.com

Wow factor: ♦♦♦♦
Choice: ♦♦♦♦
Service: ♦♦♦♦♦
Price: £££££

Classic
Green Park, Bond Street LU, 10 min walk
Mon-Sat, 10am-6pm, Thurs, 10am-7pm
Own label
Sizes: Women 4-16

Strikingly immaculate shop window display and the beautifully laid out interior makes this store a pleasure to visit. The DVF shop launch party was one of the highlights of London Fashion Week in September 2007 and it was great to see Di-

ane von Furstenberg completely in her element, sashaying elegant and chic, bright eyed around the shop like it was the good old Studio 54 days.

DVF is the famous creator of the iconic wrap dress and here at wrap-central you can choose between many styles of wraps with different combinations of sleeve, empire lines and waisted from £250. In addition there are lots of graphic prints and long silver versions in sequins.

Inside the shop, it's long and white, opening to a circular bright room at the back that features swimwear collections with long seating in the centre of the main shop. Service is excellent, honest and they certainly know their stock. In the changing rooms are large seats, circular mirrors, hooks and heavy white satin curtains. Also good on jewellery and sunglasses.

Other stores are at 83 Ledbury Road, Notting Hill, W11, tel 0207 221 1120 Mon-Sat 10-6pm, Sun 12-6pm.

56 High Street , Wimbledon Village, London SW19 0208 944 5995

Dover Street Market
17/18 Dover Street
London W1S 4LT
tel: 020 7518 0680
www.doverstreetmarket.com

Wow factor: ☆☆☆☆☆
Choice: ☆☆☆☆☆
Service: ☆☆☆☆☆
Price: £££££

> Glam, cool
> Green Park LU, 5 min walk
> Mon-Sat, 11am-6pm, Thurs, 11am-7pm
> Own label; Designer Mix
> Sizes: Women 6-14; Men: S-XL

Compelling environment that creates emotional bonds across many genres. Displays are art exhibitions and change every six months. At Rei Kawakubo of Comme des Garcon fame's dream concept there are surprises at the turn of every corner. DSM has collections unique to them from designers around the world. There's a warm welcome on each floor and at ground level a store guide.

On Women's: To-die-for top new names such as Mario Schwab, Christopher Kane, Gareth Pugh,. Established designers Martin Margiela, Azzedine Alaia, John Galliano plus several upcoming foreign labels and of course signature pieces from Commes des Garcons. Men's and women's are mixed on the different floors, plus many other interesting labels including Andrew Logan's art jewellery pieces. Of note are the selection of Nicolas Kirkwood signature high heel shoes.

The witty Gold Birdcage changing room is the most eccentric in London and has a red velvet seat and interior complete with a small round mirror. Service is good.

On Men's: Head turning styles come in the form of Commes des Garcon (CDG) Black Play men's t-shirts at £110, Polo's £70, Cotton woven Fred Perry long sleeve shirts £145, printed striped polos £145. The CDG speedo bathing shorts are totally cool. Other designers include Raf Simons and a hot capsule collection of Stephen Jones hats.

On top floor is the Rose Café where fashionistas hang out. Great quality food.
See page (259)

Electrum Gallery

21 South Molton Street,
London W1K 5QZ
tel: 020 7629 6325
www.electrumgallery.co.uk

Wow factor:🏠🏠🏠🏠
Choice:🏠🏠🏠🏠🏠
Service:🏠🏠🏠🏠
Price: £££ upwards

> Cool, jewellery
> Bond Street LU, 1 min walk
> Mon-Sat, 10.00am-6pm,
> Designer mix

Treasure trove of a hundred on-trend jewellery designers. Looks like a small shop with a couple designers in the window but inside there are cabinets each with a different collection. Three assistants retail for all the designers. The designers can be commissioned to design a piece for you which will be unique. Also if a ring doesn't fit it can be made in your size .

The door is locked with a sign to knock. When I arrived there were two other people trying to be let in. It did take a few minutes before staff realised that there were customers outside. Once in, you can browse around for as long as you want without being pestered by staff. When you want assistance you get it in a helpful, friendly way. The collections are exceptionally good and do make you forget about the surroundings that have a bland gallery ambience with office desks.

On Women's: Josef Koppmann does a chunky mix of sterling silver, 24 carat gold and gemstones to produce outstanding abstract shapes (www.josefkoppmann). Olivier Schlevogt specialises in gold bands with silver circle with gap and diamond detail. Marianne Anderson does filigree earrings. Also names to watch out for are Zwetelina Alexieva, Nikolay Sardomov, T.+Munsteiner and David Goodwin. Wooden sculptural jewellery is on offer for something a little different.

On Men's: Huge choice in creative contemporary cufflinks of which Kamilla Ruberg is worth a check out.

Etro

14 Old Bond Street
London W1
tel: 020 7495 5767
www.etro.it

> Glam
> Green Park Tube, 5 min walk
> Mon-Sat, 10am-6pm,
> Own label
> Sizes: Women 40-46; Men: 48-56

Fantastic for vibrant colour, striking stripes and gorgeous patterns, this plush shop décor-wise has a real rich feel to it. For women there are wide legged trousers, jumps suits and one shoulder dresses that make these clothes easy to wear anywhere. Downstairs there are lots of good quality men's jackets with signature coloured linings and often coloured details on the sleeves and collars and some excellent trouser to choose from. For the summer, there's fine holidaywear with South East Asia design influences Service here is always efficient and the changing rooms good. The colour combinations on the shirts are legendary and there's a good selection of sunglasses, ties, bags and accessories too.

Etro is also available in Harrods.

 Top 200

Fenwick
63 New Bond Street
London W1
tel: 020 7629 9161
www.fenwick.co.uk

Wow factor: ⌂⌂⌂⌂
Choice: ⌂⌂⌂⌂
Service: ⌂⌂⌂
Price: £££

Classic, sophisticated
Bond St LU, 3min walk
Mon-Sat, 10am-6.30pm except Thurs 10am-8pm
Designer mix
Sizes: Women: varies; Men: varies

Whilst at the classic end of the fashionable looks with prices high end high street – low end designer, Fenwick is particularly strong on accessories. Each Fenwick has their own buyer so no two Fenwicks are the same. Here there are three bright floors of women's and one basement men's.

On Women's: Home in on handbags, jewellery (try Georgina Scott), scarves and hats with a ground floor that has wonderful fake fur fashions in winter and sandals and cover-ups for the Summer. The staff on handbags possess a good recall of individual customer needs and are stock knowledgeable. Fenwick has an exciting label mix that's unavailable in the other stores. The top floor has an enormous selection of jeans and casual labels such as Sonia.

Elsewhere, level of contact is not good. Having wanted to try on trousers £145 reduce to £45 in the sale on the women's first floor. Nobody came over to me when I was trying on the trousers, got back changed without anybody asking me and then handed back to another assistant who merely asked "is it any good" . Store is thus variable. Still, as store goes Fenwicks is well equipped, looks slick and in places rather glitzy. There are lots of changing rooms around and these are good sized with two mirrors to see back and front. Has Carluccio's Caffe in basement, a popular stop off point for tired feet , see page (258) for review and does special events other than just Sale Days.

On Men's: Also in the basement are micro-ranges including Nicole Fahri and , Paul Smith and there's a big choice of ties as well as shoes and mainstream accessories.

Also at Brent Cross.

Kurt Geiger
65 South Molton Street
London W1K 5SU
tel: 020 7758 8020
www.kurtgeiger.com

Wow factor: 👠👠👠👠
Choice: 👠👠👠👠
Service: 👠👠👠👠
Price: £££

Glam
Green Park Tube, 5 min walk
Mon-Sat, 10am-7pm, Thurs, 10am-8pm, Sun 12-6
Own label and designer mix
Sizes: Women shoes 3-8; Men: shoes 7-11

For review of this chain see page (225)

L.K Bennett
31 Brook Street
London W1K 4HF
tel: 020 7629 3923
www.lkbennett.com

Wow factor: 👠👠👠
Choice: 👠👠👠👠
Service: 👠👠👠👠👠
Price: ££££

Classic
Bond Street LU, 7 min walk
Mon-Sat, 10am-7pm, except Thurs 10-8, Sun 11-6pm
Ready to wear

For review of this chain see page (226)

Georgina Goodman
44 Old Bond Street,
London W1S 4GB
tel: 020 7493 7673
www.georginagoodman.com

Wow factor: 👠👠👠👠👠
Choice: 👠👠👠👠
Service: 👠👠👠👠👠
Price: ££££

🛈 **DesignerRunBoutique**

Glam, ready to wear and bespoke
Green Park LU, 5 min walk
Mon-Sat, 10am-6pm, Thurs, 10am-7pm
Own label
Sizes: Women shoes 35-42

Exquisite use of colours and shapes, signature hand-painted stripes and irregular geometric high heels makes compelling viewing at this unique shoe shop situated in a small Grade II listed building. The door handle is a gold shoe and inside the orange and gold chairs, gold metal ceiling centrepiece with lights are quite conducive. I tried on a delightful satin court shoe with frills (£350) and discovered a very friendly personalised service. Boots are from £400 and there are also a few pumps. Bespoke available too involving three fittings and from £600.

JC de Castelbajac
50-51 Conduit Street
London W1S 2YT
Tel 0207 287 6406
www.jc-de-castelbajac.com

Wow factor: ✿✿✿✿✿
Choice: ✿✿✿✿
Service: ✿✿✿✿✿
Price: £££- ££££

Cool, edgy
Oxford Circus LU, 7 min walk
Mon-Fri 10.30am-6pm, Thur 10.30am-7pm
Own Label
Sizes: Women 6-16; Men: 48-54

Super Wow idiosyncratic self-referential fashion gallery. Startlingly vibrant windows and inside, bold colour flashes hit you from every direction, and oh yes, there are mannequins with multicoloured mohicans. One wall has chalked words by JC documenting his life, others have Union Jack pictures and the changing rooms have a white mural of the sea with faces of a men including Edgar Allen Poe and graffiti on the wall. A marriage of postmodern art and fashion the place buzzes with clubby music with a resonating staff.

On Women's: Sensational is the belted coat in grey or black with red heart on the chest £495. Straight legged trousers with gold button details £194 and matching long belted jackets are eye-popping as are the sequined football patterned shift dresses whilst jeans, velvet sportswear and trousers at £199 are worth a visit,

On Men's: If you're unsure of the meaning of fashion logo take a look at the lining of the silver jackets that give the definition written on it. T-shirts are more casual as are the cardigans at £195.

Clientele are said to include: Peaches and Pixie Geldof, Kelly Osborne, and rock celebrities. Staff infected by JC's very own enthusiasm for playful fashion experience. They let you browse uninterfered. Accessories of bags, jewellery, sunglasses, shoes and hats are equally intriguing.

John Richmond
54 Conduit Street
London W1S 2YY
tel: 020 7287 1860

Wow factor: 🔔🔔🔔🔔🔔
Choice: 🔔🔔🔔🔔
Service: 🔔🔔🔔
Price: £££££

Glam
Oxford Circus LU, 5 min walk
Mon-Sat, 10am-6pm, Thurs, 10am-7pm
Own label
Sizes: Women 8-12, shoe 4-8; Men: 36-46, shoes 7-12

Destination venue for your rock star makeover. Rock star chic in this high gloss store with minimalist rock star mannequins -laden window, automatic glass sliding doors walk along the glass walkway into the shop proper. Emblematic "Life is Rock and Roll" chairs. Women's on ground floor and then down a glass staircase. Don't forget to let your hand slide down the minimalist white groove that will be your banister of the day.

On Women's: Black with gold buttons Military style jackets £900 has good cut and good material, cords £210, rock diva shoes with chunky crystal top £320, clothes are mostly black with glitz, just a few splashes of purple, ivory. Jewellery bow necklace, earrings, bags and purses £90. Good selection of street chic Eyewear also. Female changing rooms are black glass, black curtain and a black Philip Starck-style chair. Clientele include Madonna, Mick Jagger and Annie Lennox.

On Men's: Homage to punk was in evidence the day we visited with a large Warholesque painting of Sex Pistol's Sid Vicious at far end wall whose face also appeared in the linings of purple velvet jackets at about £750 with the black pin stripes looking very snazzy too. Excellent in quality and design is cashmere with leather trim coat at £1125 with also a good selection of leather jackets, trenchcoats, shoes and T's and tasty silver lamé roll neck.

Service is surprisingly a bit formal and reserved. Seemed more at home serving men than women, the sales assistants being a little unsure of female sizings.

John Rocha
15a Dover Street
London W1S 4LR
tel: 020 7495 2233
www.johnrocha.ie

Wow factor: 🔔🔔🔔🔔🔔
Choice: 🔔🔔🔔🔔
Service: 🔔🔔🔔🔔🔔
Price: £££

Glam, cool
Green Park LU, 5 min walk
Mon-Sat, 10am-6pm, Thurs, 10am-7pm
Own label
Sizes: Women dress 6-14, shoes 36-40; Men: 34-48, shoes 40-45

Zen white tranquility provides the perfect ambience for this art display-led lovingly designed fascinating fashion corner shop. Formerly a pub, it's the mix of Rocha's beautifully cut clothes, his dramatic fashion statement pieces and art on the walls that is intoxicating. Set on three floors with stone and timber and original 1930's French ceramic tiles, it's very much a work in progress concept as Rocha adds objects he has collected on his travels to show off his fashions. Clientele also pleased to show off his clothes include Natalie Press, Anna Friel, Gavin Rosdale, Jamie Hince and Henry Conway.

On Women's there's swing jackets (£520), irregular shape skirts with structured hems, colours soft and natural with bright splashes of colour. Of note are hand-knits, crochet and hand-painted fabrics whilst the handbags, flat shoes, scarves and hats are well worth checking out. In 1997, Rocha expanded his horizons to include contemporary jewellery, crystal and interiors.

On Mens: Black linen trousers with a shiny coating felt great and there are also skinny cut offs for holidays. Service is congenial and attentive, changing rooms are wooden, white and simple with satisfsactory mirrors, hangers and a chair. Also designs ranges for Debenhams.

 Top 200

Jil Sander
72 New Bond Street,
London W1
tel: 020 7495 0076
www.jilsander.com

Wow factor: ⌂⌂⌂⌂⌂
Choice: ⌂⌂⌂⌂⌂
Service: ⌂⌂⌂⌂⌂
Price: £££££

> Classic, men's ready to wear, made to measure
> Bond Street LU, 5 min walk
> Mon-Sat, 10.00am-6pm, Thurs, 10.00am-7pm
> Own label
> Sizes: Women dress 34-42, shoes 36-41; Men: 36-48, shoes 41-45, sneakers 40-46

What a find! Combines the classic styles of Jil Sander and new designs of Belgium designer, Raf Simons. A much smaller shop than they previously had it will be moving to the other end of Bond Street in a couple of years. White slick, minimal décor complementing the minimal classic collection of beautiful fabrics. These well made garments make admirable investment pieces that won't go out of style after one season.

On Women's: With signature architectural designs the shift dresses, coats with sculptured collars are inviting. Tried on a grey jacket with hidden buttons and long scarf neck detail. The assistant that helped me on with the jacket then started wrapping the scarf around me several times as if I were a maypole!

Alterations are included in the price, that is if you can find the price. Maybe it's because they are so high at £1500 for a jacket that their customers don't find price an issue. Shoes start around £600 and the black bugle beaded ankle boot is quite sensational and costs £1110. In a new sunglasses range some have strikingly vibrant blue rims and all are smart.

On Men's: Raf Simons input is clearly signatured over the collections. Relaxed two/ three toned suit jackets with bold sections of colour from the waist down are inspiring as are the zip details. Suits are from £860-£1500. Whilst classic grey and black colour palettes are in evidence, a jacket runs at £750 whilst some bright colours also prevail. Shoes, however are pretty classic at £355. Does offer a made to measure service and a you can choose a few individual details but not full-on bespoke The new Aviator sunglasses with tortoise shell sides at £150 are tasty.

Service is excellent throughout and they remember your face and what your penchant is.

Top 200

Jimmy Choo
27 New Bond Street,
London W1S 2RH
tel: 020 7493 5858
www.jimmychoo.com

Wow factor: ☺☺☺☺☺
Choice: ☺☺☺☺
Service: ☺☺☺
Price: £££££

Glam,
Green Park Tube, 5 min walk
Mon-Sat, 10.00am-6pm, Thurs, 10.00am-7pm, Sun 12-5pm
Own label
Sizes: Women 36-40½

Red carpet Oscar shoewear with a celebrity following that includes Kylie Minogue, Helen Mirren, Katherine Heigl and Emily Blunt. The understated distinctiveness that's classic and sexy is a big hit amongst ladies-that-lunch and sophisticated fashionistas with the Jimmy Choo name almost becoming synonymous with fashion shoes. Shelves and tables elegantly display to-die-for shoes and boots in this shoe heaven. Lots of colour and crystallised shoes in satins. Jimmy Choo, a quiet unassuming designer is often around the fashion show circuit himself with so many of his shoes finishing off so many designers outfits. Londoner, Tamara Mellon the company's founder and president has made an incredible impact on the success of the company and is the perfect shoe ambassador who really does walk the talk.

The Leather Platform Court Shoes £425 are stunningly elegant and are very comfortable indeed. The service here is great and they pay attention to making sure the fit is right. Whilst there, the sales assistant made an extra hole for me on the strap to ensure perfect fit. With several branches in Sloane St, Selfridges, Harvey Nichols and Harrods, there is also a couture boutique at 18 Connaught Street, London W2 (Tel 0207 262 6888). Also has a good selection of leather slouch bags and clutches.

John Smedley
24 Brook Street
London W1K 5DG
tel: 020 7495 2222
www.johnsmedley.com

!Mustvisit

Classic
Bond Street, 5 min walk
Mon-Sat, 10am-6pm, Thurs, 10am-7pm, Sun 12-5pm
Own label
Sizes: Women S-XXL ; Men: S-XXL

The John Smedley name may conjure up a traditional look but this flagship store is contemporary contemporary and sleek with a top notch wide range of pullovers with a variety of sweater fits for both men and women of which 98% are Made in England. Must-have colours of the season mixed with classic shades that are timeless pieces for every wardrobe. Range also includes shirts, socks, hosiery, women's dresses and coats. Men's pullover £112; Women's cardigan £137.

Linda Bee
26 South Molton Lane,
London W1K 5AB
tel: 020 7629 5921

Wow factor: ♤♤♤♤
Choice: ♤♤♤♤
Service: ♤♤♤♤♤
Price: ££

①DesignerRunBoutique

Vintage
Bond Street LU, 3 min walk
Mon-Sat, 1pm-6pm, Thurs 1pm-8pm
Own label and designer mix

Unusual, witty, pretty, collectable and wearable vintage and fashion jewellery Highly revered and a delight to be served by, Linda and her assistant give a very personalised service with excellent stock knowledge. Located in Gray's Antiques Market in a first and foremost position, Linda Bee's concession is a blast of colour and sparkle that draws you in to look closer. Indeed here celebrity clients include Gwyneth Paltrow, Kate Moss, Vanessa Paradis, Daphne Guinness and Ralph Fiennes.

As well as vintage jewellery, she also has her own range including great hoop earrings in a multitude of colours, elaborate necklaces that can really transform a outfit Don't let your sight miss out at the periphery of the concession as there are excellent handbags that may include great names as Dior. You'll get great advice if you are seeking to match jewellery to a particular outfit. Also 30'40 hats and shoes.

Louis Vuitton
160 New Bond Street
London W1
tel: 0207 399 4050
www.louisvuitton.com

Wow factor: ♤♤♤♤♤
Choice: ♤♤♤♤♤
Service: ♤♤♤♤♤
Price: £££££

Classic
Piccadilly LU, 5 min walk
Mon-Sat, 10am-7pm
Own label
Sizes: Women varies; Men: varies

Unashamedly expensive refined travelwear and home to one of most sought after collections on Bond Street designed by Marc Jacobs,. On entry, first visible are the handbags the focal point where most people are looking and buying. Here too you'll find members of staff whispering about waiting lists for the latest bag collection. Panic! Will you get one? Styles like the Montorgeuil GM in their famous monogrammed canvas will set you back £445, others are credit card busters . Still, you can buy into the brand at their wall of more affordable variously smart styled sunglasses and capsule clothes and shoe collections.

On Women's: Louis Vuitton never disappoints on service. When I tried on a grey jacket at £1800 that was quite bulky the assistant who gave impeccable advice was honest enough to say this was not the right style for me. Women's are on the ground floor.

On Men's: Based on the first floor there's an excellent assortment of nylon bomber jackets, wool peacoats, slimfit wool trousers, viscose sweaters, cashmere rollnecks, patent Derby shoes, lambskin gloves and of course their legendary selection of briefcases and leather and canvas bags . Elegant watches and pens are pure luxe.

Stages high profile events including exhibitions of artists at the Serpentine Gallery such as Richard Prince and the introduction of a limited edition bag.
Also at 190 Sloane St, SW1; 6 Royal Exchange Buildings EC3 with large concessions in Selfridges and Harrods.

Top 200

Luella
25 Brook Street,
London W1K 4HB
tel: 020 7518 1830
www.luella.com

Wow factor: 🏠🏠🏠
Choice: 🏠🏠🏠
Service: 🏠🏠🏠
Price: ££££

Glam, cool
Bond Street LU, 5 min walk
Mon-Sat, 10am-6pm, Thurs, 10am-7pm
Own label
Sizes: Women 36-44

The Traditional English Rose, urban edged, handbag heaven with influences of aristocratic equestrian meets rock music. Horses, hearts and crown motifs abound.

The outside is small fronted with her name heart shaped in lights. Inside the décor is old traditional home with a witty twist. Mini mounted animal heads on wall and classic paintings with the Luella logo in it. Two rooms. At the front it's handbags; one style of shoes in a couple of colour choices. Skirts £385, dresses £895; small collection of styles in a choice of different colours and fabrics. Even in the changing rooms there's no escape from the animals. In this small curtained off space is a mini-deer head hook to hang your garments; a mirror, seat and unfortunately not enough places to hang clothes.

To drool over are signature handbags with heart fobs from £395. The service is good but staff are not always there when you need them especially if Sienna, Kylie, Kelly Osborne or Kim Cattrall are passing through. Also at Harvey Nichols see page (132).

Top 200

Mascaró
33 South Molton Street
London W1
tel: 020 7493 8224
www.jaimemascaro.com

Wow factor: ▢▢▢▢
Choice: ▢▢▢▢
Service: ▢▢▢▢
Price: £££

Glam,
Bond Street LU, 5 min walk
Mon-Sat, 10am-7pm, Sun 12noon-6pm
Own label
Sizes: Women 36-41;

Opened in July 2008, Mascaró have been making ballerina shoes and pumps for 90 years. Whilst small and chic outside, inside it's shocking pink décor with velvet seats and fuchsia carpet and rows of fascinating shoes, bags and boots. Pretty Ballerinas are upstairs.

At Mascaró, you'll discover high strappy leathers, suedes, or patent shoes and boots around £165. Taking it up a level are dual-coloured sequined boots and shoes plus bags to match. Staff are very attentive and were ready to bring many different styles to try on as needed.

Pretty Ballerinas excel in pumps in all styles and colours including croc pumps with square toes at £119. Cutesy ones even have faces on. From my own ballet days I can vouch for the quality of these.

Clientele include Lily Allen, Kimberley Stewart, Kelly Osbourne, Donna Air, Anna Friel and, Lindsay Lohan.

Other Pretty Ballerinas shops are at 34 Brook Street, W1;30 Royal Exchange EC3; 7 Pont Street, SW1 Stop Press: Bespoke service now available at Pont Street; Mascaró, with a Pretty Ballerinas concession is also at 13a Marylebone High Street W1.

 Top 200

Matthew Williamson
22 Bruton Street,
London W1
tel: 020 7629 6200
www.matthewwilliamson.com

Wow factor: ⌂⌂⌂⌂⌂
Choice: ⌂⌂⌂⌂
Service: ⌂⌂⌂⌂⌂
Price: £££££

> Glam
> Green Park LU, 10 min walk
> Mon-Sat, 10am-6pm
> Own label
> Sizes: Women 6-14;

Super- glam fashion meets tropical garden setting at this outstandingly designed showcase for one of England's premier designers. Not to be missed is the under glass garden displaying clothes situated towards the shop's rear. Celebrated for his vibrant colour combinations, Williamson doesn't disappoint with a shop ablaze with paradisal confections.

Giant floral inspired prints appear on superb maxi dresses and whilst peasant style dresses are around £675, most of the beaded are north of £1550. On jackets and coats, Williamson explores tantalising silhouettes featuring sleeves billowing out from the elbow. Also has a bijou collection of shoes.

Trying on one of the peasant dresses one can enjoy the satisfying ambience of the voluminous changing rooms decorated with butterflies on cream wallpaper, a Louis XIV –style fluorescent pink chair, gold twig hook, and large pink tassels on door. Staff are eager to help and service goes with the high quality of the shop.

Mauro Shoes

Grays Mews, Stand M14
Mayfair, London W1K 5AB
tel: 020 7629 8692
www.mauroslompshoes.co.uk

(!) Designer Run**Boutique (!) Must**visit

> Glam
> Bond Street LU, 2 min walk
> Thurs, 11am-7.30pm, Fri 11am-6pm and by appointment
> Own label

Hot and sexy! Elegant and sophisticated! Commissions from Agent Provocateur and Coco De Mer. Opened October 2008. Brazilian shoemaker Mauro Slomp. Shoes about £155, bespoke £300-£500 four week turnaround. Worth investigation, crimewriter Martina Cole is a big fan.

Top 200

Miu Miu

123 New Bond Street,
London W1
tel: 020 7409 0900
www.miumiu.com

Wow factor: 🏠🏠🏠🏠🏠
Choice: 🏠🏠🏠
Service: 🏠🏠🏠🏠
Price: ££££

> Glam
> Bond Street LU, 4 min walk
> Mon-Sat, 10.00am-6pm, Thurs, 10.00am-7pm
> Own label
> Sizes: Women 38-44, shoes 34-41

Witty, creative, edge of fashion, full-on colour and style narrow shop that is youthful and exuberant. Check the statement feather jackets, skirts at £315 and guaranteed to intrigue footwear with unusual heels and sensational use of colour from £250. Handbags and sunglasses are peachy too.

Prada-owned, it's expensive but not Prada-expensive. If you can tear yourself away from the bags as you walk in, there's a wealth of sumptuous clothes and shoes at the back. The huge changing rooms are well on the wow side with a gold clothes horse, green embossed wallpaper, two nice seats and thick pile gold carpet. Ever busy, service is good but you may have to wait a bit .

Top 200

Mulberry

41-42 New Bond Street,
London W1
tel: 020 7491 3900
www.mulberry.com

Wow factor: 🏠🏠🏠🏠
Choice: 🏠🏠🏠🏠
Service: 🏠🏠🏠🏠
Price: £££££

> Classic
> Bond Street LU, 4 min walk
> Mon-Sat, 10am-6pm, Thurs, 10am-7pm
> Own label
> Sizes: Women 6-16; shoes 35-42; Men: 36-48 jackets, 30-40 trousers

Luxurious, understated, confident, iconic leather handbags in large burgundy fronted emporium. To-die-for handbags on ground floor, whilst on the first floor there are shoes and clothes in a highly inviting area with a large round pouffe, tables and purple rugs. With a long history of collaboration, each month it becomes a gallery space for emerging artists and designers. In July 2008, they invited Jonathan Kelsey to create a first capsule collection of women's shoes that are well worth a look.

On Women's: Handbags with waiting lists, a mix of re-interpreted classics and a modicum of edge with iconics that include "The Bayswater" and "The Roxanne". Bags start at £600 with purses and luggage to match. On show too are unstructured, feminine dresses, suits, trousers and skirts and good value denim pencil skirts at £97.

On Men's: Collections veer on the retrospective and have previously included a well interpreted early 90's Kurt Cobain style. Parkas, duffles and pea coats are featured that are all good quality tailored with a suave individuality. Bags, briefcases, wallets, cufflinks, keyrings, organisers come with a true touch of class.

Expect an okay welcome and departure, attentive service, good changing rooms. Celebrity clientele includes Kate Moss, Kate Bosworth, Kiera Knightly,, Scarlett Johanssen, Orlando Bloom and Daniel Craig.

Also 171 Brompton Road, Knightsbridge SW3; 199 Westbourne Grove, Notting Hill W11; Mulberry Men's Store, 38 Floral St, Covent Garden, WC2; 11-12 Gees Court, St Christopher's Place, Marble Arch W1, and at Harrods and Harvey Nichols.

 Top 200

Nicole Farhi
158 New Bond Street,
London W1
tel: 020 7499 8368
www.nicolefarhi.com

Wow factor: ☖☖☖
Choice: ☖☖☖☖
Service: ☖☖☖☖
Price: £££££

Classic,
Bond Street LU, 7 min walk
Mon-Fri, 10am-6pm, Thurs, 10am-7pm, Sat 10am-6.30pm, Sun 11-5pm
Own label
Sizes: Women 8-16, shoes 37-42, Men's: 38-44 and a few 46's, shoes 41-45

For years been consistently good value, quality casual designwear both in-store and on the London Fashion Week catwalks. As you enter this large store with wooden floors, big wooden framed mirrors, great images of models in Nicole's latest collection, downstairs is the restaurant and on the ground floor is first the menswear leading through to womenswear. The large bright white room at the rear houses further collections.

On Women's: Signature heavy knits, coats, floral dresses with 50's influences. Reasonable doorman and staff welcome and departure. Can take a couple of minutes to find a staff for service on some occasions but when they come over they are

very knowledgeable. Tried on shorts at £299 that felt fine and can vouch for the changing rooms being well equipped. Finish off you outfit with a neat choice of handbags, jewellery, sunglasses, shoes scarves and belts.

On Men's: Excellent leather jackets, relaxed casuals make a sound investment as do the well made knitwear, cotton shirts and lounge jackets.

Extend your luxury experience downstairs at Nicole's, a very pleasant bar and restaurant see page 259 for review.

	Top 200

Oliver Sweeney
66 New Bond Street,
London W1S 1RW
tel: 020 7355 0387
www.oliversweeney.com

Wow factor: 🁢🁢🁢🁢🁢
Choice: 🁢🁢🁢🁢
Service: 🁢🁢🁢🁢
Price: £££

> Glam
> Bond Street LU, 5 min walk
> Mon-Sat, 10am-6.30pm, Sun, 12am-5pm
> Own label
> Sizes: Men: shoes 6-13

We've always been a big fan of Oliver Sweeney shoes that always standout and speak volumes of individuality. The modern installation format presents ready to wear on the left with the new style "Pointer" geometric toed shoes prominently displayed. Casuals are £95-£135, smarter shoes are around £240. In the centre can be quite good sales reductions.

Also sells leather belts, wallets, gloves and keyrings and on the right are casual leather jackets in chocolate and tans at around £650. Service is attentive, friendly and very obliging. Clientele include Brad Pitt, Paul Weller, Will Smith and Noel Gallagher.

Also at 133 Middlesex Street, Bishopsgate, E1. Also at Harvey Nichols, Knightsbridge, House of Fraser, Harrods, Selfridges and Jones the Bootmaker.

 Top 200

Pringle
112 New Bond Street,
London W1S 1DP
tel: 020 7297 4580
www.pringle-of-scotland.com

Wow factor: ⛾⛾⛾⛾
Choice: ⛾⛾⛾⛾
Service: ⛾⛾⛾
Price: ££££

> Glam, cool
> Bond St LU, 5 min walk
> Mon-Sat, 10am-6.30pm, except Thurs, 10am-7.30pm
> Own label
> Ready to wear, Unique designs, Sizes: Women XS-XXL; Men: S-XXL

Heritage knitwear from a company that has been knitting cashmere since the 1870's and actually coined the term knitwear when a knitted garment was worn as outerwear. Today, this voluminous store exudes tranquility with classic styles and a continued tradition of innovation and glamour. Impressive in décor there's a large spiral staircase with square hook sculpture on it.

With regard to service it's a store of two halves. Men's great: women's average. The menswear staff have the patience of angels and you can drive them mad trying different items on to your hearts content. On women's, service although it is not always forthcoming, but it is good. Pringle is a hugely popular brand amongst celebrities and is worn by Madonna, Guy Ritchie, Ewan McGregor, Nicole Kidman and Scarlett Johanssen.

On Women's: the ground floor flourishes with signature woolen jumpers in array of colours and cardigans from £235 as well as a plethora of non-knitwear.

On Men's: The first floor is a real treat of jackets, trousers and knitwear. I was magnetically drawn to try a beautifully designed roundneck black cashmere jumper with self-pattern and holes so an underneath shirt colour would show through. It was beguiling how my credit card came out. Exceptional too are the cashmere and merino wools and there's some impressive ties to choose from. Conventional cotton and wool jumpers are available. Changing rooms are absolutely fine and staff are perfectly charming. Would definitely visit again.

Also at 141 Sloane Street, SW1, plus individual boutiques sell capsule collections such as Hub in Stoke Newington (see page 171) and several large stores.

Poste
10 South Molton Street
London W1
tel: 020 7499 8002
www.friendsofposte.com

Wow factor: △△△△
Choice: △△△△
Service: △△
Price: £££

Glam, cool
Bond St LU, 4 min walk
Mon-Sat, 10am-7pm, Sun 11.30am-6pm
Own label, Designer Mix
Sizes: Men: Shoes 6-12

This funky standalone shoe boutique hardly puts a foot wrong with it's own great value on-trend fashion range plus a superb edit of big name designerwear with a formidable roll call of Martin Margiela, Dior, Prada and Paul Smith. Margiela's shoes at £360 - £500 are wow as are Dior's patents, although Poste's Chelsea boots at £120 are good value going up to a very stylish chisel toe at £340 and a wicked selection of sneakers.

Quirky whimsical, grab the Burgundy Chesterfield sofa or armchairs and try on. The historical busts, an old clock, vintage boxing gloves and the funny little man front door stop catches your as eye as you scan the shelves collections that have a handy informative synopsis about each label's designer. Service can come down to being given a giant shoe horn and to get on with it. However, they know their stuff here and you can be sure what you buy is hot. Fans include Paul Weller and Noel Gallagher.

Poste is also available at Harvey Nichols, Knighsbridge

Prada
16-18 Old Bond Street
London W1
Tel 0207 7647 5000
www.prada.com

Wow factor: △△△△△
Choice: △△△△
Service: △△△△
Price: £££££

High Glam
Green Park LU, 5 min walk
Mon-Sat, 10am-6pm, Thurs, 10am-7pm, Sun 12-5pm
Own label
Sizes (continental): Women 34-42, shoe 35-41 ; Men: 44-56, shoe 41-44.5

Leading edge fashion, directional for many designers and high street chains, this large store attracts celebrity A-list and world people. Supermodel, Claudia Schiffer whisks in for a new handbag whilst the paparazzi eagerly wait outside by the front window for more shots. Inside it's spacious, with all the collections easily seen a great credit to designer Mucci Prada..

On Women's: Designs are totally feminine. Expect a VIP welcome and farewell. Prada shoes are always interestingly designed and I bought a pair of patent anklestrap shoes at £295. On the ground floor are accessories and to- die- for handbags that are beautifully displayed, top whack jewellery, butterfly sunglasses, shoes and scarves. The upstairs is minimally designed in light green décor and pink carpets. Sensational lace dresses at £2000.

On Men's: On the ground floor are suits, shirts and ties. Upstairs you'll find more casual collections such as signature casual shoes for example blue patent leather upper and rubber soles at £225 that are excellent and very original. Tried on black cool funky zip up plastic pleated jacket at £525. Although not my size the assistant located my size at Selfridges or suggested that it could be delivered to the store for me which was excellent. At the back was a small sportswear section.

Service is helpful and one feels as if one can take one's time and try on to make sure of the right decision. The service is friendly but not OTT although if you are a regular favoured customer or celeb then they do go overboard and bring out items not on show that they might think you are interested in.

Top 200

Rigby and Peller
22a Conduit Street
London W1
tel: 0845 0765545
www.rigbyandpeller.com

Wow factor: 🛍🛍🛍
Choice: 🛍🛍🛍🛍
Service: 🛍🛍🛍🛍🛍
Price: ££££

> Classic
> Oxford Circus LU, 7 min walk
> Mon-Sat, 9.30am-6pm, Thurs, 9.30am-7pm
> Own label
> Sizes: Women 30A-48

See Rigby and Peller, Westfield, Shepherd's Bush for review page (164)

Top 200

Rupert Sanderson
33 Bruton Place,
Mayfair
London W1J 6NP
tel: 0870 750 9181
www.rupertsanderson.com

Wow factor: 🛍🛍🛍🛍
Choice: 🛍🛍🛍🛍
Service: 🛍🛍🛍🛍🛍
Price: £££££

❗ Designer Run**Boutique**

> Glam
> Bond Street LU, 10 min walk
> Mon-Fri, 10am-6pm, Sat 11am-6pm
> Ready to wear
> Sizes: Women shoes: 34½-42

Hidden down a quiet mews just off Berkeley Square waves the brown flag of Rupert Sanderson, award winner of the Accessory Designer of the Year at the 2008 British Fashion Awards. The shop's elegant wooden slatted walls, beige armchairs and floor are clearly overshadowed by the show stopping shoes. Perfect courts in different materials and colours kick in at £350 with a vast array of styles of ankle or shoe boots from £450. Delectable are the shoe boots with geometric fronts and the ankle boots with mac fabric overlaying black patent for a shinier effect. A graduate from Cordwainers College in East London and trained with Sergio Rossi and Bruno Magli, Rupert Sanderson is definitely a name to watch. Top notch service with complimentary coffee or water. Very good place.

Also at 2a Hans Road, Knightsbridge, London SW3 1RX. Tel 0207 584 9249

Top 200

Sonia Rykiel
27/29 Brook Street
London W1 4HE
tel: 020 7493 5255
www.soniarykiel.com

Wow factor: ☖☖☖☖☖
Choice: ☖☖☖☖
Service: ☖☖☖☖☖
Price: £££££

Glam
Bond St LU, 5 min walk
Mon- Sat 10am to 6.30pm, Thursday, 10am to 7pm
Own label
Sizes: Women dress sizes 36-4 (French Size), shoe sizes 36-41;
Men: 34-48

Well worth a visit is this Parisian Queen of knitwear's label of creative démode/un fashion, characterised by inside-out stitching, zero-hems and unlined pieces. Key visual statements are black, stripes, lace, rhinestone and message-rich sweaters.

Double fronted outside the store has an attractive window display. Inside, it's spacious with two rooms with accessories at the front, clothes at the back and down stairs. At the rear of the downstairs there's also sportswear.

On Women's: Loud and clear bling is in abundance with most items having crystal – even the umbrella handles and handbags (£661) that will certainly standout in the crowd as will the platform high and chunky suede shoes at £673.
The changing rooms are black and white with a good mirror, seat and hook.

The knitwear is bold and beautiful. A woolen coat, large yellow and black check with yellow fur sleeves costs £1085. Complete your outfit with a splendid choice of handbags, jewellery, sunglasses, shoes scarves, hats and belts.

Unique are the incredibly large crystal motifed brooches with bows, and butterflie and also small butterfly rings.

Expect to be greeted on entry. As I walked to the back of the room a member of staff walked with me and showed me what was on the rails and followed me downstairs to explain further. Although I didn't feel pushed I tried a signature woolen skirt on with elasticated waist at £265 and were shown other items. It's a personalised service with customers coming in knowing staff by name and who know exactly what to show them. Good stock knowledge pleasant hellos and goodbyes. Celebrity clientele includes Sarah Jessica Parker, Sharleen Spiteri and Brett Anderson and they also do special event previews.

On Men's: Urban chic, sharp suits, stripey jumpers, well crafted, particularly strong on evening suits, Summer on-trend shorts. Lots of blacks and greys but bold colours such as neon also well in evidence. Shoes and accessories also available.

Smythsons

22a Conduit Street
London W1
Tel: 0845 0765545
www.smythson.com

!MustVisit

Classic
Bond Street LU, 4 min walk
Mon-Fri, 9.30am-6pm, Thurs, 10am-7pm, Sat 10am-6pm
Own label

Heritage personalised stationery meets fashion at this seriously sophisticated shop where the men in suits and ties still don't seem at ease in selling handbags. They should do because this "it's who you know" shop has recently been sharking it's way up the fashion ladder with high quality understated product designed by Conservative Party leader's wife, Samantha Cameron who in 2007 created the famous Nancy Bag.

Service is extremely formal and the place doesn't feel like a fashionable shop. But then perhaps sticking to old school values of quality and Savile Row standards isn't such a bad thing either.

On Women's: Extremely smart and desirable canvas and leather handbags with a small clutch costing around £495. Check out the Maze Bag. There's also a good selection of purses, organisers and keyrings as well as some men's accessories too.

Also, 135 Sloane St, SW1; 214 Westbourne Grove, Notting Hill, W11; 7 Royal Exchange EC3. Plus Selfridges, Harrods and Harvey Nichols.

Stella McCartney
30 Bruton Street
London W1
Tel 020 7518 3100
www.stellamccartney.com

Wow factor: 👠👠👠👠👠
Choice: 👠👠👠👠
Service: 👠👠👠👠
Price: £££££

Cool, ready to wear and Bespoke
Bond Street LU, 5 min walk
Mon–Sat 10am–6pm, Thurs 10am- 7pm
Own label, Unique designs
Sizes: Women 36-42; shoes 36-40 Men: Bespoke

Always with sensational windows this upscale designer store in four storey Georgian Townhouse opened in 2003 by Stella McCartney, leading fashion designer, a fervent vegetarian and a patron of the Vegetarian Society. Consequently, all her clothes and shoes are totally vegetarian-friendly and the perfume range is organic.

Dress to impress when you come as there's security on the door. Once you're inside, the atmosphere is relaxed and the service slick and sophisticated.
Through the elegant hallway is a drawing room adorned with a wall of marquetry panels. On display are a wonderful range of accessories, sunglasses, handbags and don't forget to peruse the marquetry drawers that can be pulled out to yield arrays of further product.

Next on is a glasshouse garden with a beautiful maple tree surrounded by works of art and furniture. At the rear of the ground floor is the Shoe Room that houses a circular display of exclusive shoes completely suitable for vegetarians. Particularly good are the stretch over the knee boots at about £550 and the patent sustainable wood wedges at around £700.

Ready to Wear Collections are on the first floor and at the rear is an organic Lingerie Boudoir. A McCartney bonded wool strapless is about £1000 and looks terrific whilst the long flowing cotton/silk dresses will set you back about two grand. On trying on clothes the staff's help is impeccable and friendly whilst further upstairs is a bespoke tailoring service for men and women under the watchful eye of a Savile Row master tailor.

Strongly eco-conscious, Stella McCartney has her own organic line of women's clothes that she intends to expand as well as introducing a men's clothes range. The shop also stocks her fast growing organic unisex skincare range that's 100% organic and boasts that all formulae exclude synthetic preservatives, silicone and any ingredients of animal origin. Stella McCartney designed a range of vegetarian-suitable trainer shoes for Adidas, although not available at his shop is available at the Adidas's main shop in Oxford Street.

Stella McCartney also has shops within Selfridges and Harvey Nichols as well in New York and Los Angeles. However, true to her British designer roots, the flagship shop is here in Bruton Street.

Vivienne Westwood

44 Conduit Street
London W1
tel: 020 7439 1109
www.viviennewestwoodonline.co.uk

Wow factor: ⬛⬛⬛⬛
Choice: ⬛⬛⬛⬛
Service: ⬛⬛⬛⬛
Price: £££££

Glam
Oxford Circus LU, 5 min walk
Mon-Sat, 10am-6pm, Thurs, 10am-7pm
Own label
Sizes: Women XS-L, 6-14; Men: S-XL

Fashion anarchy by the rail at ever breaking the rule book Dame Vivienne Westwood, queen of punk's world famous - always being snapped by Japanese tourists - store. When your sales assistant wears a VW gold lamé dress suitable for the Oscars you know this is a shop where something is going down big time.

Modesty isn't in Westwood's vocabulary and her iconic fashion items are boldly framed a la classic art gallery whilst the central staircase has a rather nice tree trunk sculpture.

On Women's: Heavily historically referenced tailored statement clothes such as skirts with bustles at £220 and designs where material lays twisted, tucked, ruched to give new lines to body shape. For logo-lovers there's an abundance from logo buttoned coats and logo clasped bags to orb jewellery. Of note too are the Anglomania Patchwork T-shirts and cabinets with jewellery, sunglasses. And the terrific range of shoes and belts. Service wonderful and they will search the shop to track down the right items for you. Strangely changing rooms have no mirrors so you'll have to view yourself outside presumably so sales staff can advise and complete the sale. On the outer walls, are palatial interior photos whilst inside there's the typical Westwood twist, a red plastic stool.

On Men's: Downstairs, there's very well made coats with brown logo buttons at £800, political statement T-shirts £80, unusual shirts, logoed jumpers and striped ties with Westwood's logoed embroidered orb at £50. Good service, reasonable changing rooms.

Wolfords

3 South Molton Street,
London W1K 5Q13
tel: 020 7499 2549
www.wolfordboutiquelondon.

Wow factor: ⬛⬛⬛
Choice: ⬛⬛⬛⬛
Service: ⬛⬛⬛⬛⬛
Price: £££

Glam, elegant
Bond St LU, 5 min walk
Mon-Sat, 10am-6pm
Own label
Ready to wear
Sizes: Women 6-14;

Renowned tight spot and the shop is quite small too. An example of each piece is on display after which you pick size and colour from the shelves choc full of boxes. Lingerie section is at the back with two small okay changing room cubicles with seat, mirror and hooks.

Figure hugging bodies, skirts, dresses and tights. Cashmere range from about £150. Signature tights, stockings at about £20 and leggings. Do experiment with the lycra tubes in different lengths and colours. Check out the Fatal Dress, £89 that is one long tube that can be worn with versatility as an evening dress ruched up into a shorter dress, doubled up into a skirt or even a top. Tried one on and it was so good I bought one in white. Great! Pleasant staff were very knowledgeable on stock and immediately knew the size that I would need. Expect a great goodbye when you leave.

Also in Shepherd's Bush at Westfield ,Village H6 Level 1

MountStreet

Mount Street is one of the most upcoming fashion streets in London with Balenciaga, Christian Louboutin and Marc Jacobs. Luxury abounds and here you can shop without the hustle and bustle of most other London streets.

Alfred Dunhill
Bourdon House
2 Davies Street
London W1K 3DJ
tel: 0845 458 0779
www.dunhill.com

Wow factor: 🏠🏠🏠🏠🏠
Choice: 🏠🏠🏠🏠🏠
Service: 🏠🏠🏠🏠🏠
Price: £££££

Classic,
Green Park Tube, 5 min walk
Mon-Sat, 10am-7pm
Own label, ready to wear and bespoke
Sizes: Men's jackets: 36-50, shoes 6-11

Alfred Dunhill's unashamed gentleman's classic luxury retail lifestyle mansion house set back through an arch on the corner of Bourdon Street and Davies Street. Opened in August 2008 it focuses on cultivating customers over a period of time. On your first visit expect a smooth welcome and as you turn the corners of the maze of rooms on the ground floor there's coats, leather jackets, ties, and massive collection of cufflinks through to countrywear casuals and shoes. Staff graciously enquire if they can help. Check out the snazzy signature driving jacket made from lambswool and their excellent selection of driving gloves all part Alfred Dunhill's motoring heritage. If you want, get a show round of the whole mansion as I did. Down the wooden staircase there's a coffee bar, armchairs and newspapers to chillout, leading through to a humidor well stocked with cigars and cigarettes for which they are so famous for. In a separate room there is a small cinema with a film showing but alas no takers when I visited. However, you can book the place out for a film screening or a promotion. Dunhill is particularly strong on chunky pens and exquisite quality bags, belts and wallets.

On the first floor a large room has more jackets and trousers. Masculine accessories abound, think Thomas Crown, master of the universe big boy toys. A silver metal propeller blade, stereoscopic telescopes for spying on the streetwalkers below and a further collection of rare antique Dunhill gold pens. Behind a closed door there's a barber shop with a man having a cut and blow dry for £35-£50. and next door there is a spa too. Tried on a hand finished cashmere jacket at £1695 that felt very good and they leave the sleeve buttons out so that you can choose what you want. Changing rooms are naturally good.

Also on this floor there is a separate room Bespoke, made from scratch, measurement made from your body about £2400 (allow 8-10 weeks). Custom tailoring service, makes a new pattern from your size about £1400 (allow 6-8 weeks). Ready to wear suits from £800, tuxedos £2500. Designer Kim Jones trained at St Martins first collection with Dunhill available from Spring 2008 uplifts the menswear even further. Clientele at Dunhill's include Jude Law and Daniel Craig and they special event evenings are also held.

They also have Alfred's an invitation-only club with a bar and restaurant. For the rest of us mere mortal customers you do get access to the two Bentley's to be ferried around town for further shopping experiences!

With charming first class service this place is Total Wow!

Alfred Dunhill concessions are also at Selfridges, Harvey Nichols and Harrods. But these concessions are no substitute for the Bourdon House experience.

Balenciaga

12 Mount Street,
London W1K 2RD
tel: 020 7317 4400
www.balenciaga.com

Wow factor: ☺☺☺☺☺
Choice: ☺☺☺
Service: ☺☺☺☺☺
Price: £££££

MountStreet

> Glam, cool
> Green Park Tube, 5 min walk
> Mon-Sat, 10.00am-6pm,
> Own label
> Sizes: Women 6-14

Fantastic shopping experience in what may be described as a spaceship that has landed on Mars. Nicolas Ghesquière, designer for the collections and store concept has created an awesome décor with real silverleaf on the walls, an orange ceiling, an Egyptian mirror sculpture, clashing coloured carpet and columns from which music emanates from. From the central pod changing rooms are rails protruding out of it in a circle with garments displayed in colour themes. There are also twelve pieces taken from Balenciaga archives such as the Summer of '52 look.

Balenciaga is one of London's "Just for people in the know" shops. So much so that the window slats obscure the shops' interior and we were told "they do not want walk in trade, no mannequins are used at any of their stores, people go on destination".

The material and sculptural look of the pieces are beautiful in silk, satins and chiffons. There is only one of each piece in the size it comes in and also in the stock room some catwalk pieces that don't appear on the rails. The assistant didn't have the item I wanted to try in the size but brought out a selection of other pieces for me see and try. As the door pods opened he waved his hand inside and a light came on. "Enjoy" he said. I felt he was genuinely enthused with the shop itself and was happy to share it with the customers. Skirts cost about £800 but are terrific quality and the full skirt that I tried was most certainly beautifully sculptured. A small delectable selection of handbags, jewellery and sunglasses are available.

Also in Superbrands in Selfridges, Harvey Nichols and Harrods. Menswear is available at Browns.

Christian Louboutin

17 Mount Street,
London W1K 2RD
tel: 020 7491 0033
www.christianlouboutin.com

Wow factor: ☺☺☺☺
Choice: ☺☺☺☺
Service: ☺☺☺☺
Price: £££££

> Glam
> Green Park Tube, 5 min walk
> Mon-Fri, 10am-6pm, Sat 11am-6pm
> Own label
> Sizes: Women ; Start at 34 but not many through to 42

Flagship store that's to Christian Louboutin's famous skyscraper strappy red sole shoes. With a great cut, there are also glamorous wedges, flats, courts and boots

There are great, wedges, flats, courts and boots all with signature red soles and some handbag to match. The dramatic window display boasts a massive Fabergé egg and a mannequin dressed in a tutu emerging from the egg of course an amazing pair of shoes. Inside, shoes are displayed in frames like pieces of art or in church like window alcoves. High heels start from £300 going up to sky high prices.

Service is friendly, but with a tinge of sniffyness. However, expect a warm welcome from all staff and a please come back departure. There's also a VIP room hidden by mirrors with further exquisitely creative designs. Laboutin has a strong celebrity A-list following including Lily Allen.

Shops are also on 23 Montcomb Street, SW1. Capsule collections in Harvey Nichols and Harrods.

Top 200

Jenny Packham
3a Carlos Place
London W1K 3AN
tel: 020 7493 6295
www. jennypackham.com

Wow factor: 🏠🏠🏠🏠🏠
Choice: 🏠🏠🏠🏠🏠
Service: 🏠🏠🏠🏠🏠
Price: £££££

Glam
Green Park Tube, 5 min walk
Mon-Sat, 10am-6pm, Thurs, 10am-7pm
Own label
Sizes: Women 6-16

Whilst most people think of a Bureau de Change as a place to change money, at Jenny Packham's it's where you change your clothes. For this former small bank has been converted into the currency of delectable fashion items of which her statement pieces are full on glamour. Each dress has exquisite crystal beading work. There are a good selection of shapes, from figure hugging and plunging backs to 1920's flapper. Striking colours make these dresses to be seen in. There are of course blacks, ivories and a great selection of white minis, Dress are from £1500 to £7000 for fully beaded. The reason to come here is for a stunner of an evening dress.

Being in a peachy part of Mayfair, a stones' throw from Mount street the décor luxuriates with a single small window, but full of sparkle, displaying gold tree trunks with two evening clad mannequins. Inside reflective black marble, there is a gold tree wall mural. The other wall has black shelves with gold vases and other

pieces. There is a large black sofa in the centre and a plasma screen displaying fashion shows. The rails around the walls have clothes of different colour schemes. Glass cabinets have accessories of Judith Leiber crystal evening bags, Erickson Beamon crystal statement jewellery; earrings £300 and rings by Electric.

The changing room only had a single hanger. I tried on a black beaded fringe mini with shoulder detail £1550. Service was attentive but not pushy and genuinely interested in customers. Celebrity clientele in Kiera Knightley, Beyonce, Mariah Carey and Hilary Swank.

Harry's of London
59 South Audley Street,
London W1K 2QN
tel: 020 7409 7988
www.harrysoflondon.com

!) Must Visit

Classic
Green Park Tube, 7 min walk
Mon-Sat, 10am-6pm, except Thurs, 10am-7pm, Sun 11am-6pm
Own label
Sizes: 6-12

Opened September 2008. Shoes hand stitched in Italy with a penchant to timeless styles. Very small shoe shop so that the three store staff plus a few customers makes the place look busy.

English designer. Cappuccino or water whilst you are being served. Does special event evenings. Strong on slipper selection. Brush calf shoes £350 , boots £325, loafers and trainers £275, stitch detailed and high quality slippers around £325. Some shoes such as the Downing Penny Loafer have rubber outsoles for waterproofing against London puddles! Whilst other boots have injected rubber islands. Service is super duper.

 Top 200

Marc Jacobs
24-25 Mount Street,
London W1K 2RR tel: 020 7399 1690
www.marcjacobs.com

Wow factor: ♙♙♙♙
Choice: ♙♙♙♙♙
Service: ♙♙♙♙♙
Price: £££££

Glam, cool
Green Park Tube, 5 min walk
Mon-Sat, 11am-7pm, Sundays 12noon-6pm
Own label
Sizes: Women 6-14; Men: 34-48

Large very eye-catching windows displays in this double frontage shop with flowers in the window. Inside luxurious carpet that you sink into. The shop is divided into small rooms that focus principally on women's although there's good menswear at the back of house. But the shoes and accessories are equal strong in women's and men's.

On Women's: Leading edge of fashion, Marc Jacobs the American designer who also designs for Louis Vuitton sets trends. Great use of colour and fabric. Sizes tend to come up a size bigger and those looking for small sizes should put their skates on as they sell quick to the point that mid-season you may not find anything. Hot on handbags, a small selection of jewellery, sunglasses. All staff welcomed when one walks through. Shop was easy to navigate and see collections and the staff made you feel comfortable to do so in your own time.

On Men's: Tried on a fluorescent stripped black wool and acrylic cardigan £699 and even better a cashmere jumper £729. Changing rooms are large with a big chair, rail and huge mirror. The service is helpful with good sales technique and was offered a Diet coke. Shirts such as a light blue with a yellow stripe look good but are pricey at £249.

SavileRow

Home to bespoke tailoring, Savile Row stretches from Conduit Street to Burlington Gardens and is one of the most historic retail districts in the world Great names include Kilgour, Gieves & Hawkes and Huntsman plus newer arrivals Ozwald Boateng and Lanvin.

Abercrombie & Fitch

7 Burlington Gardens,
London W1S 3ES
Tel: 0844412 5750
www.abercrombie.co.uk

Wow factor: ☺☺☺☺☺
Choice: ☺☺☺
Service: ☺☺☺☺☺
Price: ££

Casual, classic, American-style
Piccadilly LU, 5 min walk
Mon-Sat, 10am-7pm, Sun, 12am-6pm
Own label, ready to wear
Sizes: Women XS-L; Men: 34-48

Could be described as Savile Row on viagra. The atmosphere is smouldering, sizzling and sexy, nightclub-esque. With an enormous pillared entrance you pass through the security guys on the door, past the Chippendale-style model stripped to the waist being photographed by female customers until you reach the "David " statue that stands proudly at the approach of the disco inferno's darkness. Clothes are stacked on tall shelving units and the music is high on decibels, bass and beat. Do take the long sweeping staircases up and check the faux renaissance paintings of contemporary muscular men and the stores panoramic inferno view. Although targeting the teenage young clubbers market, at Abercrombie & Fitch there were multitudes for different ages.

At A&F it's All-American lifestyle clothing for every guy and girl. Sales assistant that look like male models welcome you. Indeed, some get to go on A&F's model shoots. They and the female staff shake to the music and truly look like they enjoy their work. Unique is that they were like waitpersons in a club or like your friend there to look after you. They have a good stock knowledge and even when one leaves if they meet you in the street they say "How you doing?" Ambience was busy and brilliant. Changing rooms are security locked. No chair but two coat hooks.

On Men's: Polo shirts come in many types. The "Muscle" polo shirt I tried was cut tight fit with high cut sleeves to enhance the biceps, that will leave you ready to hit the dance floor. Polo £50 orange –white horizontal stripe with labels of authenticity. On offer too are vintage distressed polo shorts with aged fronts as well jeans, underwear and fragrances.

On Women's: Upstairs there's an excellent selection of shirts, T's, and jeans with some great outerwear including some excellent fleeced, hooded zip ups at £60. Sweaters and camisoles/tanks £30 are there as are totes at about £70 and lightweight scarves in many colours for £40.

B Store

24a Savile Row
London W1S 3PR
Oxford Circus LU, 10 min walk
Tel 0207 734 6846
www.bstorelondon.com

Wow factor: 🖤🖤🖤🖤🖤
Choice: 🖤🖤🖤
Service: 🖤🖤🖤🖤
Price: £££

Cool
Mon-Sat, 10am-7pm,
Own label, designer mix, ready to wear
Sizes: Women 6-14; Men: 34-48

So cool, you may have to be prepared to be initially ignored by the busy manage on the phone whose attention can be obtained by frantically waving a shoe o shirt. After profuse apologies, you will get great silky smooth schmoozey attentive service. The shoes here are own brand and at around £159 were good with the all leather with grey metallic patent top particularly likeable. They certainly know their stock here and connect well with customers. Strong on men's shirts, cardigan and a smattering of oddball hats. Established labels include Ann-Sofie Back, Pete Jensen trainers, Jens Laugesen, Linda Farrow Eyewear, Raf Simons, Opening Cer emony as well upcoming designers such as Spijkers en Spijkers all of which attrac a high celebrity quotient and quirky fashionista fandom.

B Store has great sales. I bought a pair of Oscar 4 metallic and leather at £155 a a bargain £85. And the accessories are good too. The End of Season Sale can b tremendous. Located at the Conduit Street end of the Row, B store has an ex pansive window, nice round armed chairs for trying out shoes and definitely oka changing rooms. Marvellous shop!

Henry Poole & Co.

15 Savile Row
London W1S 3PJ
tel: 020 7734 5985
www.henrypoole.com

(!) **Must**Visit

Classic, Bespoke
Piccadilly LU, 6 min walk
Mon-Fri, 9am-5.15pm
Own label
Sizes: Men: bespoke

Essential viewing for any man thinking about purchasing his first bespoke suit Having initiated the long tradition of the Savile Row suit and created the tuxedc jacket these are tailors of distinction. Established in 1806 in Everett Street, Bruns wick Square, since 1982 Henry Poole & Co now resides in the Victorian building at No.15 with a showroom and cutting room on ground floor with over 2000 cloth swatches to choose from. The definition of bespoke comes from "bespoken" giving the characteristic of choice and they say here no two suits are alike. At a whopping £2808.10 for a two piece suit and a further £835.72 for an extra pair of trouser taking 10-12 weeks you'll be one of the privileged few who can say they share the same Savile Row tailors as Charles Dickens and Sir Winston Churchill. Whilst less of an exquisite purchasing experience than some other tailors on the Row, service is very reasonable. Some military uniforms are on show, livery – cocked hats and dress swords.

Huntsman

11 Savile Row,
London W1S 3PS
tel: 020 7734 7441
www.h-huntsman.com

Wow factor: 🏠🏠🏠🏠🏠
Choice: 🏠🏠🏠🏠🏠
Service: 🏠🏠🏠🏠🏠
Price: £££££

Classic, Bespoke, Made to Measure, Ready to wear
Piccadilly LU, 6 min walk
Mon-Fri, 9.30am-5.30pm, Sat, 10am-5pm
Own label
Sizes: Men: 34-48

For an old world journey experience into the finesse of the perfectly balanced single buttoned jacket, Huntsman is a hard one to beat. Established in 1849, Huntsman seems a place of anecdotes. At the front of house is a grand old fireplace and two stag heads said to have been left behind by a customer on his way to lunch. At the back of house and clearly visible are the cutting rooms, where they work on measurements, patterns and the long mahogany tables where as tradition has it your "sales advisor" will unroll the cloths for you to choose materials. The main work room is below ground and should you declare to go bespoke you will be invited for a full show round and an insight into the intricacies of their skilled techniques. Here too is the Patterns Room with it's historical fascinating archive of five thousand patterns of the great and the good.

Most clientele decidedly go for the Huntsman house-style of single buttoned, hybrid of a classic riding coat and dinner jacket hallmarked with firm shoulders and an elegant sculpted waist. However, on bespoke, double breasted and dare we say a two or three buttoned jacket can be knocked up too.

In ready to wear there are basically four materials still maintaining their legendary style of single button, well balanced and waistband adjusters or side straps (no real belts here). The fitter pushes me towards made to measure. Bespoke is made on the premises whilst the made to measure are sent to the factory. If you have a posture problem then bespoke is the best bet I was told.

I tried on a dark grey hopsack jacket and trouser that also comes in blue (£1450) and quoted about £50 for small alterations. Frankly, neither this nor the three other material choices were much of a switch on. Nevertheless, they would make fine everyday suits. It had a good feel to it but did explain charmingly it's shortcomings such as the trousers being too tight and explained they could be let out and the jacket length too long. Made to measure suits are £1850-£2000 and there is flexibility to move to 2 or 3 button jackets and takes about 6-8 weeks to finish. Bespoke 3-4 fittings over a minimum of 12 weeks. Two piece from about £3,840. A Women's Bespoke service has just been launched by appointment Mon-Fri 10am-3pm.

The changing room I was directed to was large and rich in wooden panelling, a leather armchair and on the wall personal pattern sheets of Sir Laurence Olvier, Gordon Banks and others. Also hand-made shirts including those made from West Indian Sea Island cotton of outstanding quality, plus ties, handkerchiefs and braces.

A valeting service is available where the resident presser spends over an hour reshaping a jacket or coat virtually restoring it back to it's original 's appearance when it was first made.

Kilgour
5&8 Savile Row
London W1
tel: 020 7734 6905
www.kilgour.eu

Wow factor: 👔👔👔
Choice: 👔👔👔👔👔
Service: 👔👔👔👔👔
Price: £££££

Bespoke, Ready to Wear, Cool
Piccadilly LU, 5 min walk
Mon-Fri, 9am-6pm, Thurs to 7pm, Sat 10.30am-6pm
Own label

Forward thinking fashionistas should head for The No5 store, renowned for unstructured tailoring with a seasonal fashion driven look suitable for dressing up and down. Balance, proportion and provenance are part of their exacting ethos. An unstructured Jersey wool jacket will set you back around £1000 and can be worn with an optional gilet for about £325. The assistant said it aimed to be a kind of cardigan of a jacket and felt quite good on. Leather jackets here are very tempting and trousers are fine quality at £225.

Whilst No. 5 has a more art gallery feel and service with a high charm quotient, No8 is modernist/minimalist in décor and parallels the more classic regular type of suit on offer. At No8 they call it their contemporary look and here too service is polished. Bespoke suit service is 8-12 weeks and does shirts as well. Staple Kilgour designs are also available.

Gieves & Hawkes
No1 Savile Row
London W1
tel: 020 7434 2001
www.gievesandhawkes.com

Wow factor: 👔👔👔👔👔
Choice: 👔👔👔👔👔
Service: 👔👔👔👔👔
Price: £££££

Classic,
Piccadilly LU, 5 min walk
Mon-Thurs, 9.30am-6.30pm, Fri, 9am-6pm, Sun 11am-5pm,
Own label
Sizes: Men: 34-48

Temple, par excellence of sartorial gentlemanly elegance. The windows preface the chapters with mannequins featuring modern design and historic military tailoring pedigree. Inside, the ground floor high ceilinged imbues nostalgia of a bygone era of genteelness. Red armchairs, shirtmaking service. Lots of staff patiently waiting and ready to serve. Chandeliers vary from room to room, one made from antler, each room offers a further charming surprise.

On the first floor gallery there are sumptuous cashmere coats then follow round to the dinner suits and evening shirts. As a James Bond film theme plays I begin to feel the masculine idealism suffuse through me and my credit card itching to purchase. Further round the gallery are Naval Office Pocket books, naval buttons and military ties. On the first floor, an exhibition space displayed historical naval uniforms, military books, tricorne hats and various historical documents and paraphernalia, a picture of George V hangs on the wall.

Tried on a £175 pair of grey wool trousers that came up very wide fitting. In the changing rooms: be prepared to change in front of the Bengal Lancers (a picture that is). The room, quite charming, has a nice tartan chair, hook, mirrors and military pictures around the walls. Service was reasonable but as the assistant was mulitiple serving when it was finished it was finished. Ties, cufflinks are in abundance as are jumpers. Gieves & Hawkes aims for a slim silhouette and tapered waist for a modern dapper classic look.

Gieves & Hawkes is also at 33 Sloane Square SW1, Selfridges, Harvey Nichols and House of Fraser-City, 68 King William Street, EC4.

 Top 200

Lanvin
30-32 Savile Row
London W1S 3PT
tel: 020 7434 3384
www.lanvin.com

Wow factor: 🏠🏠🏠🏠🏠
Choice: 🏠🏠🏠🏠🏠
Service: 🏠🏠🏠🏠🏠
Price: £££££

Glam, cool, ready to wear and bespoke
Oxford Circus LU, 8 min walk
Mon-Sat, 10am-6.30pm
Own label
Sizes: Men: 34-50

Highly inventive, classy leading edge menswear fashions and not for die hard conservative dressers. Maybe it's the little wooden men climbing down the mirror in the window that offers a clue that this is no ordinary menswear shop. For here the signature is the teenage boy who has grown too fast for his clothes. So what you get are oversized bowties, cut off trousers, shortened jacket sleeves, materials normal on the inside appearing outside and vice versa. The collections at Lanvin Men's flagship store are designed by Lucas Ossendrijver under the influence of the now legendary Alber Elbaz. Of note also are the collaborative collections with Acne jeans, tailored fronted pleated trousers, classic blazers and macs.

The shop has a relaxed atmosphere although with the inventive designs and the fast beat play list, the fashionista's pulse does get racing. I tried on a tuxedo (£1500) to wear with denim jeans or grey trousers and it felt excellent. The changing rooms are plush and service is excellent with alterations included in the price. Beautiful set on a ground floor and basement it's a pleasure to browse round. Quality tailored trousers are £450, Trilby hats are about £220 and there are also scarves, insect-themed cufflinks, waistcoats and shorts and a superb range of coats. A feast for the eyes are the selection of metallic patent coloured shoes in quilted satin as are the ties part -embroidered with green feathers catch the eye. One of the best menswear's shops in London.

Top 200

Ozwald Boateng

30 Savile Row,
London W1S 3PT
tel: 020 7437 0620
www.ozwaldboateng.co.uk

Wow factor: ☺☺☺☺☺
Choice: ☺☺☺☺☺
Service: ☺☺☺☺☺
Price: £££££

> Cool, ready to wear and bespoke
> Oxford Circus LU, 5 min walk
> Mon-Sat 10am-6pm, Thurs, 10am-7pm
> Own label
> Sizes: Men: 34-48

Style conquers functionality in this store's design. Whilst the exterior and windows of this large corner shop radiates attention, inside there's brightly coloured collections displayed against black walls with lighting that's too dark. To view the colours properly you may have to search out somewhat more illuminating lighting within the store. Signature fabrics are his two-toned effects with a wool/mohair mix and about 80% of the fabrics are specially commissioned for Ozwald Boateng. Of note are the coloured suits with brightly clashing linings, plain and shot silk shirts, shot suits and ties. Ready to wear signature purple two piece suits start at £999.

Expect a friendly welcome. The changing rooms are concealed behind a wall of mirrored doors and are pretty good although inside there are not enough hooks. Has an on-site atelier with tailoring team adept at Savile Row craftsmanship to produce for bespoke clients. In addition, Boateng goes beyond traditional Savile Row tailoring design with a diffusion line inspired by the "Old School Tie ", British public school heritage look.

Also showcases, jeans, casual trousers, jackets, overcoats and a range of inventive knitwear that can be accessorised with a range of trainers, socks, belts, ties and cufflinks. Service here is very good. Great place.

Norton & Sons
16 Savile Row,
London W1S 3PL
tel: 020 7437 0829
www.nortonandsons.co.uk

Wow factor: ⬠⬠⬠⬠⬠
Choice: ⬠⬠⬠⬠⬠
Service: ⬠⬠⬠⬠⬠
Price: £££££

Bespoke Tailors, classic
Green Park Tube, 5 min walk
Mon-Fri, 9am-5.30pm, Sat,1pm-5pm
Own label,
Sizes: Bespoke

The staff at Norton & Sons may well form part of the customers' extended family by the time the suit is finished. The service is so friendly and personalised and the way you get shown round and introduced to the staff members – this is a true sartorial experience. Established in 1821, the modern country home style décor features a prominent Deer's head. With only a few suits on display, the workshop is at the back with cutter and shirtmaker. According to Head Cutter, David Ward, "Norton and Sons have all the classical styles with a modern approach to style, but will customise to clients. There's a fantastic amount of detailed sewing work. On bespoke tailoring there's sixty hours of handwork that takes several months to complete. "

Three-piece suits start at £3500 and they create about 200 suits a year. Also makes overcoats and woolen jumpers, can be ordered bespoke in 40 colours. They work with Scottish woolen mills. Has a small accessory range.

On tailoring, there's simple classically proportioned clothes made from a choice of 3000 British cloths. One, two or three button single or double breasted suits lounge suits, overcoats, trousers, short trousers. Daywear is made from merino wool, cashmere and vicuna. Also classic dinner suits, dress coats, morning coats and waistcoats. Norton & Sons has a reputation as long as your arm as a Sporting Tailor. They are highly adept in cutting and tailoring tweeds for functional sporting clothing including plus two and fours, safari jackets and field coats.

Service is exemplary. Norton & Sons have worked on clothing collections for Kim Jones, Giles, House of Holland, Richard Nicholl.

OxfordCircus

At the heart of this area close to the underground station is the world famous Top Shop home to Kate Moss's collections as well French Connection, Urban Outfitters and Mango. Renowned for its department stores, towards Marble Arch is Debenhams, John Lewis, Selfridges as well as the Reiss flagship store and Arrogant Cat. Nearby is Marylebone High Street area with Matches and KJ Laundry. Walking from Oxford Circus to Piccadilly are the beautiful stores of Liberty, Jaeger and Aquascutum.

Almost Famous

3-4 Percy Street,
London W1T 1DF
tel: 020 7637 2622
www.AFLondon.com

Wow factor: 👠👠👠👠
Choice: 👠👠👠👠
Service: 👠👠👠👠
Price: ££

Glam
Goodge Street or Tottenham Court Road LU, 5 min walk
Mon-Sat, 11am-7pm, except Thurs, 11am-8pm
Own label
Sizes: Women 6-16; shoes 4-7

Romance is in air at Almost Famous with its feet still touching the ground. Modern day meets old love stories along the rails situated in two rooms of mostly dresses. Feminine and glamorous with a good selection of on-season colours it's great value at around £100. Floral printed macs, rose appliquéd dresses and floatiness abounds.

The shop has a pretty-girly feel about it with lots of mirrors around the place, a light blue divan in the centre, a sweet mirrored dressing table and some retro wooden cabinets displaying very delightful clothes.

Service was good when asked but didn't bother you as you browsed around. I tried on a £199 ivory wool coat with satin tie-up that can be interchanged. Also has a nice selection of short jackets, trousers, sunglasses, shoes and black patent wedges with ankle strap £68 and some interesting jewellery as well. Changing rooms are elegant in blue and white with floral curtains and a pouffe. Danni Minogue buys here.

Top 200

Arrogant Cat

31a Duke Street,
London W1U 1LS
tel: 020 7487 5501
www.arrogantcat.com

Wow factor: 👠👠👠
Choice: 👠👠👠
Service: 👠👠
Price: ££

Glam
Marble Arch LU, 5 min walk
Mon-Sat, 10am-8.30pm, except Thurs,10am-9.30pm
and Sun11.30am-6pm
Own label
Sizes: Women 6-12

A stone's throw from Selfridges, for review of this chain see page (217)

Also at 311, King's Road SW3 tel 0207 349 9070, 18 Great Portland St, W1; 12 Kensington Church Street, W8; 4 The Square Richmond on Thames, Surrey.

 Top 200

Anne O'Dowd
21 New Quebec St
London W1
tel: 020 7402 5292
www.anneodowd.com

Wow factor: 🛍🛍🛍🛍
Choice: 🛍🛍🛍
Service: 🛍🛍🛍🛍🛍
Price: ££

Glam
Marble Arch LU, 8 min walk
Mon-Fri, 11am-7pm, Sat, 11am-6pm
Designer Mix
Sizes: Women 8-16, shoes 4-7

Seen on the red carpets, worn and loved by Strictly Come Dancing Professional Dancers these elegant satin Nicolangëla special occasion dresses ingeniously wrap around to fit and flatter all shapes and sizes. Starting at £350, if the colours aren't what you are looking for, relax on the sofa and look through their sample book and they will order the style in the colour of your choice. At the rear of the boutique is a shoe studio with designs exclusive to Anne O'Dowd enabling you to complete your outfit for a bargain £150.

 Top 200

Aquascutum
100 Regent Street
London W1B 5SR
tel: 020 7675 8200
www.aquascutum.com

Wow factor: 🛍🛍🛍🛍🛍
Choice: 🛍🛍🛍🛍🛍
Service: 🛍🛍🛍🛍🛍
Price: ££££

Classic, glam
Piccadilly LU, 3 min walk
Mon-Sat, 10am-6.30pm, Thurs, 10am-7pm, Sun 12-5pm
Own label
Sizes: Women 6-14; Men: 36-48

Raining champions for macs and trenchcoats, Aquascutum not only invented the first waterproof cloth in 1853 but also created the raincoat itself. A massive corner shop, with vibrant window displays, Aquascutum doesn't just rest on it's laurels of World War I and II trenchcoat designs and iconic 1940's rainwear chic, it's now becoming ever more forward thinking whilst still revering it's heritage. The luxurious feel as you walk in makes you think more Bond Street than Regent Street. The ground floor is ladieswear, the 1st floor men's classics and 2nd floor men's contemporary and a joy to visit.

On Women's: As you stroll around the ground floor, you think you've seen the collection but then you discover different areas tucked away. The main collection is quite classic; the couture collection and a vintage collection are a re-interpreted version using styles from 20-30 years ago that are proving currently very popular. There's a whole room dedicated to their signature macs that start at £500. The changing rooms are deluxe with a large Venetian mirror and side table, seat, hooks and hangers. I tried on a bright pink couture suit of pencil skirt with cummerbund waist £350 and a three frill peplum backed jacket with frill collar at £995 that was excellent. Service is attentive, friendly and helpful and there are plenty of accessories and lots more to tempt you here. Collections are also at The Shop at Bluebird as well as concessions at Browns and Harrods.

On Men's: Aquascutum have always been on the expensive side but the extra quality is worth it. Entry point foldaway macs will get you the Aquascutum label for £275. For the full monty, check out the Kingsgate an iconic derivative of the World war II trenchcoat is cotton polyester and a silicon "shower-proofing treatment for £750. With more cash to splash, on their Limited Editions range, of note is the Camberley lambswool coat £3995 and the Nayland off-white raincoat £995. Two piece personalised tailored suits are also available from £700.

Bargain tip: Spend over £195 and get 2 hours free parking or 4hours at the weekend. See website for full details.

Collections can also be found at Start and The Shop at Bluebird, whilst menswear concessions are at Moss Bros, 8 King Street, Covent Garden and Selfridges.

Top 200

Armani Exchange
244 Regent Street,
London W1B 3BR
tel: 020 7479 7760
www.armaniexchange.com

Wow factor: �☐☐☐☐☐
Choice: ☐☐☐
Service: ☐☐☐☐☐
Price: ££

Glam, cool
Oxford Circus LU, 3 min walk
Mon-Sat, 10am-8pm, Thurs, 10am-9pm, Sun, 12am-6pm
Own label
Sizes: Women XS-XL; Men: XS-XXL

Armani on an urban budget, this impressive store has bargain jeans on a diffusion label and certainly cheaper jeans than the Emporio Armani's at £180.
With large well displayed windows there's an enticing mannequin display as you walk in and in the centre. The urban-techno décor with silver metal and mesh covered walls, grey slabbed floors, massive photographic imagery and pulsating bassy playlist creates a good vibe. Changing rooms are consistent with shops' theme.

On Women's: Jackets with great cuts, dresses for clubbing, special occasions and day, jeans T-shirts and shorts are all on-trend. Staff were service proactive around the store when I tried on a £119 jacket. Good value handbags, sunglasses, small hats, belts are on offer.

On Men's: Good welcome on the ground floor and they happily will explain the difference between A/X and Emporio. Popular are their J35 range at £95 whilst those at £75 are good too. Logoed belts, graded coloured swimshorts, summer

Flip-flops, inexpensive aviator sunglasses, dip-dyed cotton embroidered shirts are available. Unfortunately, no short lengths on jeans and trousers.

Overall the service is very good, knowledgeable and not pushy.

 Top 200

Banana Republic

224 Regent Street
London W1B 3BR
Tel: 020 7758 3550
www.bananarepublic.eu

Wow factor: 🏠🏠🏠🏠🏠
Choice: 🏠🏠🏠🏠
Service: 🏠🏠🏠
Price: ££

Classic
Oxford Circus LU, 7 min walk
Mon-Wed 10am-8pm, Thur 10am-9m, Fri 10am-8pm, Sat, 9am-8pm, Sun, 12noon-6pm
Ready to wear
Sizes: Women XS-XL, shoes 4-6; Men: XS-XL, shoes 7-11

For excellent value for money smart clothing, Banana Republic makes a very good choice. Bright attractive windows emanate from this corner voluminous store whilst inside it has a luxurious hotel lobby feel about the place with dark wood and chrome fitting and a staggeringly impressive sweeping staircase upwards. A pleasure to browse round, womenswear is on the ground and first.

On Women's: The wardrobe staples look classy and won't break the bank. Check out their L.B.D. £75, trousers in different cuts at £85, V-necks and the short sleeve t-shirts £9.50 and short Mac £95 for well made fashion classics. Handbags are around £125 whilst jewellery, sunglasses, shoes, scarves, hats and belts are reasonably priced for a quality look. Changing rooms are good and note that women's clothes come up on the big size and you may need to have a size smaller than usual. Staff are helpful and friendly but not always forthcoming.

On Men's: Good quality understated classic three pieces suits, overcoats, shirts jumpers and ties that are very reasonably priced. On men's shoes 7-11 but they come up one size larger than normal.

Benetton
255 Regent St
London W1U 1LS
tel: 020 7647 4220
www.benetton.com

(!) Must Visit

Classic
Marble Arch LU, 5 min walk
Mon-Sat, 10am-8pm, except Thurs, 10am-8.30pm and Sun 11.30am-6pm
Own label
Sizes: Women 38-46, shoes 2-8; Men, 34-48

For review of this chain see page (218)

For review of this chain see page (218)

Also at 23 Brompton Road, Unit 10 Brunswick Centre, 488 Brixton Road, 116 Putney High Street.

 Top 200

Coast
262-264 Regent Street
London W1R 5AD
tel: 020 7287 9538
www.coast-stores.com

Wow factor: 🛍🛍🛍
Choice: 🛍🛍🛍🛍
Service: 🛍🛍🛍
Price: ££

Glam, classic
Oxford Circus LU, 2 min walk
Mon-Sat, 10am-8pm, Sun 12noon-6pm
Own label
Sizes: Women dress 8-18 ; shoes: 3-8

For review of this chain see page (219)

Top 200

Crimson
7 Porchester Place
London W2 2BS
tel: 020 7781 1115
www.crimsonclothes.com

Wow factor: 🛍🛍🛍
Choice: 🛍🛍🛍
Service: 🛍🛍🛍🛍
Price: £

Glam, Retro
Marble Arch LU, 5 min walk
Mon-Sat, 11am-6pm,
Designer Mix
Sizes: Women 8-16

Value for money, Top Shop prices with one-on-one full on service and exclusive items in this treasure trove of trinkets and trifles. Bijou in size it's a homage to the American '50's specialist shop run by owner, Anmarie McDonald. The American owner befriends you straight away and is extremely passionate about what she does. The counter has an eclectic selection of jewellery, rings from £5, bracelet

£10. Anmarie has an office in the back where she writes plays in between serving customers. Who knows you might be her next character...

The changing room is a curtained cubical with a jumble of cushions on the floor, hangers, mirror and of course Anmarie's bicycle! Gershwin music get you in the mood.

New clothes with a 50's era vintage feel by designers from America, exclusive to that shop. Great valued strapless dresses with full skirts at £55, three –quartered sleeved Macs £40, classic T-shirts £12, Sarah Donegon individualised vintage fabric small handbags with bows £55. Also hessian casual larger bags, casual hats and belts. Altogether there's six different labels that change seasonally and there's lots to see in this compact space. Once a month she hosts late evenings with champagne that's a great opportunity to chat with her and designers. Service is very good, knowledgeable about designers, friendly and helpful.

 Top 200

Debenhams
334-348 Oxford Street
London W1C 1JG
Tel: 0844 561 6161
www.debenhams.com

Wow factor: ▯▯▯▯
Choice: ▯▯▯▯
Service: ▯▯▯
Price: ££

Classic, Glam
Bond Street LU, 2min walk
Mon-Sat, 9.30m-8pm except Wed 10am-8pm, Thurs 9.30am-9pm,
Sun 12pm-6pm
Designer mix and own label
Sizes: Women: varies; Men varies

Debenhams gives an awesome choice of big name British designers at low prices. Attractive window displays and four gloriously bright floors although it does get cluttered on sale days.

On Women's: Key concessions are Kookai, Jane Norman, Principles, Phase Eight Warehouse and Oasis whilst shoe concessions include Dune, Faith Principles and their own brand. Arrays of well designed handbags, jewellery such as Swarovski and Jon Richard together with sunglasses, belts, scarves wraps and hosiery are in full force.

Top designers have Debenham labels with collections especially for the store at high street prices. These have less expensive materials but nevertheless retain the style of the main collection. I tried on one such piece, a black pencil skirt for £35 by Rocha John Rocha that was quite good but actually opted for a cute Red Herring pink frilly skirt at £16. Other hot names that you can affordably try are Julien Macdonald, Ben de Lisi, Jasper Conran, John Richmond, Janet Reger Lingerie and Philip Treacy hats. Changing rooms are good, well lit, two mirrors for different views, service button and seats outside.

On Men's: Jasper Conran's stylish overcoats, trousers and bag accessories are particularly delectable. Rocha John Rocha casual black linen jackets, dark grey trousers and jeans are worth checking out as are the Mantaray checked shirts and white linen trousers. St George by Duffer olive sweaters are good value as are shoes here especially the brown boots at £75. Service is usually very helpful.

Top 200

Dune
28 Argyll St
London W1F 7EB
tel: 020 7287 9010
www.dune.co.uk

Wow factor: 🛍🛍🛍
Choice: 🛍🛍🛍
Service: 🛍🛍🛍
Price: £

Cool
Oxford Circus LU, 4 min walk
Mon-Wed, 10am-7pm, Thurs -Fri, 10am-8pm, Sat 10am-7pm,
Sunday, 12am-6pm
Own label
Sizes: Women shoes 3-8; Men: 6-12

Flagship store. For review of this chain see page (220)

Emeline 4 Re
9 Princes Street,
London W1B 2LQ
tel: 020 7495 3503

!! Must Visit

Ethical
Oxford Circus LU, 5 min walk
Mon-Sat, 10am-6pm, Thurs, 10am-7pm
Own label
Sizes: Women 10-14, shoes 37-41

Designer-led ethical mix of lines not easily found elsewhere such as Uncommonly Beautiful, Feng Ho, Amira, Skura as well as Beyond Skin's shoe vegetarian range. Strong on recycled clothes and new clothes made from organic fabrics. They will make new clothes to your size on request.

 Top 200

French Connection

249-251 Regent Street
London W1
tel: 020 7 493 3124
www.frenchconnection.com

Wow factor: ⛊⛊⛊
Choice: ⛊⛊⛊
Service: ⛊⛊⛊⛊⛊
Price: ££

Classic
Oxford Circus LU, 2 min walk
Mon-Sat, 10am-7pm, Sun 10am-6pm
Own label
Sizes: Women dress 6-16; shoes: 36-41; Men sizes S- XL, shoes 41-45

For review of this chain see page (220)

House of Fraser

318 Oxford Street
London W1C 1HF
tel: 0844 800 3752
www.houseoffraser.co.uk

 ! **Must**Visit

Classic, glam
Must visit
Oxford Circus & Bond St LU, 5 min walk
Mon-Sat, 10am-8pm, Thurs 10am-9pm, Sun, 11.30am-6pm
Designer mix
Sizes: Women: varies; Men: varies

This smart popular department store is always worth a visit for it's vast selection of clothes and accessories. Sale time can get a little manic.

On Women's: Basement has a young feel with clothes concessions such as Miss Sixty and All Saints. The ground floor is the most stylish predominantly accessories and the handbag display deserves special mention. The next two floors up has Karen Millen, Coast, James Lakeland, Wallis and is also particularly strong on evening dress, lingerie and hats.

On Men's: Has great names such as Ted Baker, Paul Smith and Kenneth Cole. Liked their own label, Linea, especially the wool herringbone trousers and there's an interesting collection of square ended ties and bow ties. Also good woolen suits and bags by Diesel.

House of Hanover
13-14 Hanover Street
London W1S 1YH
tel: 020 7629 1103
www.houseofhanover.co.uk

Wow factor: ⌂⌂
Choice: ⌂⌂⌂⌂
Service: ⌂⌂⌂⌂⌂
Price: £££

Classic
Oxford Circus LU, 5 min walk
Mon-Sat, 10am-6.30pm, Sun, 12am-6pm
Designer mix
Sizes: Women varies; Men: varies

Don't be deceived by the old fashioned busy window display: there's some rea
yummy designer end of ranges to be found here. Spacious, it's easy enough to
browse round and see the accessory collections on the ground floor and first floo
of ladies clothes.

On Women's: Ideal for last seasons' designer collections at greatly reduced prices
up to about 75% off big designer names including Chloe, Gucci, Prada, Missoni
Max Mara, D&G, Jimmy Choo, Stella McCartney and Fendi. Fresh waves of collections arrive every few weeks. Signature items include cashmere jumpers £29.95 in
many colours whilst handbags, sunglasses jewellery, shoes, scarves and belts and
hats come as top brands. Changing rooms are small with a locked door, mirror and
hangers. Outside there's an armchair for a companion and a viewing mirror. Service is very good and they are always on hand to help. Tried on a Max Mara jacke
£275 reduced to £160 and assistant agreed it was the wrong size and searched
the store to find other jackets I might like. They were pleasant about it when they
hadn't what I wanted.

On Men's: Situated at the rear of the store are plenty of top ranking designe
jackets, coats, shirts and trousers and well-priced ties. I found a bargain Ozwald
Boateng heavy gauge ivory linen trousers finessed with a subtle navy thread detai
that fitted perfectly. Terrific and excellent service.

Well worth a look in from time to time – you never know what you might find!

Jaeger
200-206 Regent Street,
London W1B 5BN
tel: 020 7979 1100
www.jaeger.co.uk

Wow factor: ⌂⌂⌂⌂⌂
Choice: ⌂⌂⌂⌂
Service: ⌂⌂
Price: £££

Classic
Oxford Circus, 5 min walk
Mon-Wed, 10am-7pm, Thurs-Sat, 10am-8pm, Sun, 12am-6pm
Own label, ready to wear
Sizes: Women 6-14; Men: 34-48

A glorious store with a beautifully designed classic elegance combined with fresh
innovativeness that is proving irresistible to Regent Street shoppers. The large spi-

ral staircase, the glass lift, the white, black, glossy columns and chandeliers are just a few of the luxurious features of this store that counts Kate Moss, Kate Bosworth, Katie Derham, Kylie Minogue, Alexandra Shuman as their fans.

On Women's: Whilst Jaeger's traditionally core customer is 25+, the new Jaeger London range definitely has a younger appeal and looks great. For more understated looks, amongst the main collection are very classic dresses, suits, t-shirts and evening dresses. Outstanding are Jaeger's "Black Label", their top end collection that makes a great tailored investment buy and Jaeger's capsule collection, "Limited Edition". Handbags, jewellery, shoes, scarves, belts and hats are also available. For a shop of this calibre, service was disappointing. I tried on a jacket and couldn't find anyone to ask about sizing. Eventually someone came along and although she had a good stock knowledge and showed me to the changing room, I didn't see her or anyone else after that, not even to give the jacket back to. Changing rooms were a comfortable size with two mirrors for different angles, a seat but alas nowhere to hang anything.

On Men's: Impressive on suits, jackets, trouser, shirts and coats, Jaeger has always had a strong upper echelon business executive following. Chinos and jeans, crew neck sweaters and polo tops are excellent quality are also well worth a look at.

Also in Westfield and collections in Selfridges and Harrods.

Top 200

Heaven & Earth

216-217 Tottenham Court Road
London W1T 7PT
tel: 020 7596 2020
www.heavenandearthclothing.co.uk

Wow factor: ⍝⍝⍝
Choice: ⍝⍝⍝
Service: ⍝⍝⍝⍝
Price: ££

Glam
Tottenham Court Road LU, 3 min walk
Mon-Sat, 9am-7pm, Sunday 11am-6pm
Ready to wear
Sizes: Women 8-10

This little peachy find enables you to dress unique at a relatively low cost. The pretty feminine collection has short skirts, macs at £120, dresses £150 and belts at £35 that are all short production runs. Located in a massive 20-20 Optical Store loaded with the latest designer glasses collections, Heaven and Earth have created a shop type atmosphere within small amount of that space with just a few rails.

Originating from Korea different designers fall under the umbrella of the Heaven and Earth label. Expect one of each piece, usually size 8 or 10. The collection is certainly worth a look at if you fit into their narrow size range. To try on, walk a short distance away from the unit near their window display and up two stone steps are two curtained off changing cubicles with full length mirrors. Whilst only one person is usually on, service is quite good. Handbags, belts, jewellery and sunglasses are in the main store,

Jigsaw
St Christopher's Place
London W1 1AF
tel: 020 7493 9169
www.jigsaw-online.com

Wow factor:👗👗👗
Choice:👗👗👗👗
Service:👗👗👗👗
Price: ££

> Glam
> Marble Arch, Bond Street LU, 5 min walk
> Mon-Sat, 10am-6.30pm, Thurs, 10.30am-8pm, Sun, 12am-6pm
> Own label
> Sizes: Women 8-16, shoes 41-36

For review of this chain see page (223)

John Lewis
278- 306 Oxford Street
London W1
tel: 020 7629 7711
www.johnlewis.co.uk

Wow factor:👗👗👗
Choice:👗👗👗👗
Service:👗👗👗👗
Price: ££-£££

> Classic
> Oxford Circus LU, 5 min walk
> Mon-Fri, 9.30am-8pm, Thurs 9.30am-9pm Sat 9.30am-7pm, Sun 12am-6pm
> Ready to wear
> Sizes: Women dress mostly 10-16, occasion wear 8-20; others 8-18;
> shoes: 2½-9
> Men: S- XL ; shoes 7-11 with their own brand in whole sizes only 7-12.

This store is fashionably but conventionally understated with a reputation for quality as solid as a rock. On the ground floor, a staff greeter helpfully directs shoppers to relevant departments. Accessories on ground floor, women's clothes and shoes first floor, men's on ground floor. The modern escalator system and a further eight lifts makes travel very easy.

Handbags include Radley's collection complete with doggie logos and an assortment of different labelled evening bags from as low as £10. For jewellery check the classic labels such as Monet plus a huge selection of very large colourful genuine vintage pieces, whilst on shoes notably there's a Rainbow range of satin shoe that can dyed to match your outfit. Also stocks Dune, Garbor and Cavella and a good choice of scarves, wraps, fake furs and sunglasses together with a classic range of hats and belts.

On Women's: Stocks many labels including Warehouse, Mexx, Coast, Whistles, White Stuff and z plus John Lewis's own classic JL range that has some outstanding knitwear. Also there's Betty Barclay and distinguished lines from Paul Costelloe renowned for his dressage jackets teamed with skirts and trousers, a range not readily available elsewhere in London.

In the shoe department, I tried on ankle boots that were too big but a very helpful assistant went around all the stock whilst I sat and waited. For changing facilities there are many cubicles with doors that lock, a mirror on two walls to see different views, whilst outside were armchairs and giant mirrors.

John Lewis has a huge lingerie department with fitting specialists. It is also renowned for their fabrics and haberdashery. Although regrettably it has shrunk somewhat, this can be just the ticket for those elusive items that other shops do not stock.

Men's: Has good value ready to wear Chester Barrie jackets at £150, Balmain suits £330, a reasonable selection of Barbour and a smart Hackett concession. On casuals to choose are Tommy Hilfiger, Lee Jeans, and some rather nifty Crew and Co. shirts at £60. John Lewis's own JL brand steers on the very conventional. Does special event days. A previous "Gentleman's Day" (Lingerie Academy for Men) was well attended!

Service is generally very friendly and they seem genuinely glad to help. Queues up to five minutes sometimes to pay.

Also at Brent Cross, and the Sloane Rangers favourite store Peter Jones, Sloane Square

 Top 200

Karen Millen
229-247 Regent St
London W1
tel: 020 7629 1901
www.karenmillen.com

Wow factor: 🏠🏠🏠🏠
Choice: 🏠🏠🏠🏠
Service: 🏠🏠🏠🏠🏠
Price: ££

> Glam
> Oxford Circus LU, 5 min walk
> Mon-Wed, 10am-8pm, Thurs, 10am-8.30pm, Sat 10am-7.30pm, Sun 11.30am-7.30pm
> Own label
> Sizes: Women 6-16, shoes 36-41

For review of this chain see page (225)

KJ Laundry
74 Marylebone Lane
London W1
tel: 020 7486 7855
www.kjslaundry.com

❗ Must Visit

> Cool
> Bond Street LU, 5 min walk
> Mon-Sat, 10am-7pm, Sun, 11am-5pm
> Designer mix
> Sizes: Women varies

Style magnet, this hot edit of much talked about labels has gained this friendly woodeny boutique in a very short space of time a sparkling reputation. Names include Richard Ruiz, Alice Ritter, S-Sung, Rebecca Taylor, Carl Kapp and Sphere One.

Liberty
210-220 Regent Street,
London W1
tel: 020 7734 1234
www.liberty.co.uk

Wow factor: 🏠🏠🏠🏠🏠
Choice: 🏠🏠🏠🏠🏠
Service: 🏠🏠🏠
Price: £££££

Glam
Oxford Circus LU, 3 min walk
Mon-Sat, 10am-7pm, Thurs, 10am-8pm, Sun, 12am-6pm
Own label, designer mix
Sizes: Women, varies; Men: varies

London's quaintest department store that successfully combines a sense of history with a sense of modernity. Outside it's a wooden beamed Tudor-style building with rivetingly compelling contemporary window displays. The interior too is that of a exquisitely traditional building coupled with modern touches, gothic wall lights and some amusing sculptures of arms emerging from a wall. Wooden floors and wall panelling compete for your attention with a giant aluminium chandelier that changes colour.

On Women's: A minestrone of collections from big name designers rubs shoulders with newer names. Head for the first floor that stocks Matthew Williamson, Jean Paul Gautier, Alexandra McQueen, "See Chloé", Sonia, Louise Goldin and Vanessa Bruno plus a large array of Vivienne Westwood and her Anglomania label. I tried on Vivienne Westwood black top at £295 and found it took some time to get assistance. Once one gets served they are helpful and very knowledgeable. In addition, there's also an interesting room of more unstructured collections in neutral shades. Vintage is now situated in it's own circular space with emphasis on occasionwear priced quite high but the labels are Chanel, Dior and Versace and thus worth checking out as is the new lingerie department.

Not to be missed are the signature items of Liberty Prints, Liberty Swimwear, from £99, Liberty handbags at £600. Also there are handbags from Marc Jacob, Prada and Vivienne Westwood.

The Jewellery Department is on the ground floor and sports small collections unavailable in most other stores including Christopher Kane whose pieces can be added to turn any outfit into a show stopper. Here too Dinny Hall has a concession. Overall this floor is absolutely delightful.

On the 2nd Floor, in September 2008, a sensational new triple room women's shoe department opened around where homeware is sold. Hence several shoes are displayed on a dinner table set complete with white and gold dinner service. The edit includes London designers Nicholas Kirkwood, Rupert Sanderson and Georgina Goodman and also Mui Mui, Prada, Dolce and Gabbana and Marc Jacobs. The Fabric and Haberdashery department is on the third floor.

On Men's: Descend to the lower ground floor and head for the rooms with Alexander McQueen, Jil Sander, John Smedley and Rick Owen. Also there's Savile Row –style tailoring with Kilgour and ready to wear from Paul Smith. The store's own Liberty Print shirts are around £85 and if you can't find the ties you want from their huge assortment, there's a capsule collection from Duchamp in startling colours. A separate room has further men's accessories, nightwear, belts and hats whilst at the rear is a large handsome shoe selection encompassing Martin Margiela, Prada and Kurt Geiger.

For refreshments try the ground floor tea room. Set teas are from about £10.75 to £29 and there's a big choice of tea varieties to choose from. There are two further restaurants.

Great store! Great sales!

 Top 200

Mango
225 Oxford Circus
London W1D 2LP
tel: 020 7534 3505
www.mango.com

Wow factor: ☆☆☆☆☆
Choice: ☆☆☆☆☆
Service: ☆☆☆
Price: £

Glam
Oxford Circus LU, 5 min walk
Mon-Sat, 10am-8.30pm, Thurs, 10am-9pm,Sun 11am-6pm
Own label
Sizes: Women S-XL, 8-16, shoes S-XL; Men: S-XL, shoes 6-10

Fashionistas clothes on a budget. For review of this chain see page (226)

Also at 106 Regent St; 8-12 Neal St, Covent Garden

Margaret Howell

34 Wigmore Street
London W1U 2RS
tel: 020 7591 2255
www.margarethowell.co.uk

Wow factor: ☺☺☺☺
Choice: ☺☺☺
Service: ☺☺☺
Price: £££

Classic
Bond Street LU, 8 min walk
Mon-Sat, 10am-6pm, Wed 10am-7pm, Sun, 12am-6pm
Own label
Sizes: Women 6-14

After the hustle and bustle of Oxford Street, turning off into Wigmore Street the scene is more subdued and on entering Margaret Howell, it's like a tranquilliser. The staff float past and you are not sure if they have seen you or not. A long wooden floored shop with rails on each side, it's half women's at front of house with men's to the rear and high white display units to the middle. The conservatory style ceiling at the back, however, gives the place an urban feel.

On Women's: All the clothes are extremely wearable and are good quality like the T-shirts at £65. They have the air of comfortable cosiness of a very English bygone era. Shoes are flat masculine lace-ups. There's also a small delicate collection of jewellery at the counter, as well as candle and their own brand homeware.

Had to look for someone to ask if I could try on a woolen skirt with large plaid pattern £225. Staff were pleasant when spoken to but not very forthcoming in service. They seemed to be in the Margaret Howell tranquility zone!

On Men's: For a well-made understated look, check out the slate grey wool jackets, trousers, cotton shirts, leather belts and very good navy wool and cotton car coat.

Margaret Howell has regular in-store architecture exhibitions here and was awarded Royal Designer for Industry in 2007. Also at 111 Fulham Road, London SW3 and 1 The Green, Richmond.

Top 200

Marks and Spencer

458 Oxford Street
London W1N 0AP
tel: 020 7935 7954
www.marksandspencer.com

Wow factor: ☺☺☺☺
Choice: ☺☺☺☺☺
Service: ☺☺☺
Price: ££

Glam
Marble Arch LU, 3 min walk
Mon-Fri, 9am-9pm, Sat 8am-8pm, Sun 12 noon-6pm
Own label
Sizes: Women 8-20; Men: S-XXL

This flagship has a great layout, attractive, easy to see and walk around. Giant pictures of celebrity models used to advertise the clothes including Twiggy and, Erin

O'Connor. Café Revive has some good coffee and snacks for tied feet.

For review of this chain see page (227)

 Top 200

Matches
87 Marylebone High street
London W1U 4QU
tel: 020 7487 5400
www.matchesfashion.com

Wow factor: ☗☗☗☗
Choice: ☗☗☗☗☗
Service: ☗☗☗☗☗
Price: ££££

> Glam
> Baker St or Bond St LU, 5 min walk
> Mon-Sat, 10am-7pm, Sun, 12am-6pm
> Designer mix
> Sizes: Women varies; Men: varies

Top name fashion collection edit situated in plush airy shop that's a big hit with Marylebone celebrity residents and presenters from nearby BBC.

On Women's: Rails of superb clothes from Herve Leger of bandage dress fame at £828, Reda, Ossie Clark, Diane von Fustenberg, Alexander McQueen. Tried on a black short Ossie Clark silk jacket with leather details (£725) which had it been in the right size would be tempting. Certainly the service was top notch, the changing room well equipped small white and bright, and you do get offered orange, juice, water or coffee as you browse together with some good resting areas to relax at.

On Men's: Inspired edit of completely on-trend collections highlighted by Philip Lim round neck cashmere jumpers, Lanvin preppy cardigans, Balenciaga polo knit jumpers with zip detailed collar. These are just a few of the big name labels at Matches and with the help of further lines from Alexander McQueen, Kilgour and Prada this is superb one-stop venue to create your own wow top end individual look.

 Top 200

Monsoon
498-500 Oxford Street
Marble Arch
London W1C 1LQ
tel: 020 7491 3004

Wow factor: ☗☗☗
Choice: ☗☗☗☗
Service: ☗☗☗☗
Price: ££

> Glam
> Marble Arch, 3 min walk
> Mon-Fri, 9.30am-8pm, Thurs, 9.30am-9pm, Sun, 12am-6pm
> Own label
> Sizes: Women 8-18 but also some 20 and 22's and a petite range, shoes 4-8; Men S-XL

For review of this chain see page (228).

New Look
500-502 Oxford Street
London W1
tel: 020 7290 7860
www.newlook.co.uk

Wow factor: 🏠🏠🏠🏠
Choice: 🏠🏠🏠🏠🏠
Service: 🏠🏠
Price: £

Cool
Marble Arch LU, 3min walk
Mon-Sat, 10am-6pm
Own label
Sizes: Women dress 6-18; shoes: 3-8, Men's S-XXL, shoes 6-12

One the best designed stores in London. For review of this chain see page (229).

Oasis
292 Regent Street,
London W1
tel: 020 7323 5978
www.oasis-stores.com

⚠️ **Must**Visit

Classic
Oxford Circus LU, 3 min walk
Mon-Sat, 10am-6pm
Ready to wear
Sizes: Women dress 8-16; shoes: 36-41

For review of this chain see page (230)

Paddy Campbell
8 Gees Court
St Christopher's Place
London W1U 13Q
tel: 020 7493 5646
www.paddycampbell.co.uk

Wow factor: 🏠🏠🏠
Choice: 🏠🏠🏠
Service: 🏠🏠🏠
Price: £££

Classic
Marble Arch LU, 5 min walk
Mon-Fri, 10am-6pm, Thurs, 10am-7pm, Sat 10.30am-6pm
Own label
Sizes: Women 8-16

Timeless, successful sophistication combines with mature gracefulness at designer Paddy Campbell and daughter Rebecca's shop. Small in size, but with an airy feel it has a garden bench as you walk in. Originally an eighteenth century tea ware house, Paddy set up shop in 1979 and upstairs is the design studio, with most clothes made in the UK. Whilst this is the flagship, a second shop in Beauchamp Place opened six years later that is also very popular.

A treat for the eye are the classic cut shift dresses in pure silk with matching coats; suits, skirts with trousers, well cut jackets with pretty sash waists and rose print dresses. Perfect outfits for a wedding in subtle but rich colours and a touch of individuality and there's some smart jewellery to match.

The 1930's statement pieces are styled in lace, soft wools and cashmere and embroidered fabric. Daywear, think slightly vintage Liz Taylor, James Bond's Miss Moneypenny grey flannel and printed wool dresses. Occasionwear, think long silver cobweb dress £599, pleated flapper dress in ice with a large graceful bow at £549, brocade jackets and dresses and Ottoman swing jackets at £369.

At season end, Paddy Campbell sells off the remainders of materials downstairs and their samples get snapped up at greatly reduced prices.

With a cheery welcome, I tried on a silk jacket with bows on the waist in silver-grey. The changing rooms consisted of two curtained off spaces at the back with chairs, mirrors and hooks. Staff are a touch on the reserved side but were knowledgeable and helpful when asked. The jacket looked better than I anticipated and if you don't want the full-on Campbell-look, the little jackets can be dressed down with a jean or more casual trouser.

Also at 17 Beauchamp Place,London SW3 1NQ,Tel 020 7225 0543
Mon-Sat 10am-6pm except Wed 10am-7pm and Sat 10.30am-6pm

 Top 200

Primark
499-517 Oxford Street,
London W1K 7DA
Tel: 0207 495 0420
www.primark.co.uk

Wow factor: ṭṭṭṭ
Choice: ṭṭṭṭṭ
Service: ṭ
Price: £

Casual, classic
Marble Arch LU, 2 min walk
Mon-Fri, 9am-9pm, Sat, 9pm-8pm, Sun 12noon-6pm
Own label
Sizes: Women varies; Men: varies

Every bargain hungry fashionista in London shops here. For review of this chain see page (231)

Also at East Ham, Hackney, Kilburn, Leytonstone, Tooting, Wandsworth and Hammersmith.

Reiss
9-12 Barrett Street
London W1U 1BA
tel: 020 7486 6557
www.reiss.co.uk

Wow factor: 🏠🏠🏠🏠🏠
Choice: 🏠🏠🏠🏠
Service: 🏠🏠🏠🏠🏠
Price: ££

Glam
Marble Arch LU, 5 min walk
Mon-Wed 10am-7pm, Thurs -Sat, 10am-8pm, Sun, 12am-6pm
Own label
Sizes: Women 6-14; Men: S-XL

This is their dazzling flagship store. For review of this chain see page (235)

Russell and Bromley
109 New Bond Street,
London W1
tel: 020 7629 4001
www.russellandbromley.co.uk

Classic
Bond St LU, 5 min walk
Mon-Sat, 10am-6.30pm, Thurs, 10am-7.30pm, Sun, 12am-6pm
Own label
Sizes: Women 3-8; Men: 6-12 and sometimes 13

This prime position revered family business corner shoe store has windows al
round stylishly crammed with their latest collections. For review of this chain see
page (236)

River Island
301-309 Oxford Street,
London W1C 2DN
tel: 0844 395 1011
www.riverisland.com

Wow factor: 🏠🏠🏠🏠
Choice: 🏠🏠🏠🏠
Service: 🏠🏠🏠
Price: £

Urban
Oxford Circus LU, 2 min walk
Mon-Sat, 10am-8pm, Sun, 10.30am-6pm
Own label
Sizes: Women 6-18, Shoes 3-8; Men: XS-XXXL, shoes 6-12

For review of this chain see page (233)

Swarovski Crystallized Cosmos and lounge
24 Great Marlborough Street,
London W1F 7HU
tel: 0207 434 3444
www.crystallized.com

Wow factor: ☐☐☐☐☐
Choice: ☐☐☐☐☐
Service: ☐☐☐☐
Price: ££- ££££

> Glam, glitzy
> Oxford Circus LU, 2 min walk
> Mon-Sat, 10am-7pm, Thurs, 10am-8pm, Sun 12am-6pm
> Own label

Sparkle up your day with this "exhibition" space showcasing dazzling affordable jewellery. Staff wearing black suits greeted you on entry and if a newcomer give a full tour to show how the store works. The first floor café has low cut modernist beige armchairs, displays of dresses, shoes, bags illustrating ways the Swarovski product has been used by top designers. A fresh exhibition arrives every two months.

Pendants are from £20 although there are also very big elaborate pieces. The walls are choc full of crystals to buy in different shapes and sizes with the colours graded in shades around the shop.

What's terrific is that you can DIY your own jewellery. If you buy a three drop pearl earring ready to wear it's £19. But if you buy the same earring in kit form it's only £9. Similarly a necklace ready to wear is £42; do it yourself is £18. Swarovski also run their own creativity classes from beginner to advanced at £20-£55 to make your own designs.

Also has a café lounge for coffee and alcoholic drinks see page (262) for review.

Selfridges
400 Oxford Street,
London W1
tel: 0800 123 400
www.selfridges.com

Wow factor: ☐☐☐☐☐
Choice: ☐☐☐☐☐
Service: ☐☐☐☐☐
Price: £-£££££

> Classic
> Marble Arch and Bond Street LU, 5 min walk
> Mon-Wed, 9.30am-8pm, Thurs-Sat, 9.30am-9pm, Sun, 12am-6pm
> Designer mix and own label
> Sizes: Women varies, Men: varies

One of the most outstanding fashion department stores in London, Selfridges is an impressive trendsetter for sensational window displays, in-store fashion presentation, special themed events and in-store entertainment. Always a pleasure to visit, it covers the complete price spectrum so there's always something for everyone.

On Women's: The second floor designer room is the place to head for, proceed through a red tunnel to the Superbrands concession to be amazed by the Gucci, Stella McCartney, Dolce Gabanna and Alexander McQueen collections. In the main section on this floor too are not only other concessions but also rails of comparatively lesser known designers such as Ashish and Future Classics as well as rails of well known labels including Matthew Williamson, Diane Von Furstenberg and Issa. The third floor offers less expensive more classic brand lines with an ever-decreasing hat department, whilst the ground floor has a lively high street chain line-up of Topshop, Karen Millen,, Miss Selfridge, All Saints and Mikey. On the ground floor too are handbags from Fendi, Gucci, Marc Jacobs and many others, a mixed jewellery designer room and a further Wonder Room of even more upscale jewellery and watches.

As you browse the different departments staff greet you and are mostly helpful. On the second floor, the large changing room is decked completely in gold with a large mirror with winged sides. Service is of an excellent standard.

On Men's: The first floor has a stunning array of leading designers covering virtu-ally all styles. Of note is Alexander McQueen and Paul Smith plus a good value own label. Don't miss the men's Superbrands section it's awesome. A huge range of shoes are available including Oliver Sweeney.

For the many in store restaurants and cafés to enjoy during your shopping experi-ence see page (262).

Top 200

Ted Baker
245 Regent Street,
London W1B 2EN
tel: 020 7493 6251
www.tedbaker.com

Wow factor: ☖☖☖☖
Choice: ☖☖☖☖
Service: ☖☖☖
Price: £££

Urban
Oxford Circus LU, 2 min walk
Mon-Sat, 10am-8pm, Sun, 10.30am-6pm
Own label
Sizes: Women 6-18, Shoes 3-8; Men: XS-XXXL, shoes 6-12

For review of this chain see page (236)

Also at 9 Floral Street, Covent Garden; 234 King's Road, SW3; South Molton St; Victoria; Westbourne Grove; Canary Wharf; Cheapside; Monument and Wimbledon.

 Top 200

Top Shop
214 Oxford Street,
London W1
Tel: 020 7636 7700
www.topshop.com

Wow factor: ☐☐☐☐☐
Choice: ☐☐☐☐☐
Service: ☐
Price: £

> Glam, at the edge of fashion
> Oxford Circus LU, 30 sec walk
> Mon-Sat, 9am-8pm, Thurs, 9am-9pm, Sun, 12am-6pm
> Own label and designer mix
> Sizes: Women varies; Men: varies

Legendary flagship store. For review of this chain see page (237).

Also at 42 Kensington High St, London W8; 32 The Strand, London WC2, Unit 3 Canada Square, London E14 plus concession in Selfridges and many other stores.

Uniqlo
311 Oxford Street,
London W1
tel: 020 7290 7701
www.uniqlo.co.uk

!MustVisit

Street Casual
Oxford Circus LU, Bond St LU 5 min walk
Mon-Wed, 10am-8pm, Thurs-Sat, 10am-9pm, Sun, 12am-6pm
Own label
Sizes: Women XS-XL; Men: S-XL

For review of this chain see page (239)

 Top 200

Urban Outfitters
200 Oxford Street,
London W1D 1NU
tel: 020 7907 0815
www.urbanoutfitters.

Wow factor: ⌂⌂⌂⌂
Choice: ⌂⌂⌂⌂
Service: ⌂⌂
Price: £

Urban
Oxford Circus LU, 3 min walk
Mon-Sat, 10am-8pm, Thurs, 10am-9pm, Sun, 12am-6pm
Designer Mix
Sizes: Women varies; Men: varies

Successful, contrived American corporation attempt at 18-30 year old emotiona retail bonding fix that on the whole is a ton of fun. Inside the décor is wooden with an iron central staircase and a cool playlist ambience. It gets busy as there's a huge choice of "I've just thrown this outfit together" looks and irreverent signature ironic T-shirts that in the past have overstepped the mark of good taste towards offensiveness.

On Women's: The three floors of women's clothes are choc full of floral dresses £45, printed dresses, T –shirts, jeans, shorts, coats and macs. The top floor has the bigger names such as Religion, Thomas Burberry, Vanessa Bruno, Paul & Joe plus another seven other great brands. The changing rooms have girly blue and white wall paper and are well equipped. Handbags, jewellery, sunglasses, shoes, hat and belts are available.

On Men's: Of the 37 brands stocked, highlights include Duffer of St George reversible hoody £39.99, Oxford Shirts £19.99, Full Circle Socan Smart Shorts £55, Stussy Strand Polo £50 and MHL by Margaret Howell casual shirts. Also stocks G star and Born Free and plenty of chinos and denims.

Staff tend to have a minimum contact approach with customers on the shop floor but really walk the talk with the clothes being totally enamoured with what they are wearing. At sales time clothes just pile upon the floor with no one clearing them up. Now that's what we call laid back! In-store events are on their website Also at 25 Neal St, Covent Garden WC2, Kensington High Street.

Whistles
12 St Christopher's Place
London W1U 1NQ
tel: 020 7487 4489
www.whistles.co.uk

Wow factor: 🛍🛍🛍🛍
Choice: 🛍🛍🛍🛍
Service: 🛍🛍🛍🛍🛍
Price: ££

Cool
Marble Arch LU, 5 min walk
Mon-Fri, 10am-7pm, Sat , 10am-6pm, Sun, 12am-5pm
Own label as well as Pink Soda, Michael Stars, Paige denim
Sizes: Women 8-16

For review of this chain see page (240)

Zara
333 Oxford Street
London W1
tel: 020 7518 1550
www.zara.com

Wow factor: 🛍🛍🛍🛍
Choice: 🛍🛍🛍🛍🛍
Service: 🛍🛍🛍
Price: £

Glam
Bond Street LU, 0.5min walk,
Mon-Sat, 10am-8pm, Sat 10am-6pm
Ready to wear
Sizes: Women clothes XS-XL 6-14; shoes: 36-41; Men S-XL/XXL

For review of this chain see page (241)

Soho/CarnabyStreet

The ever increasing influx of new designers into the Carnaby area and Soho has made this area a hotbed for creativity. Established names such as Designworks and John Pearse Shop continue to offer leading edge whilst Harriet's Muse, Nico D, Anna Lou and Victim are names to watch.

Anna Lou of London

11 Newburgh Street,
London W1F 7RW
tel: 020 7434 1177
www.annalouoflondon.com

Wow factor: ☐☐☐
Choice: ☐☐☐☐
Service: ☐☐☐☐☐
Price: ££

! **Designer**Run**Boutique**

Cool
Oxford Circus LU, 7 min walk
Mon-Sat, 10am-6pm, Thurs, 10am-7pm
Own design jewellery

Blue bijou shop for accessory addicts focusing on cutesy girly retro kitsch. Launched in 2004, Anna Scaife is its founder and creative director. Designed and handmade in the UK, of note are the initial necklaces at £17.50, the heart necklace £25, rose bracelets at £22, kaleidoscope lucite bracelets at £25. Look out for the collection with Laura Lees.

Service is switched on and everything comes in matching sets of plastic necklace, bracelet, earrings, hairslides and rings and often in a choice of colours and often with crystals. Headbands are priced a touch higher at £35. Followers include Kate Moss, Kylie Minogue, Kelly Osborne, Minnie Driver and Madonna. Capsule collections are also available at Fenwick, Harvey Nichols and Urban Outfitters.

Beyond the Valley

2 Newburgh Street,
London W1F 7RD
tel: 020 7437 7338
www.beyondthevalley.com

Wow factor: ☐☐☐☐☐
Choice: ☐☐☐
Service: ☐☐☐
Price: ££

Edgy
Oxford Circus LU, 7 min walk
Mon-Sat, 10am-7pm, Sun 12.30pm-6pm
Designer mix and own label
Sizes: Women: varies

Stepping stone for 100 new designers to platform creative ideas before they develop them for larger scale production. Beyond the Valley gets much exclusivity and the production runs are limited so you know you are getting something rather special. Also has a Side Room gallery for art exhibition bookings from emerging creative talent. Don't be deceived by the small frontage of the shop, it's bigger than you think. The layout here is ladieswear at the front; menswear to the right and further women's downstairs at the rear. Also does pop-up events detailed on their website.

Beyond the Valley is Jo Jackson, Kate Harwood and Kristyana S. Williams, Central St Martin graduates who wanted to create an alternative pathway for young designers in transit from academia to the fiercely competitive commercial world of fashion.

Tried on a silk mini-skirt, high waisted with a bright graphic design (£80) that also comes in plain colours and denim. Loved it. However, the changing room, a cupboard with a lopsided door; was a bit weird because it really was like being in a cupboard ! The two guys running the shop were flapping around frantically on mobiles. But once you got their attention, service-wise they were great.

Around the shop are various novelty signifiers such as a tea service with cup handles sculptured in the shape of women's legs sporting gold high heels, as well as cloud cushions and a scattering of books. Also stocks Labour of Love.

Top 200

Dahlia
5 Fouberts Place
London W1
Tel: 020 7287 7117
www.dahliafashion.co.uk

Wow factor: 🏠🏠🏠
Choice: 🏠🏠🏠
Service: 🏠🏠🏠🏠🏠
Price: £

(!) DesignerRunBoutique

> Glam, cool
> Oxford Circus LU, 5 min walk
> Mon-Sat, 10am-7pm, Sun, 12am-6pm
> Own label
> Sizes: Women S-L; shoes 36-41

With it's soft edged pink and beige Union Jack logo, Dahlia portrays it's take on contemporary Swinging London, Carnaby Street –style in the form of this very pretty shop. Says Dahlia owner and designer Tracy Mitchell at the shop opening in July 2008, "It's girly clothes that are fun to wear."

Dahlia is a shop that has developed from a Portobello Market stall. In the road between the high street stores of Regent Street and the boutiques of Carnaby Street, Dahlia is positioned well for a small London brand that has big ideas on expansion. Collections are regularly refreshed offering emerging trends at high street prices with a sense of individuality.

Key items are the coats £85 and floral dresses whilst at the rear are shoes that are excellent value and a sprinkling of well-priced handbags. Service is good, friendly and knowledgeable.

Also available at Portobello Market (W11), The Laden Showroom (Brick Lane E1), Topshop Oxford Circus and Brent Cross

Top 200

Designworks
42-44 Broadwick Street,
London W1F 7AE
Tel: 020 7434 1968
www.designworkslondon.co.uk

Wow factor: 🏠🏠🏠
Choice: 🏠🏠🏠🏠
Service: 🏠🏠🏠🏠
Price: £££££

> Cool
> Piccadilly Circus LU, 7 min walk
> Mon-Fri, 10.30am-7pm, Sat 12-7pm
> Own label and designer mix
> Sizes: Men: 36-42, shoe 6-11

This chic corner boutique in Soho opened in 1995 is conceptually described a "New-Brit" style, a kind of hybrid of elegant brashness and classics with a twist. Consisting of their own ranges and collection edits including jumpers from Veronique Branquinho, leather zip-up jackets from Santacroce, DNL shirts, Le Magnifique graphic T-shirts and bags from Zufi Alexander. Prices-wise, the leather jackets are £500-£1000 but are good value as they are tremendously stylish and good quality, whilst snazzy sneakers cost £150 and are boots around £310.

Fashion sophisticated staff like to let you browse around the many rails and quite pleasantly friendly when you need them. Changing rooms toward the rear are quite comfortable. Gives discounts of up to 60% in their sales – but you've got to be quick because items get snapped up extremely quick.

Irregular Choice
39 Carnaby Street
London W1
tel: 020 7494 4811
www.irregularchoice.com

(!) MustVisi

Edgy
Oxford Circus LU, 5 min walk
Mon-Sat, 10am-7pm, Sun, 12am-6pm
Own label
Sizes: Women S-L, shoes 35-43; Men: shoes 40-46

There's a clue in the name as to what to expect in this shop. Quirky fashion orientated this shop is one on it's won in Europe. On show are wearable but witty pieces veering up to wicked flamboyance. Visible are a few colourful clothes here but the main attraction is the footwear. Shoes range from a staggering £30 with most expensive reaching £180. Décor, you have to see it to believe it. Cartoons collide with flashing lights, planets and roses. We told you it was an irregular choice!

Top 200

Jess James
3 Newburgh Street
Soho
London W1F 7RE
tel: 020 7437 7001
www.jessjames.com

Wow factor: 🏠🏠🏠🏠
Choice: 🏠🏠🏠🏠🏠
Service: 🏠🏠🏠🏠🏠
Price: £££££

Edgy
Oxford Circus LU, 7 min walk
Mon-Fri ,11am-6.30pm except Thurs, 11am-7pm, Sat 11am-6pm

There's something fishy about this creative jewellers for men and women. Unconventional without counters, the central cabinets have a long fish tank running through the middle of them. This futuristic sleek shop with a wall mounted LCD screen beams out imagery of some of their more extravagant pieces. Wall cabinets showcase over 30 designers, mostly British, from classic to the extraordinary and of course their made to order specials. At the rear is their own collection including lots of watches. Customer movement activated lighting illuminates their displays.

On Women's: Katie Clark's feather earrings £54, cherry pendants by Tina Lilienthal from £85 are just a few of the standouts here.

On Men's: High points are Chris Hawkins silver rock surfaced rings and cufflinks, silver stingray necklace at £294 together with classy William Cheshire "branded" ring and cufflinks at £102 and £120.

Expect faultless and enthusiastic service. Great Shop.

Top 200

Joie
37 Marshall Street,
London W1F 7EZ
tel: 020 7434 3423

Wow factor: ◌◌◌◌
Choice: ◌◌◌
Service: ◌◌◌◌
Price: ££

①DesignerRunBoutique

Glam
Oxford Circus LU, 7 min walk
Mon-Sat, 11am-7pm, Sun, 12am-6pm
Own label
Sizes: Women: mostly one size

One of the prettiest boutiques for clothes in London. Green grass-like carpet and the colourful clothes lay planted like flowers. The theme is signature ultra feminine with oodles of frills and floaty floral tea-dresses from £130. They make no more than 20 of each style and there's a nice selection of frill skirts at £45. Matching frilly handbags at £180 are available as well as cuffs. The short frilly skirt with an elasticated back that I tried felt good.

The one changing room is intriguing. When it closes it is like a gift box complete with lid. When it opens you pop out! Service is sweet and if you want the skirt longer they can add another frill. Some items also available at Top Shop, Oxford Circus.

Top 200

John Pearse Shop Soho
5 Meard Street
London W1
tel: 020 7434 0738
www.johnpearse.co.uk

Wow factor: ◌◌◌◌
Choice: ◌◌◌
Service: ◌◌◌◌
Price: £££££

①DesignerRunBoutique

Bespoke tailors, English Eccentric
Tottenham Court Road, 5 min walk
Mon-Fri, 10am-6pm, Sun, 12am-6pm
Own label and Ready to wear
Sizes: Men: 34-48, Women 6-14

In 1966, he co-founded Granny Takes A Trip, a hot ticket boutique in the Swinging London era where he counted The Who, Hendrix and Cream as his customers and Mick Jagger and Alex James to this day.

This rather secret type of a shop defines itself as a salon. The difference being that in a salon there is no hard sell that you get in a shop. White, bright and airy with a blazing fire, a garish tailors dummy and Francis Bacon painting conjures up a refined creative atmosphere.

On Men's: Original clothes designs are predominantly made to measure with suits £1700 although some ready to wears at £1000. Impressive are the denim suits with red striped stitching. The hand painted ties, some made to order, are very good indeed and the white cotton shirts striped down one side at £118 are quite inspired. A moleskin ready to wear funnel necked coat at £700 fitted well whilst the made to measure version will set you back £900. Black cord jackets, flat caps and belts are also available. Of particular note are his inventive styled coats.

On Women's A smaller part of the shop is dedicated to women's wear featuring denim jackets, coats plus jackets and shirts also made to order.

Once you get passed the social barriers, service is quite good. But first you must press the intercom to be let in and if they are having one of their "tailoring meetings" you will be ignored for some time. John Pearse will approach you if he deems a prospective sale is imminent. Whilst initially he may have a frosty air as the conversation progresses he can be quite charming and eventually friendly. He is there most of the time so you do get the services of a London Fashion legend.

Top 200

Leluu
8 Newburgh Street,
London W1F 7RJ
tel: 020 7734 3113
www.leluu.com

Wow factor: 🏠🏠🏠
Choice: 🏠🏠🏠
Service: 🏠🏠🏠🏠
Price: £££££

! DesignerRunBoutique

Glam
Oxford Circus LU, 7 min walk
Mon-Sat, 11.30am-7pm, except Thurs, 11.30am-7.30pm, Sun 1pm-6pm
Own label
Sizes: Women XS-L

Central St Martins fashion graduate, Uyen Luu offers good quality, non-mass market designs at a high street prices with a clientele that includes Fern Cotton, Peaches Geldof, Katie Holmes and Helen Mirren.

Opened in May 2008, this boutique has black lattice framed windows and a white stripped out interior with shoes lined up on the floor and handbags and signature hand printed dresses on show.

The Mildred 50's inspired trenchcoat with frill collar and bow back (£175) that tried on comes in a range of colours and is an excellent buy. We found the changing rooms very basic, just a curtained-off area, but the service very good. Impressive is the handmade cotton tea-dress at an amazing £49 and a well made Frankie silk shirt dress at £75. All the clothes are own label but there are accessories from other designers and lots of shoes. A good little shop.

Also at Earlham St, near Seven Dials in Covent Garden and also Praed St, Paddington.

 Top 200

Nico D
16a D'Arblay Street
London W1F 8EA
Tel 020 7287 0207
www.nico-d.com

Wow factor: ⛶⛶⛶⛶⛶
Choice: ⛶⛶⛶⛶⛶
Service: ⛶⛶⛶⛶⛶
Price: ££

❶ DesignerRunBoutique

> Glam, cool
> Tottenham Court Road LU 5 min walk
> Mon-Sat, 10am-6pm, Thurs, 10am-7pm
> Own label, Ready to wear:
> Sizes: Women 1-5 (8-16); Men: 1-5 (36-44)

Refreshingly original designs in this boudoir chic boutique under the helm of designer Nico Didonna who may be in the back workroom and come out if needed. With an excellent welcome from staff their proficient stock knowledge will set you straight. Especially interesting is that Nico who shows on the catwalk at London Fashion Week will customise to meet your requirements.

On Women's: Coats with oversized collars and interesting hemlines are worth a whirl. Of note is the black crystal organza wrap jacket at £220. Clothes are tailored with a contemporary twist. Luxurious fabrics are used such as lama, alpaca as well cashmere, wools and silks.

On Men's: Detailed tailoring flared trousers with zip on leg bottoms £195, jacket £360, waistcoat £140. Also interesting shirts, T-shirts, jumpers, very good leather clutch bags, ties, belts, shoes (£260) and jewellery. There's no charge for alteration on the suits

With an ambience of relaxing music, amicable service, spacious changing rooms this is a pleasant shopping experience.

 Top 200

Number 22
22 Carnaby Street,
London W1F 7DB
tel: 020 7 734 1690
www.numberstores.com

Wow factor: ⛶⛶⛶
Choice: ⛶⛶⛶
Service: ⛶⛶⛶⛶
Price: ££

> Cool
> Oxford Circus LU, 5 min walk
> Mon-Fri 11am-7pm,Sat 10.30am-7pm, Sun, 2pm-6pm
> Own label
> Sizes: Women 28-34, Shoes 38-41, Men shoes 41-46

Cool, cool and more cool. S***R or Swear are the shoes; People's Market are the clothes, Thom York from Radiohead, A-list indie artists, musicians and actors are the clientele.

Shoes are the main event especially the men's. Although, the shop appears narrow it goes keep going around the corner where there's more stock and changing rooms with mirrored doors.

On Men's: Black patent, silver or gold leather are persuasive. Black shoes with studs all over are statement standouts. All these are priced around £100 and more casual ones are even less. Check out the Dean designs, pointed toes with rubber soles and the £90 red pairs in the window.

On Women's: Clothes are street casual and likeable is the T-shirt dress with cowl neck and flower appliquéd sleeves. If you are not dressed in the style of the shop you could get a frosty reception. But staff do warm up if you do show interest in the merchandise.

Also in Westfield under the concept store, Number.

Top 200

Two See
21 Fouberts Place,
London W1 7QE
tel: 020 7494 3813
www.shoptwosee.com

Wow factor: ⬛⬛⬛⬛
Choice: ⬛⬛⬛
Service: ⬛⬛⬛⬛⬛
Price: £££

Cool
Oxford Circus LU, 5 min walk
Mon-Sat, 11am-7pm, Sun, 12am-6pm
Designer Mix
Sizes: Women: varies; Men: varies

Vibrant showcase of avant garde collections combining urban cool with a touch of edginess. The two mannequins in this white fronted boutique preludes the inventive designs within this popular distressed decored boutique perfect for Carnaby fashionistas.

On Men's: Service is style informative and friendly. Tried on a pair of Jean Pierre Braganza black narrow fit trousers that hugged superbly. Highlights include J-C Castelbajac veni, vidi, voici bag and Burfitt.

On Women's: Sexy silhouettes from Preen, check out the silk polo neck dress with one-sided draping at £185, unusual structured shapes from Hussein Chalayan and the gorgeously wearables from Jean Pierre Braganza.

Victim
33 Marshall Street,
London W1F 7EX
Tel: 020 7494 4044
www.victimfashionst.com

Wow factor: 🏠🏠🏠🏠
Choice: 🏠🏠🏠
Service: 🏠🏠🏠
Price: ££

❗ Designer Run**Boutique**

Glam, cool
Oxford Circus LU, 7 min walk
Mon-Sat, 11.30am-6.30pm
Own label clothes
Sizes: mainly one size but can make to order in 1-2 weeks;

Victim is self-styled Mei-Hui Liu brainchild who walks the talk of her own designs. It's Victoriana meets anything goes, styles change monthly. Mei-Hui Liu is often around and so you get the real benefits of talking to the designer herself.

Silk dresses have patterns of different coloured fabrics interestingly arranged on them and often overlaid with antique lace pieces. Full net skirts at £150 in the same theme are available. Bespoke skyscraper shoes with extreme high platforms completes the look.

On service, you may need to take your French phrase book as the shop assistant is working from an English phrase book. Otherwise it's pretty friendly. Changing rooms are basic. Just a curtain that goes round. The shop, small and woodeny is one of a kind. Marvellous.

CoventGarden

Theatreland district with entertainment that spills out onto the street. Often mobbed with people there are huge number of fashion shops to choose from. Amongst the most famous is Stephen Jones in Great Queen Street, Duffer of St George in Short Gardens and Fenchurch in Earlham Street. For glam with edge there's Unconditional, for cool with prettiness there's Fifi Wilson and for goth with attitude, All Saints.

All Saints
57-59 Long Acre
London EC1
tel: 020 7836 0801
www.allsaints.co.uk

Wow factor: 🖤🖤🖤🖤🖤
Choice: 🖤🖤🖤🖤
Service: 🖤
Price: ££

> Cool
> Covent Garden LU, 1 min walk
> Mon-Sun 9.30am-9.30pm, except Thurs, 9.30am-10.30pm and
> Sun 12am-6pm
> Own Label
> Sizes: Women XXS-L; Men: 36-44

For review of this chain see page (217)

Also at Foubert's Place, Market Place, Selfridges Womenswear, South Molton Street all in W1 plus Islington, King's Road, Kensington and Harrods.

Duffer of St George
29 Short Gardens
London WC2H 9LH
tel: 020 7379 4660
thedufferofstgeorge.com

Wow factor: 🖤🖤🖤🖤
Choice: 🖤🖤🖤
Service: 🖤🖤🖤
Price: £££

> Street Casual
> Covent Garden LU, 7min walk
> Mon-Fri, 10.30am-7pm, Sat 10.30am-6.30pm, Sun 1pm-5pm
> Own Label
> Men: S-XL

A big name famous for it's quirky take on traditional English clothing. In 1989 they started the "Old School Movement" and now concentrate on the three distinct categories, "Shield Tailoring", "Shield Casual" and "Duffer Sportswear" For such a big label, this is a small sized flagship. Set on two floors, the changing rooms are okay and service is friendly and laid back especially on a Sunday afternoon.

Noted for their 1950's comic imagery on T-shirts, also prominent are the Duffer logoed T's. Good jackets, sweatshirts, reversible hoodies and windcheaters are nicely displayed. Conservative shirts, narrow ties and striped knitwear are also available and we liked the hooped cotton t-shirt at £40 that had a great feel when I tried it on. Has a small collection of women's as well. Stocked at Urban Outfitters and Debenhams.

Fenchurch
36 Earlham Street,
London WC2H 9LH
Tel: 020 7240 1880
www.fenchurch.com

Wow factor: 🏠🏠🏠
Choice: 🏠🏠🏠
Service: 🏠🏠🏠🏠
Price: ££

Ethical
Covent Garden LU, 5 min walk
Mon-Sat, 10am-7pm, Sun 12am-6pm
Own Label
Sizes: Women XXS-L; Men: S-XXL

Original designs and graphic signature prints meets organic fairtrade with a big following amongst eco-fashionistas. The ethical element is not overtly apparent within the shop but there is a reassuring ethical ethos permeating through the company. Urban in décor, brick walls, wooden floor the place has a good on-trend feel and adequate changing rooms with mirrors and very good, friendly, chatty service.

On Women's: Bijou collection of T-shirt and T-shirt dresses with small patterned print designs, V-neck jumpers around £38 and a tasty selection of hoods and sweats.

On Men's: Liked the striped shirts with large contrasting coloured embroidery across the back of shoulders at £40 reduced to £28 in sale and also the floral print shirts. Fenchurch fans have lots to choose from with many items having their logo of which some logos are made in heavy metal. Check their detailed denims, hoods, sweats and belts.

Fifi Wilson
38 Monmouth Street,
London WC2H 9EP
Tel: 020 7240 2121
www.fifiwilson.co.uk

Wow factor: 🏠🏠🏠
Choice: 🏠🏠🏠
Service: 🏠🏠🏠🏠
Price: ££

Cool
Covent Garden LU, 1 min walk
Mon-Sun 9.30am-9.30pm, except Thurs, 9.30am-10.30pm
and Sun, 12am-6pm
Own Label

Have a try-on fest in one of the most yummilious changing rooms in London. This cup cake of a shop comes in sugar pink and white whose large boudoir chic changing room is adorned with pretty sequined hearts on the wall and two rather nice angled mirrors. For a door stop, take the satin stuffed toy duck and place in front of the door.

With a carefully compiled designer mix encompassing Biba, Manoush, Cacherel, Laundry Industry and Sonia by Sonia Rykiel, this boutique is a major hit with Covent Garden locals and those working in theatreland. Tried on a pure silk dress that was amazing value at £60. Large bags in Chinese silk are also tempting as is the jewellery and appealing lingerie. Service is amiable and very good.

Also at 51 Abbeville Road, Clapham, London SW4
Tel 0208 675 7775
Mon-Sun, 10am-6pm

1 Godfrey Street, Chelsea Green, London SW3
Tel 0207 352 3232
Mon-Sat,10am-6pm, Sun 12pm-5pm (only in the summer months)

Koh Samui
65-67 Covent Garden
London WC2H 9DG
tel: 020 7240 4280
www.kohsamui.co.uk

!) Must Visit

Classic
Covent Garden LU, 10 min walk
Mon-Sat, 10am-6.30pm,
except Tue, Wed, Fri, 10.30am-6.30pm, Thur 10.30am-7pm
Sun 11.30am -6pm
Designer Mix
Sizes: Women: varies

One of London's prettiest boutiques themed around shells, pearls, butterflies, sequins, feathers and beautiful embroideries. Service is friendly, frequented by film and pop stars and a popular haunt for fashion editors inspired by the one-off big name and upcoming designer items as well as and the 1920-40's period pieces.

Top 200

Unconditional
16 Monmouth Street,
London WC2H 9LH
tel: 020 7836 6931
www.unconditional.uk.com

Wow factor: 🛍🛍🛍🛍
Choice: 🛍🛍🛍
Service: 🛍🛍🛍🛍🛍
Price: £££

!) Designer Run**Boutique**

Glam
Covent Garden LU & Leicester Square LU, 5 min walk
Mon-Sat, 11am-7pm,except Thurs, 11am-8pm and Sun, 12am-6pm
Designer mix & own label
Sizes: Women's XS-XL; Men's XS-XL

English eccentricity meets rock. Striking windows magnetically pull you in. Opened in July 2008 on the former B&O site, the Bladerunner designed décor mixes traditional with contemporary looks. With men's at the front, it's a fierce mix of hard edge urban and eveningwear oozing with class. Quirky mounted rabbits head with antlers adorn the walls upstairs in the women's section and arranged around the place are grey velvet armchairs and sofas.

On Women's: Imaginative are the mustard wrap dresses, black leather coats, black and white skirts, red and white striped dresses. They were quite honest when tried on an A-line skirt that it didn't quite fit me right but as I was served by their catwalk shows stylist, I was shown several great possibilities from around the shop. Changing rooms are luxurious in grey and white although the armchair in the middle does take up rather a lot of the space.

On Men's: Deconstructed shapes always full of surprises. Think Jude Law styling with bold signature statement clothes. Well sculptured white shirts with original cuts and details are worth checking out as are the coats and very high collared leather jackets.

London designer Philip Stevens started in 1996 with menswear and has now extended to womenswear. The A-list clientele include Will Young, Skin, Tori Amos, Kasabian and David Bowie. Does have a new season preview evening.

Also available at their sister shop Concrete, 25 Fouberts Place, London W1 Tel 020 7434 4555, Harrods, Selfridges and The Shop at Bluebird (see page (140)

Pop
5 Monmouth Street,
London WC2H 9LH
Tel: 020 7497 5262
www.pop-boutique.com

! **Must**Visit

Vintage, retro
Covent Garden & Leicester Square LU, 5 min walk
Mon-Sat 11am-7pm, Sun 1pm-6pm
Sizes: Women's: varies; Men's: varies

Frenzy of printed dresses, stripes, spots and flowers in every colour combination. Pop's own-label dresses are around £20 the rest are all vintage. The wooden rails are crammed with clothes. Also at the Vintage Clothing at Top Shop, Oxford Circus.

The Loft
35 Monmouth Street,
London WC2H 9DD
Tel: 020 7240 3807
www.the-loft.co.uk

! **Must**Visit

Vintage
Tottenham Court Road or Covent Garden LU, 7 min walk
Mon-Sat, 10am-6pm, Thurs, 10am-7pm
Own label
Sizes: Varies

Many celebrities come to buy and sell clothes at this packed store a stone's throw from Seven Dials. Vivienne Westwood, Paul Smith, Jimmy Choo, Prada, Gucci. Clothes are about one-third of the original price.

Poste Mistress

63 Monmouth Street,
London WC2
tel: 020 7379 4040
www.postmistress.co.uk

⚠ Must Visit

Cool
Leicester Square LU, 5 min walk
Mon-Sat, 10am-7pm, Thurs, 10am-8pm, Sun 11.30am-6pm
Own label and designer Mix
Sizes: Women shoes 3-8

Women's mirror image of the Poste men's shoe shop,. Here in addition to their excellent own label the designer line up includes Alexander McQueen, Vivienne Westwood, Dries Van Noten, Emporio Armani, and new labels such Finsk and Rae John. No wonder big celebrity name clientele shop here.

Top 200

Stephen Jones

36 Great Queen Street
Covent Garden
London WC2B 5AA
tel: 020 7242 0770
www.stephenjonesmillinery.com

Wow factor: ⛶⛶⛶⛶
Choice: ⛶⛶⛶
Service: ⛶⛶⛶⛶⛶
Price: £££££

Cool
Holborn, Covent Garden LU, 5 min walk
Tues-Fri 11am-6pm,Thurs, 11am-7pm
Own label
Sizes: Women varies, Men's varies

Set in a Georgian townhouse, it consists of a small hat boutique, design studio and workroom. Inside the décor is a subtle pretty lilac with a couple of classic dressing tables and a small sofa. The majority of the shop is women's all of which are quite beautiful and proudly displayed and at the rear is one of Jones's signature small whimsical ladies cocktail top hats. On the right, as you enter are a fascinating collection of men's hats with a unisex bias. Inspiration comes from clubbers, flower girls around Covent Garden and attracts a celebrity clientele of Pink, Beyoncé Knowles, Gwen Stephani and Alison Goldfrapp. Stephen Jones's creations are also in the permanent exhibition at the V&A Museum in South Kensington.

On Women's: Stephen Jones produces remarkable millinery creations and for model millinery, prices start from about £500 and a minimum of three weeks to make. Materials and straws can be dyed to match your outfits. The Miss Jones diffusion line collection are from £95 whilst a capsule diffusion for men's also kicks in at the same price point. Alice bands are £180-£330. A scarves range are by Alps Kamura.

On Men's: More Boy George than Daniel Craig, it has a fine array of witty knitted bus caps, beanies and trilby variants. I tried on a unique designed felt black trilby-style hat called Wild Street and good value at £330 from his "Jonesboy" range that fitted perfect and had a novel resin crystal on a chain that hung in front of my eye. Whilst very interesting this wasn't exactly for me. Other shapes were presented also, such as a unisex orange wide brimmed hat for £275, a style made for Madonna and some unfinished ones in suede felt that could be made up for me in a few days. Stephen Jones hats always have a creative twist   Overall the service is charming, extremely knowledgeable and an enjoyable experience.

JermynStreet

This famous street is home to some of most renowned shirtmakers in the world. Established in 1885, Turnbull & Asser is the one to head for. Possibly one of the best kept fashion secrets in London is waistcoat makers, Andy and Tuly in Princes Arcade. For men's hatters you'll spoilt for choice between Bates in Jermyn Street and Lock and Co a short stroll away in St James's Street.

Andy and Tuly

12 Princes Arcade,
Jermyn Street
London SW1
tel: 020 7494 3259

Wow factor: ♙♙♙♙♙
Choice: ♙♙♙♙♙
Service: ♙♙♙♙♙
Price: £££

(!) DesignerRunBoutique

Classic, specialist
Piccadilly Circus LU, 5 min walk
Mon-Sat, 10am-7pm
Own label
Ready to wear and bespoke
Sizes: Men's: S-L

Greatest waistcoat shop in London with fantastic cuff link selection. Set a stone's throw from Fortnum and Mason along an opulent shopping arcade, this husband and wife run bijou Aladdin's cave is packed to the rafters with mouthwatering waistcoats from the exquisitely embroidered (£250) to conservative plain silks (£125).

For something uniquely flashy, I bought my own material from Soho Silk (tel 020 7434 3305) that cost £21 and tailor Andy measured me up and turned the whole thing around in 24 hours with their express service for just £100 - a bargain for a bespoke waistcoat! Service was courteous and efficient and it fitted great. Andy even handed me back half the unused material that he said was enough for another waistcoat and made me a matching hanky for £5 – now how's that for honesty. Andy and Tully also stock and make special occasion brocade Nehru jacket and a small selection of ties.

Bates

21a Jermyn Street
London W1
tel: 020 7734 2722
www.bates-hats.co.uk

(!)MustVisit

Classic
Piccadilly LU, 5 min walk
Mon-Fri, 9am-5.15pm, Sat, 9.30am-4pm
Own label
Sizes: Men: 34-48

You may feel you've been through a time portal inside this highly revered gentlemen's hatters crammed full with shelves with anything from wool tweed flat caps, soft felt racing hats, trilby's, homburgs and Panama's, to top hats and plaited straw boaters all of which are of the finest quality.

As soon as you enter, you'll be asked what style and colour you want and in no quicker time than you can say black fedora you will be tape measured up and the said item arranged upon your head. The wide brimmed one I tried felt excellent and at £149.50 represented good value although when I asked if there were any others in my size, one for £112 was produced that was also very good but not quite as superb a fit. Whilst traditional hats such as The Deerstalker may have an rarified appeal to country gentry, fashion lovers still flock to Bates for its clear authenticity. Service is quick, efficient and formal and with it's old world atmosphere, historical military hats on display, those wanting their hat buying experience with a whimsical sense of history, Bates offers great value.

 Top 200

Lock & Co

6 St James's Street,
London SW1A 1EF
tel: 020 7930 8874
www.lockhatters.co.uk

Wow factor: ⌂⌂⌂⌂⌂
Choice: ⌂⌂⌂⌂⌂
Service: ⌂⌂⌂⌂⌂
Price: £££££

Classic
Green Park LU, 8 min walk
Mon-Fri, 9am-5.30pm, Sat, 9.30am-5pm
Own label
Sizes: Men's hats: 6¾-7¾;
Women's ready to wear and fitting service available

Hat history prevails on this 1676 family owned heritage townhouse shop that's a class act whilst deeply conservative in attitude continues to be forward looking. On the ground floor a plethora of hat storage boxes and fascinating silk plush top hats (renovated £1500), Panamas and folding trilby's for holidays. I tried on a navy Fedora £190 that felt excellent. The smaller brimmed Snapbrims at £150 have a more modern twist and proving popular with guys in film, television and art. Further in, if you are to be measured up for a top hat, bowler or riding hat, is an area where they place the Conformateur, a metal measuring device that records the configuration of your head. A small white card is inserted in the machine and the heavy device placed on your head. It feels a little uncomfortable

but in a few seconds it is removed and a pin-hole pattern outline of your head is produced that forms the basis of your personalised hat pattern. On the wall proudly displayed are patterns of Laurence Olivier, Cecil Beaton and many others. At the back of the shop are a massive selection of tweed caps, wool and various riding headwear. Worth looking at near the wooden banisters at the shop's rear is Lord Nelson's cocked hat that Lock had designed in 1805.

Upstairs are well-displayed couture and ready- to-wear millinery collections by Sylvia Fletcher. Advice on style are given by a team of advisors or on certain days by Sylvia herself. A ready- to-wear Flower Beret at £245 looks perfectly charming and good value whilst fascinators are elegant (but a tad expensive) at £285 Couture starts at £420 and is a popular resource for Royal Ascot goers.

Top 200

Turnbull & Asser
71-72 Jermyn Street,
London W1
tel: 020 7808 3000
website http://80.168.52.54/index.html

Wow factor: ⌂⌂⌂⌂
Choice: ⌂⌂⌂⌂⌂
Service: ⌂⌂⌂⌂⌂
Price: £££££

Classic
Green Park LU, 5 min walk
Mon-Sat, 10am-6pm, Thurs, 10am-7pm
Own label
Sizes: Men: shirts 15-18, knitwear S-XXL

Established in 1885, Turnbull & Asser are by appointment to H.R.H. The Prince Of Wales Shirtmakers and one of the most famous shirts labels in the world. Full of British traditional style the shop has a luxuriously wooden interior. Shirts and ties are on the ground floor whilst downstairs there are lots of rooms with suits, blazers, trousers and a picture of James Bond wearing a Turnbull & Asser dinner shirt and bow tie.

All the ready to wear and bespoke shirts are manufactured in the UK. Ready to wear shirts are about £115 and the red Bengal stripe in poplin feels great. Turnbull & Asser's are always excellent to wear and the stripey ones are legendary. The bespoke service in Bury Street offers a thousand shirt fabrics to choose from.

Whilst the image here is very conservative there has been a revived interest in their brightly coloured selection of smoking jackets that can be dressed down with casual trousers or worn with skinny jeans. I tried on a velvet smoking jacket for around £800 and found the service splendidly informative and congenial.

Concessions are also in Harrods and in the City at 125 Old Broad Street.

City

The two key fashion shopping areas in the City are around Bank and Liverpool Street.

A short walk from Bank underground station along Treadneedle Street is the upscale and beautiful Royal Exchange with many famous names including Louis Vuitton, Gucci, Lulu Guinness, Karen Millen, L.K.Bennett and Agent Provocateur. At the Courtyard, Royal Exchange is Paul Smith and Prada and a little further away is Principles at 38 The Poultry, Reiss in Leadenhall Market and Ted Baker & Friends in Cheapside.

By Liverpool Street underground and British Rail is the Broadgate shopping area with Monsoon in the Octagon Arcade, Broadgate Circus; Reiss at Unit 28, Broadgate and a short walk away for shirts is Turnbull and Asser in Old Broad Street, for men's shoes is Oliver Sweeney in Middlesex Street and for womenswear Whistles in Brushfield Street.

These shops, many of them part of chains are reviewed elsewhere in the book and are in the Fashion Fabulous London Top 200. In addition reviews for Bread & Honey, Joy and Blaak are given below.

Bread & Honey
205 Whitecross Street,
London EC1
tel: 020 7253 4455
www.backin10minutes.com

Wow factor: ⌂⌂⌂
Choice: ⌂⌂⌂
Service: ⌂⌂⌂⌂
Price: ££

Urban
Old Street LU, 5 min walk
Mon-Fri, 10am-6.30pm, except Thurs, 10am-7pm and Sat 11am-6pm
Designer mix
Sizes: Women XS-L; Men: Small-XL

Devoted to the hip Hoxton/Shoreditch current look, this market street situated boutique will enhance your cred with its excellent streetwear edit. Service here is friendly, chatty and style-informative and we can vouch that they don't try to sell clothes that are unsuitable.

Art on wall is for sale, and there are two changing rooms for women, two for men. The one I used had graffiti in the men's changing room, a hat stand for putting clothes on, a not so good mirror and a big carton painting and a seat outside for a companion.

On Women's: Of note are Laura Lees label, embroidered tops, dresses and pieces with signature florals and skulls. Also worth a peruse are People's Market knitwear £65, T-shirts, dresses at £50 and an assortment of accessories.

On Men's: Has a combination of evening casualwear and off–the-football- terrace look T-shirts with a good line in 100% Shetland wool sweaters, striped shorts £50 and shirts at £70. Lee Jeans, Stussy designer trousers, shoes, baseball caps, scarves and belts are also worth a look.

Top 200

Joy
5 Paternoster Row
London EC4
tel: 020 7489 7123
www.joythestore.com

Wow factor: ⌂⌂⌂
Choice: ⌂⌂⌂⌂
Service: ⌂⌂⌂
Price: £

Cool
St Paul's LU, 3 min walk
Mon-Fri, 8am-7pm, Sat 11am-5pm
Designer mix and own label
Sizes: Women 8-14; Men: S-XL

For review of this chain see page (224)

Also at Bankside, Brixton, Brunswick Centre, Clapham Junction, Chiswick, Fulham, Greenwich and Putney.

Blaak
The Old Curiosity Shop
13-14 Portsmouth Street
London WC2A 2ES
tel: 020 7405 9891
www.blaak.co.uk

Wow factor: 🛍🛍🛍🛍
Choice: 🛍🛍🛍
Service: 🛍🛍🛍🛍🛍
Price: ££££

Edgy
Holborn LU, 5 min walk
Tue-Sat, 11am-7pm
Own label
Sizes: Men's: 46-50, shoes 40-44

Cultures clash at this Charles Dickens Old Curiosity Shop with real individuality super cool edgy designs. The small quirky asymmetric room is full of historical character, deep dark green with wooden floors and beams and an enormous gold cord style framed mirror. The service here is most definitely not Victorian but global fashion savvy.

Black trousers with a mix of wool and large areas of satin looked really amazing and cost £335. Unfortunately they were too small around the waist for me and they weren't getting any more in that size. Being a small shop availability of sizes may be problem sometimes. The one changing room also dark green was an irregular shaped room with furry style flooring. Also of note are the jackets £750 and shirts from £200-£500. Accessories include sunglasses by Oliver Goldsmith, large bags and belts made in black pony at £150. Exaggerated square toe shoes come from the atelier straight upstairs made by Daita Kimura. Intriguing.

WEST LONDON

Belgravia

One of the wealthiest areas in London, the two key fashion areas are around Pont Street and Elizabeth Street featuring the shop of the most famous milliner in the world, Philip Treacy. Nearby is designer Ben de Lisi and jewellery design boutique, Erickson Beamon. Pont Street includes superb fashions at Allegra Hicks, designer-run boutique Liza Bruce and Anya Hindmarch all in very close proximity to Sloane Street and Knightsbridge.

Agent Provocateur
16 Pont Street,
London SW1
tel: 020 7235 0229
www.agentprovocateur.com

Wow factor: 🏠🏠🏠🏠
Choice: 🏠🏠🏠🏠
Service: 🏠🏠🏠🏠🏠
Price: ££££

> Glam
> Knightsbridge LU, 10 min walk
> Mon-Sat, 10am-6pm
> Own label
> Sizes: Bras 32a-36F, some 38B-D; Shoes 36-41

This is the Belgravian socially acceptable face of smouldering risqué fashion. Some last bastions of the British Empire may frown as they pass the broad window display of sexy lingerie but our impression was that it was very much a beehive of activity for Sloane socialite women and gentleman busily browsing. Indeed, whilst there, a man was buying long red gloves "for my wife" he said whilst another bought fishnet stockings. Attractive sales assistants in pink overalls, black stockings and high heels were efficient. Service is discreet and attentive with customers put at ease.

Bras and lingerie are quite expensive for what you are getting. Still, there seems some cachet to sashay along Pont Street with their famous Agent Provocateur shopping bags. Around the shop are also various sex toy paraphernalia and special event evenings are also held.

I tried on a black lace kimono with separate tie belt at £370. The changing rooms are geisha chic and quite luxurious. Signature candy pink and black lingerie as well as usual black, red and leopard print seductives are available. Clientele include Kate Moss and Peaches Geldof.

Allegra Hicks
28 Cadogan Place
London SW1
tel: 020 7235 8989
www.allegrahicks.com

Wow factor: 🏠🏠🏠🏠
Choice: 🏠🏠🏠🏠
Service: 🏠🏠🏠🏠🏠
Price: £££££

> Glam
> Knightsbridge or Sloane Square LU, 5 min walk
> Mon-Sat, 10am-6pm
> Own label
> Sizes: Women 6-14

Queen of Kaftans with amazing prints from textile designer Allegra Hicks. Cruise liner collections with great selection of kaftan beachwear but you don't have to be sauntering off to sunny climes to wear her clothes. There's lots of eveningwear, tea dresses and casualwear. The store has two floors of clothing with house interiors. Leafy carpets, butterfly pictures and a comfortable sofa. The changing rooms here that have her big logo design on the door and are amongst the most luxurious in London.

The Allegra Hicks Teardrop logo, delicate abstracts and graphic print designs tastefully embellish beautifully dresses and scarves in varied colours such as her silk jersey turquoise dress at £395. Colour palettes focus on pinks, turquoise, coral and lemon as well as timeless neutrals with some of the prints almost having a 3D effect. I tried an ivory woolen coat with beaded buttons £575 and received friendly, helpful but not pushy service with a good stock knowledge. Especially worth a look are the classic evening dresses, handbags, jewellery sunglasses and shoes.

 Top 200

Anya Hindmarch
15-17 Pont Street,
London SW1
tel: 020 7838 9177
www.anyahindmarch.com

Wow factor: 🏠🏠🏠🏠
Choice: 🏠🏠🏠🏠🏠
Service: 🏠🏠🏠🏠
Price: ££-££££

Classic
Sloane Square LU, 5 min walk, Bus 137 or 22
Mon-Sat, 10am-6pm, Wed, 10am-7pm
Own label

Anya Hindmarch is one of the most famous designers of personalised handbags. Whether you want your picture or a favourite pet on a bag this is the place to come. Taking eight to ten weeks and starting from £115 up to £195 there are a variety of quality bag shapes to choose from.

On the ready to wear bags there are many 70's inspired shapes including Silver and Gold Disco clutch at £260, bigger clutches £695, Cobalt Blue totes £595, and the more neutral brown and beige mixes such as the Perry bag, £695. Less expensive is their logo purse at £75. On display too are cashmeres and a small shoe collection.

The outside of the shop has black framed windows giving a serious classic impression. Inside it's light and airy with charmingly helpful staff. Anya Hindmarch has a strong celebrity following including Thandi Newton, Jordon Dunn, Reese Wetherspoon and Claudia Schiffer. Samples sale events are held that you pre-register for.

Also at 63 Ledbury Road,, Notting Hill W11, 118 New Bond Street, 157 Sloane Street, Harvey Nichols and Harrods.

Augustina
11 West Halkin Street,
London SW1X 85L
tel: 020 7823 1188
www.augustinaboutiques.com

!Must Visit

> Glam, cool
> Knightsbridge LU, 10 min walk
> Mon-Sat, 10am-6pm,
> Designer mix

It is always good to see fresh new names on display. This small jewellery boutique is packed with fifteen capsule collections from relatively unknowns to the London scene. Only three pieces of any one style are stocked and in addition there's Augustina's own jewellery collection of 18ct gold, silver, gold plate charms, horses and unicorns. Handbags from about £250 and shoes are at the back.

Ben de Lisi
40 Elizabeth Street,
London SW1W 9NZ
tel: 020 7730 2994
www.bendelisi.com

!Must Visit

> Glam
> Victoria LU and BR, 7 min walk
> Mon-Fri, 10am-6pm
> Own label
> Sizes: Women 8-16

Bargain seekers will be pleased to see their window sign "We now have a permanent sale section at the rear of the shop. Includes a selection of press samples and prototypes in various colours from £50-£200". Whilst a bit of an unruly workroom at the back, there are indeed some great finds including signature long beaded dresses.

A white shop with a couple of mannequins in the window, surprisingly unlike the vivacious designer's TV personality, the shop is fairly subdued in atmosphere. Of note is that the evening dresses can be made up to size and colour for the same price of around £550 in six to eight weeks.

Erickson Beamon
38 Elizabeth Street,
London W1
tel: 020 7259 0202
www.ericksonbeamon.com

!Must Visit

> Glam,
> Victoria LU BR, 5 min walk
> Mon-Fri, 10am-6pm, Sat 11am-5pm
> Own label

Small shop with inviting window, elaborate intricate jewellery draws you in to see the rest of the collection. Large double hooped earrings with graduated pearls, crystal hearts, oversize pearl necklaces and a good choice of Edwardian- style chokers.

Top 200

Liza Bruce

9 Pont Street,
London SW1
Tel: 020 7235 8423
www.lizabruce.com

Wow factor: 🏠🏠🏠🏠
Choice: 🏠🏠🏠🏠🏠
Service: 🏠🏠🏠🏠
Price: ££££

① DesignerRunBoutique

Glam
Knightsbridge LU, 10 min walk
Mon-Sat, 10am-6pm
Own label

Desert island dreamin', Liza Bruce's boutique is a swimwear, cruisewear paradise for the well-moneyed Belgravia set and her visiting fans from all over the world. Rails upon rails of tightly packed exemplary kaftans in every colour imaginable all mostly beaded enchantedly. Beautiful fabrics, with terrific selection of swimsuits albeit smaller than one might expect and notable in gold and animal prints from around £280, bikinis £220. A celebrated designer from the '80's for swimwear Bruce was at the forefront of lycra-driven fashion and continues to innovate still today. A true London fashion designer hero.

I tried on a pink and gold mini kimono with delectable voluminous sleeves at £425. These come in one size as they tie round. The changing room is a cluster of exotic rugs, accoutrements and hanging lanterns that are visible in the mirror to help create a perfect image of you on your exotic holiday location. Bruce's jewellery are large bold ethnic colourful pieces from £1000-£5000 that are worth a look. Bags and sunhats complete the luxurious wish you were here look. Service is congenial with first class stock knowledge.

Lotus London Boutique

11 Pont Street
London SW1X 9EH
Tel: 020 7235 3550

① MustVisit

Classic
Knightsbridge LU, or Sloane Square LU 10 min walk
Mon-Sat, 10am-6.30pm
Own label and ready to wear

This pretty pink signed picture postcard of a shop has inviting cabinets of jewellery, rails with beaded kaftans at £236, elastic topped dresses in chiffon and some more expensive printed ones. Attracts a clientele that includes Donna Air, Kelly Brooke and Danni Minogue. Downstairs has more rails of styles in different colours and fabrics of their own label plus some Paul and Joe.

Service is very friendly and helpful. I tried a turquoise printed chiffon dress, £81, that you can alter to become a skirt. I was shown to a large changing room with a dressing table that had two mini hot water bottles and flowers on the seat. After a few minutes an assistant came down to see how I was getting on. They showed me more pieces that they thought I might like. It's a place I would be quite happy to return to. Supports fairtrade and local community initiatives.

Top 200

Philip Treacy
69 Elizabeth Street,
London W1
tel: 020 7738 8080
www.philiptreacy.co.uk

Wow factor: ♦♦♦♦♦
Choice: ♦♦♦♦♦
Service: ♦♦♦♦♦
Price: £££££

Glam
Victoria LU BR, 7 min walk
Mon-Sat, 10am-6pm, Sat, 11am-5pm
Own label
Sizes: Made to fit

For the world's most famous milliner, this flagship shop is surprisingly quite narrow and small. Of course the hats on display are sensational and as you ask to see more, they pull on the gold walled panelling to reveal drawers of further beautiful designs. Service is good and keen and it's not long before you're trying on and being measured up as it's more couture here than ready to wear with men's taking a week and women's a month. At Philip Treacy's they will amalgamate their existing styles with your own ideas but won't compromise their reputation with unusually bizarre requests. Hats here are expensive and continue upwards.

On Women's: Amongst the designs are felt with small asymmetric brim and tall crowns. Also sinamays with beautiful labour intensive flowers, feathers, and wedding hats. Grace Jones, Camilla Duchess of Cornwall are regular wearers and if you do get to meet Treacy himself, you'll find him charming and truly an absolute lover of not just his but beautifully created hats of others too.

On Men's: There's plenty to choose from as you enter the shop such as plain black wide brimmed hats whose stylisation is favoured by Boy George at £400, men's berets at £270 and an array of creative takes on trilby's.

Various capsule collections are at Fortnum & Mason, 181 Piccadilly; Harrods, Fenwick, selected House of Fraser stores, Peter Jones and Selfridges.

SloaneStreet

A remarkable street of two halves. The Knightsbridge end includes Dolce and Gabbana Menswear, Giorgio Armani and Sergio Rossi.

At the Sloane Square end is Maria Grachvogel, Chloé, Paul and Joe and just off Sloane Street in Ellis Street is Lulu Guinness and French Sole.

Chloé

152-153 Sloane Street,
London SW1X 9BX
tel: 020 7823 5348
www.chloe.com

Wow factor: ☐☐☐☐☐
Choice: ☐☐☐☐
Service: ☐☐☐
Price: £££££

> Glam
> Sloane Square LU, 5 min walk
> Mon-Sat, 10am-6pm, Thurs, 10am-7pm
> Own label

Spacious luxurious shop to relax and spend time in. With rails well-spaced out it's easy to see the whole collection with each item shown proudly.

Of note are the lambswool and cashmere beaded coat, several sheepskin inspired pieces, skirt with puffy uneven hem £559, jodhpurs, the small but excellent collection of boots and shoes, jewellery and of course the to-die-for bag collection in wonderful colours and a myriad of shapes. For a smaller spend check out the Chloé bag keyrings. To get changed, go through a heavy beaded curtain into an area with mirrors and several cubicles. These have heavy doors that when shut leave you in an extremely dark place and probably will spook you if you are claustrophobic. That said, it's all rather posh and there's a neat mirror with a tube light at the side, a black leather seat and a rail. Service is fine although staff are a little hard to pin down, especially when they disappear to the stock room downstairs. If there's a long wait, don't worry there's a superb big white sofa in the middle.

Chanel

167-170 Sloane Street,
London SW1X 9QF
tel: 020 7235 6631
www.chanel.com

> Glam, cool
> Knightsbridge LU, 5 min walk
> Mon-Sat, 10am-6pm
> Own label
> Sizes: Women 34-46. shoes 36-41, ballerinas 35½-42

Karl Lagerfeld brings Chanel into the 21st Century but retains the essence of the Coco Chanel design ethos. Splendid shop and expensive.

Also at 26 Old Bond Street W1; 278 Brompton Road SW3, Selfridges and Harrods

Christian Dior
31 Sloane Street
Knightsbridge
London SW1X 9NR
tel: 020 7245 1330
www.dior.com

Wow factor: 🏠🏠🏠🏠🏠
Choice: 🏠🏠🏠🏠
Service: 🏠🏠🏠🏠🏠
Price: £££££

> Glam
> Knightsbridge LU, 5 min walk
> Mon-Sat, 10am-6pm, Wed 10am-7pm
> Own label
> Sizes: Women 34-44, shoes 35-42

Palatial décor with crystal chandeliers, Louis silver velvet chairs and staircase with silver bannister cut like the bark of a tree make this a highly inviting shopping adventure. On the Ground Floor are sumptuous handbags, costume and fine jewellery, sunglasses and a cracking shoe department. Of interest are the black patent court shoes with high heels and platforms at £310. Lined up downstairs are breathtaking red carpet dresses glittering and shimmering. Others showcase less dressy in an array of mouthwatering colours. Staff are extremely helpful and friendly, and the changing room glitzy. I tried on a lilac leather short jacket with three-quarter sleeves and tie neck at £8,450 that felt incredible (and I mean the jacket, not the price). Unfortunately, guys, there's no menswear here - but down the road you'll find plenty of Dior to admire at in Harrods or at Selfridges.

Dolce and Gabbana Menswear
6 Sloane Street,
London SW1
tel: 020 7 201 0146
www.dolcegabbana.com

Wow factor: 🏠🏠🏠🏠
Choice: 🏠🏠🏠🏠🏠
Service: 🏠🏠🏠🏠🏠
Price: £££££

> Glam
> Knightsbridge LU, 3 min walk
> Mon-Sat, 10am-6pm, Wed, 10am-7pm
> Own label
> Sizes: Men: 34-48, shoes 5½-11

It's narcissus central at this shiny black, highly mirrored full on glossy store whose huge black crystal chandelier, grey slate flooring and sharp slick tailoring makes this an exuberant shopping experience. Echoes of welcome greet you from every member as you walk around gazing at the terrific tuxedos, knitwear and a showcase of superb wallets, sunglasses and accessories. Downstairs, there's more jackets, lots of cufflinks, a big selection of eye-catching logoed trainers, sportswear, ties, belts and jumpers. Staff pop out from concealed stock rooms behind the mirrored walls to greet and assist you further. Tried on a jacket (£750). Changing rooms are small but luxurious with three big silver coat hooks and whilst service is fine but a little long winded it was quite good. Trousers are £320; shirts £120.

Fendi
20-22 Sloane Street
London W1
tel: 020 7838 6288
www.fendi.com

!MustVisit

> Glam
> Knightsbridge LU, 5 min walk
> Mon-Sat, 11am-6pm, Wed, 11am-7pm
> Own label
> Sizes: Women 6-14; shoes 35-41

Home to the must-have icon Fendi bag collections, this store is a real luxe treat. Classic but striking clothes and shoes. On men's, this store only has accessories such as bags, wallets and belts. However, men's suits, jackets and trousers are available at nearby Harrods.

 Top 200

French Sole
6 Ellis Street,
London SW1
tel: 020 7730 3771
www.frenchsole.com

Wow factor: ☖☖☖
Choice: ☖☖☖☖☖
Service: ☖☖☖
Price: £££

> Classic
> Sloane Street LU, 5 min walk
> Mon-Sat, 10am-6pm,
> Own label

Extremely busy speciality shop for ballet-style pumps that come in every shape and size and made famous by the late Princess Diana who was a big fan. So busy it has seats outside for overflow. Inside there's shelves of pumps, a mirror with a monkey looking over it, armchairs and stools in mix and match materials.

Founded in 1989 by Jane Winkworth in her basement in Chelsea as a mailorder business, the company now supplies 500 outlets globally. Although semi-retired from the day to day running of the business she still designs all the shoes, packaging, advertising and original artwork for the shops' website (phew!) giving new meaning to the definition of semi-retired.

On show are plain leather pumps £65, quilted £70 and black patent £75 which purchased. Faux animal prints are signature notably leopard, snakeskin, crocodile and lizard and in force are sling backs, satin, glitter with a selection of toes in different shapes.

Be time-rich when visiting as shop is choc full with people waiting to be served and even finding a seat can be a pain. Hardened French Sole customers have developed an assortment of crowded shop tactics for obtaining seats. As I was seated, one huge woman stood straight in front of me and then backed in almost sitting on my lap until I was forced to get up or be crushed! Whilst you are waiting to be served you wonder if the two members of staff even know you are there, but when they say "who's next?" and it's you, you do get good service. Their stock knowledge is comprehensive and they don't mind showing a lot of shoes for you to try. Pumps comes up very small so you'll probably take a size bigger. None of the shoes or display are priced.

Also at their Chelsea store:
323 King's Road,
London SW3 3EP
Tel 020 7351 1634
Mon-Sat 10am-6pm, Sun 11am-4pm

51 Marylebone Lane
London W1U 2PA
Tel 020 7486 0021
Mon-Sat 10-6pm
Sun 12-5 in the Summer

Top 200

Gina

189 Sloane Street
London SW1X 9QR
Tel: 020 7235 2932
www.gina.com

Wow factor: ☆☆☆☆☆
Choice: ☆☆☆☆☆
Service: ☆☆☆☆
Price: £££££

> Glam
> Knightsbridge, 5 min walk
> Mon-Sat, 10am-6pm, Wed 10am-7pm
> Own label
> Sizes: Women: shoes 2-8

If Cinderella had seen these shoes, she would have dumped the glass slippers and gone for their crystal fairytale shoe! For Gina is crystal shoe heaven that make good classic evening shoe investments and are a big hit amongst partygoers. Also signature are the Gina flats of which the handwoven Swarovski golden crystal and black patent leather (£375) is a perfect standout as is strappy crossover four inch high heels at £385. Also there's a generous selection of plain and beaded boots from £535 and good range of perfect clutch evening bags to match.

Couture service is also available that costs an extra £150 and takes 4-8 weeks depending if it is a very crystally style or not. The service reflects the high quality of the shoes and the store counts Charlize Theron and Zara Phillips as their customers.

Also at 9, Bond Street, London W1 (Tel 0207 409 7090)

Giorgio Armani

37 Sloane Street
London SW1X 9LP
Tel: 020 7235 6232
www.armani.com

⓵ Must Visit

> Classic
> Knightsbridge LU, 5 min walk
> Mon-Sat, 10am-6pm, Weds, 10am-7pm
> Own label
> Sizes: Women XS-XL; Men: XS-XXL

Armani's finest designer collections. One of the coolest, ultramodern settings in neutral shades. Red carpet Oscar dresses and slick photogenic men's suits. Sensational and fiercely expensive.

Top 200

Gucci
18 Sloane Street
London SW1X 9NE
tel: 020 7235 6707
www.gucci.com

Wow factor: 🏛🏛🏛🏛🏛
Choice: 🏛🏛🏛🏛🏛
Service: 🏛🏛🏛🏛
Price: £££££

Glam
Knightsbridge LU, 4 min walk
Mon-Sat, 10am-6pm, Wed 10am-7pm
Own label
Sizes: Women 38-48, shoes 34-42; Men: 34-48, shoes 40-45

This famous Italian brand is noted for it's glam shoe designs in neutral colours as well as gold and silver metallics together with signature moccasins. Incredible handbags and head turning dresses in luxurious satins with draped contemporary lines. Tried on a black tailored one button jacket at £820 and received impeccable service. On browsing, expect every staff member to say hello which after the first dozen times gets a bit tedious. Otherwise everything here is top drawer. Class effort. On menswear, too, there is an excellent selection of suits, jackets, and trousers plus a wicked collection of watches.

Lara Bohnic
149F Sloane Street
(Entrance on Sloane Terrace)
London SW1X 9BX
tel: 020 7730 8194
www.larabohinc107.co.uk

❶ Must Visit

Glam, cool
Sloane Square LU, 1 min walk
Mon-Sat, 10am-6pm, Wed 10am-7pm, Sun, 12am-5pm
Own label

Since her debut at London Fashion Week in 1997, Lara Bohnic's bold modernist approach to jewellery has met with great success. Delectable is the 18ct rose gold pendant with black gold plated brass chain, £220 and spectacular is the Luna eclipse necklace £435 and similar themed earrings at £245. Wow !

Lulu Guinness
3 Ellis Street
London SW1X 9AL
tel: 020 7823 4828
www.luluguinness.com

Wow factor: 🌂🌂🌂
Choice: 🌂🌂🌂🌂
Service: 🌂🌂🌂🌂🌂
Price: ££-££££

Glam,
Sloane Street LU, 5 min walk
Mon-Fri, 10am-6pm, Sat 10am-6pm,
Own label

Castles, fans, florist basket flowerpots, a handbag in the shape of a crinoline dress and a miniature shop, these are just a few of the collectable bags at Lulu Guinness.

As you enter, there's the couture collection that includes leather bags as well as the usual signature material ones. Within the couture collection is a range of beautiful frame bags with hidden travel compartments and intricate detailing.

It all started with high glam girly bags that rose to fame with the flowerpot handbag that is a permanent part of the collection. Of the many different collections there are cotton clutches from £95, retro feel handbags, heart-shaped bags with purses to match, laminated canvas with True/ False broken heart motifs on a range from make-up bags to Tote bags. Also does clutches covered in soft black or silver snakeskin, with a pair of silver lips as the clasp.

On service assistants have the patience of angels with regard to help with matching bags with outfits. Fans of Lulu Guinness included Cherie Lunghi, Amanda Burton, Helena Bonham Carter, Liz Hurley and The Duchess of Cornwall. In 2006 Lulu was awarded an OBE for her contribution to British fashion.

Also at Royal Exchange, Threadneedle Street, London EC3V 3LR (Tel 0207 626 6391).

Maria Grachvogel
62 Sloane Street
London SW1X 9BS
tel: 020 7245 9331
www.mariagrachvogel.com

Wow factor: 🌂🌂🌂🌂
Choice: 🌂🌂🌂🌂🌂
Service: 🌂🌂🌂🌂🌂
Price: £££££

Glam
Sloane Square LU, 4 min walk
Mon-Sat, 10am-6pm, Wed 10am-7pm
Own label
Sizes: Women 8-16

For dresses with beautiful fluidity this elegant corner shop exudes styles of classic glam with timeless quality. Modern inside, it's a large airy space with red velvet heart-shaped sofa and armchairs.

The vast selection of long dresses are in a heavy satin, satin back crepe or a lighter satin that won't crease so much. The styles are graceful often with a very low back and sometimes a small train. The cut of the dresses make them flow over the body in a fluid flattering way for less than perfect body shapes.

Trying on a long dress in satin, one discovers they are cut quite small so you may need a size bigger. The assistant was on hand to tell me if it wasn't the correct size or colour and that it could be made to order. She then showed me a colour card of about thirty to choose from taking the £1500 price tag up to £2000. Changing rooms are pretty with a pink velvet curtain, red heart chair with a set of high heels in different sizes so you can see the full look. Excellent service with expertise in fabrics.

Paul and Joe
134 Sloane Street
London SW1X 9AX
tel: 020 7824 8844
www.paulandjoe.com

!MustVisit

Glam, cool
Sloane Square LU, 4 min walk
Mon-Sat, 10am-6pm
Own label
Sizes: Women 6-12, shoes 36-40

White and gold walls have giant metallic flowers with metal ball centres. Paul and Joe specialise in girly stylish clothes for women who want something just a little bit different, good quality and don't mind paying for it.

Also at 39 Ledbury Road, W11, 309 Brompton Road SW3, 38 Marylebone High Street W1. Menswear is also available at 33 Floral Street, Covent Garden and 9 King's Road, SW3.

Top 200

Roberto Cavalli
181/182 Sloane Street
London SW1X 9QP
tel: 020 7823 1879
www.robertocavalli.com

Wow factor: ☆☆☆☆☆
Choice: ☆☆☆
Service: ☆☆☆☆
Price: £££££

Glam
Knightsbridge LU, 5 min walk
Mon-Sat, 10am-6pm, Wed, 10am-7pm
Own label
Sizes: Women 6-14, shoes 36-41; Men 46-56, shoes 41-45

Bring out the animal in you in with Roberto Cavalli's signature animal prints and figure hugging slinky long evening dresses combined with pure glitz and bling. Eye-catching are the bright turquoise jackets, yellow and pink sequins and furs. I tried on a pink 50's style organza skirt at £750 in the large changing room that had an animal print covered stall and matching scarf for women to avoid getting make-up on their clothes. Initially, the service was a bit snooty but the assistant was quite honest that it was too large and needed to be altered. Otherwise it was good. Also stocks shoes, bags, sunglasses and other accessories. Roberto Cavalli's men's collection is relaxed Italian chic with notable black jackets, white suits with very wide trousers and some snazzy swimwear.

Top 200

Roger Vivier

18 Sloane Street
London SW1X 9QR
Tel: 020 7245 8270
www.rogervivier.com

Wow factor: 🌀🌀🌀🌀🌀
Choice: 🌀🌀🌀🌀
Service: 🌀🌀🌀🌀🌀
Price: ££££

Glam
Knightsbridge LU, 4 min walk
Mon-Sat, 10am-6pm, Wed 10am-7pm
Own label
Sizes: Women 34½-42

From the designer name who created the stiletto heel, this small elegant boutique is full of magnificent shoes and has a modern white table in the middle, large pouffes and a giant silver sequin mobile hanging from the ceiling.

Signatures are sculptured heels and buckles. Whilst Vivier passed away in 1998, Bruno Frisoni continues the classic buckle flats tradition made famous by Vivier. The buckled black patent high heels at £420 I tried on were great. On display too are all kinds of handbags, slimline clutchbags, sunglasses and jewellery.

With lots of staff and often three staff serving one customer the service is excellent. The only reservation is that some women may find them a little overly pushy on them getting you to try on shoes.

SloaneStreet

Sergio Rossi
207A Sloane Street
London SW1X 9QX
tel: 020 7811 5950
www.sergiorossi.com

Wow factor: ☐☐☐☐☐
Choice: ☐☐☐☐☐
Service: ☐☐☐
Price: £££££

Glam
Knightsbridge LU, 4 min walk
Mon-Sat, 10am-6pm, Wed, 10am-7pm
Own label
Sizes: Women's: shoes 2-8; Men's: shoes 7-11

Huge selection of mind blowing shoes in this long shop. Edmundo Castillo designs feminine, sexy, classic with a modern edge mostly with very high heels. Amongst the distinguished clientele here are Nathalie Imbruglia, Beyoncé Knowles and Salma Hayek.

On Women's: Tried on a croc court shoe with cut-out at the side £2650. After recovered from the price I still couldn't stand up because the heels were so high. However, there are less vertically challenging choices that I found more preferable Service is variable but on the whole friendly. Great handbags are available i you can wrench yourself away from the fantastic over the knee boots.

On Men's: The small selection features sumptuous brown leather ankle boots with zips, and a fine selection of brogues and moccasins.

Shanghai Tang
6A/B Sloane Street
London SW1X 9LE
tel: 020 7235 8778
www.shanghaitang.com

! Must Visit

Glam
Knightsbridge LU, 5 min walk
Mon-Sat, 10am-7pm, Sun 12am-6pm
Own label
Sizes: Women XS-XL; Men: 34-48

Silk Road meets Chinese contemporary in this big double fronted shop. Inside it' dark brown display units with traditional Chinese décor and lime green curtains On entry, there's the latest season styles whilst at the rear are signature authenti traditional dresses in sumptuous fabrics and colours. Of note is the cashmere with oriental buttons and mandarin collars. Like many shops in Sloane Street, prices are not always easy to find. Service, however, is spot on from the moment you enter and staff give a great deal of facetime. Changing rooms are large with green curtains that draw all the way round and there are some enchanting lantern lights.

On Women's: Shanghai Tang is well worth visiting because it's the only Chinese luxury brand in London. I tried on a purple cashmere jacket with oriental buttons and huge caped sleeves that was lined in vivid blue and gold satin at £550. and i felt good. There's also lots of silk scarves, fan shaped handbags and for something a little more special there's an exquisite Imperial Tailoring Collection that you can order to your size and colour.

On Men's: The Mandarin collar long coats and light grey trousers are quite tasty.

Versace
183-184 Sloane Street
London SW1
tel: 020 7259 5700
www.versace.com

Wow factor: 🛍🛍🛍🛍
Choice: 🛍🛍🛍🛍🛍
Service: 🛍🛍🛍🛍🛍
Price: £££££

SloaneStreet

> Glam
> Knightsbridge LU, 2 min walk
> Mon-Sat, 10am-6pm, Wed, 10am-7pm
> Own label
> Sizes: Women 6-14; Men 34-48

So famous is this thrilling Italian brand that it hardly needs an introduction. The high gloss store itself sports a prominent staircase with a glass banister and as you enter there's a marvellous array of handbags from £1000, jewellery, sunglasses and accessories all shown in colour displays.

On Women's: Despite the place being turned upside down because Versace was having a stock change day, staff were still able to give great service.
Downstairs is the main womenswear collection and shoe section. Glitzy, sexy clothes, indeed. Lots of figure hugging dresses in bold colours with matching strappy high heels shoes. I asked to try on a yellow animal print dress £995 but when the size wasn't available they offered to phone their branch at Harrods. Changing rooms are black and opulent with a white seat. Expect a good welcome and attentive service.

On Men's: High quality leather jackets, longcoats with satin lapels. Suits jackets and trousers in neutral shades with some pastels. Shirts and knitwear sometimes comes with a subtle pattern. Belts and bags are very smart indeed. Also always has a great selection of ties.

Yves St Laurent
171-172 Sloane Street
London SW1X 9NR
tel: 020 7235 6706
www.ysl.com

Wow factor: 🛍🛍🛍🛍🛍
Choice: 🛍🛍🛍🛍🛍
Service: 🛍🛍🛍🛍🛍
Price: £££££

> Glam, cool
> Green Park Tube, 5 min walk
> Mon-Sat, 10am-6pm, Wed 10am-7pm
> Own label
> Sizes: Women 36-46, shoes 35.5-40.5 ; Men: 36-48, shoes 6-11

Legendary name with a well known logo that speaks luxury. Always a good cut, the format follows quite classic shapes in neutral colours but also high octane glamour for evening wear. Deconstructed men's lambswool jackets are about £1000, women's black silk satin wrap dress is around £850.

Knightsbridge

Knightsbridge is home to two of the most famous department stores in the world Harrods and Harvey Nichols both of which have top named designers plus exclusive upcoming names too. Also in this area are highly revered names such as Caroline Charles and Bruce Oldfield as well a superb Emporio Armani.

Bruce Oldfield

27 Beauchamp Place
London SW3
Tel 0207 584 1363
www.bruceoldfield.com

!MustVisit

Classic,
Knightsbridge tube, 5 min walk
Mon–Fri 10am–6pm, Sat 11am-5pm, By Appointment
Own label, couture and ready-to-wear

Made famous by Oldfield's dressing of and friendship with the Late Princess Diana
the shop now makes all it's customers feel like princesses!   Focusing on
classic eveningwear with high glam overtones, feast your eyes on the silver columns, draped silk necklines, suits with long fitted jackets and pencil skirts that really flatter and are timeless. Pick the style you like from the rails then the fabric and
colour. Expect truly expert and personalised service that will lead to a perfect end
result. For standard size ready to wear allow approximately three weeks and £2,500
for a suit. For couture, allow 4-8 weeks and £5,000 with as many as six people work
on a dress. At the end of each season, size 10 samples are available in their sale.

Top 200

Caroline Charles

56 Beauchamp Place,
London SW3 INY
tel: 020 7589 5850
www.carolinecharles.co.uk

Wow factor: 🏠🏠🏠🏠🏠
Choice: 🏠🏠🏠🏠🏠
Service: 🏠🏠🏠🏠🏠
Price: £££££

Classic
Knightsbridge LU, 10 min walk
Mon-Sat, 10am-6pm
Own label
Sizes: Women 8-20

Having celebrated forty-five years in the business, Caroline Charles is one the most revered names on the London fashion scene. The collections, only available in the UK, are on two floors with a rich homely feel with a log fire, wooden tables and her own sketches on the walls. Upstairs the shop is a showrooom where Caroline holds fashion shows when the new season's collection arrives. These take place at 11am and 3pm for valued customers who are served champagne and canapés. However, if you are extremely enthusiastic about the label, telephone ahead and they will do their best to accommodate you.

On show are luxe classics in rich velvets, silks and satins. Take your pick of long fluted jackets, skirts with lengths below the knee, woolen belted jackets at £695 and long velvet coats for £995. Tempting also are the swing coats and chiffon tops. With more requests for larger sizes, this shop now stocks up to size 20, offering great styles for fuller figures. On accessories there are handbags, crystal flower earrings, pearl necklaces, shoes, scarves, hats and belts all to match. A one stop shop for special occasion outfits you can get fitted out from head to toe with something timeless.

We can vouch for their straight as a dye honesty with regard to fittings and suitability. Very good changing rooms are located on the mezzanine. A personal shopper is available by appointment to help you put an outfit together. Kristen Scott-Thomas and Jerry Hall are clientele.

Also at St John's Wood High Street, London NW8.

Emporio Armani
191 Brompton Road
London SW3 1NE
tel: 020 7823 8818
www.emporioarmani.com

Wow factor:
Choice:
Service:
Price:£££££

> Glam, cool
> Knightsbridge LU, 6 min walk
> Mon-Fri, 10am-6pm, Wed, 10am-7pm, Sat 10am-6.30pm,
> Sun, 12am-6pm
> Own label
> Sizes: Women dress 6-18, shoes 2-8; Men Suit: 34-48, shoes 5-12

Expect to be greeted by David Beckham in underwear, a giant photo that is. This large store is minimal in style with a big glass and chrome staircase and exudes a lot of class and best not to be viewed wearing sunglasses as it's a bit dark in places.

On Men's: Menswear is on the ground floor and as you enter, on the right is the underwear section and nearby fine logoed cufflinks and accessories. Suits (£539-£699) with tailored canvassed construction and linen jackets are well worth a look as is the knitwear such as their striped cardigan with hood in blue or grey at £235.

On Women's: The vibe here is younger than the Armani Collezione range and with a more relaxed look. Classic shift and tunic style dresses from £189-£699 make superb investment pieces whilst vintage five pocket slim fit jeans are good value at around £200 that looks great with the Shoe Boot with bow and spike heel at £319. The clothes are very well displayed and service is top drawer. Womenswear is upstairs that leads to the Armani Caffé that's open 10am-6pm, Lunch 12pm-3.30pm, for review see page (266).

Feathers
42 Hans Crescent
London SW1X 0LZ
tel: 020 7589 5803
www.feathersfashion.com

Wow factor:
Choice:
Service:
Price:£££££

> Glam
> Knightsbridge LU, 4 min walk
> Mon-Sat 10am-7pm, Sun, 12am-6pm
> Designer mix
> Sizes: Women dress 8-14

Located in the shadow of Harrods, this highly respected fashion shop offers real alternative to the large Knightsbridge department stores by providing a wonderful personalised service, in a genteel atmosphere with a great label edit that changes each season to keep it fresh.

Highlights include Rick Owen, See Chloé, sunglasses by Cutler and Gross and a small selection of accessories including jewellery, shoes, bags and hats. Tried on a Rick Owen zip jacket that changes it's look when you take the inside zip piece out, so you could say you get two jackets for £1000. Staff are amicable and delighted to let you browse or show you pieces they think you might like. The shop is easy to navigate and see all the collections that are rail displayed by designer.

Jane Norman
59 Brompton Road
London SW3 1DP
tel: 020 7225 3098
www.janenorman.co.uk

(!) Must Visit

> Glam
> Knightsbridge LU, 5 min walk
> Mon-Fri, 10am-8pm, Sat 9.30am-8pm, Sun, 10am-6pm
> Own label

For review of this chain see page (222)

 Top 200

Harrods
87-135 Old Brompton Road,
Knightsbridge
London SW1
tel: 020 7730 1234
www.harrods.com

Wow factor: 🏠🏠🏠🏠🏠
Choice: 🏠🏠🏠🏠🏠
Service: 🏠🏠🏠🏠🏠
Price: £££££

> Glam
> Knightsbridge LU, 4 min walk
> Mon-Sat, 10am-8pm, Sun 12pm-6pm
> Designer mix
> Sizes: Women varies; Men: varies

Harrods is one of the most famous stores in the world. In the side turning plush limousines wait for ambassadors, stars and royalty, whilst on the main high street it bustles with people and there's always a queue of taxis outside. Being on the tourist map, there's always an element of visitors milling around the ground floor for souvenirs. The other floors tend to attract more serious shoppers some of which will spend vast amounts of money here.

This magnificent building houses not just many big names but also labels unavailable in other London stores. Of note is the outstanding shoe department with a separate exclusive darkened shoe lounge designed to showcase the sparkling footwear at their best. The large luxurious lingerie department and vivacious hat section are also worth a visit. On the ground floor there's masses of jewellery and top named handbags.

On Women's: Highlights include Issa dresses such as the tie neck dress at £369 that you can dress up and down and a formidable line-up of John Galliano, Moschino, Velvet, Joseph, Nicole Fahri, Just Cavalli, Moncler and many others.

On Men's: The immense choice includes Paul Smith, Richard James, Etro, Canali, Brioni, Just Cavalli, Turnbull and Asser as well as made to measure from Armani, Dunhill and several others. Has an excellent selection of sleepwear, including Daniel Hanson dressing gowns from £399 to £1249 and a wonderful range of designer ties.

At Harrods, there's in-store events throughout the year and their sales days are renowned. Harrods has been a bit of a stickler for rules and currently there are nine visiting guidelines including no loud singing and a dress code of not wearing anything too revealing.

Harvey Nichols
109-125 Knightsbridge
London SW1X 7RJ
tel: 020 7235 5000
www.harveynichols.com

Wow factor: ☖☖☖☖
Choice: ☖☖☖☖☖
Service: ☖☖☖☖☖
Price: £££££

Glam, cool
Knightsbridge LU, 1 min walk
Mon-Wed 10am-8pm, Thurs-Sat, 10am-9pm,Sun, 12am-6pm
Designer mix
Sizes: Women varies; Men: varies

Luxe department store to visit for the hottest design collections. More often than not you'll see a celebrity and quite possibly royalty. This is a store where customers walk the talk and are generally well dressed. Service is consistently excellent throughout the store and the range of choice at times can be quite superb.

On Women's: On the busy ground floor is a wonderful handbag department, an extensive sunglass selection, jewellery and other accessories. Concessions include Jimmy Choo and Smythsons. Womenswear are on three floors with the 1st floor exhibiting the most prestigious labels plus their refurbished shoe department stocking great names and now some smaller brands for something more individual. Of note are collections by Stella McCartney, Roland Mouret, 7 For All Mankind and Gucci.

On Men's: Menswear casuals are in the basement with more formal collections in the lower basement. Labels include Alexander McQueen, Thom Browne, Bottega Veneta, DSquared2, Acne Jeans and D&G.

Fifth floor restaurant café and bar is a popular meeting point for fashionistas.

King's Road

World famous for it's authentic individual boutiques, the stretch from Beaufort Street to the Fire Station offers Anonymous by Ross + Bute, Austique and not to be missed The Shop at Bluebird. At the Sloane Square end of King's Road there's ethical fashions in Bamford and Sons luxuriously beautiful store, great jeans at Trilogy whilst about half way down King's Road is the superglam CM store and legendary cowboy boot specialist, R.Soles. A short distance away on Fulham Road is London designer Amanda Wakeley's superb boutique.

A La mode
10 Symons St
London SW3 2TJ
Tel 0207 730 7180

(!) Must Visit

Glam
Sloane Square LU, 1 min walk
Mon-Sat, 10am-6pm
Designer mix

A slight detour off the main shopping area, à la mode is a spacious boutique with a strong reputation for a number of rather select collections including Marni. Very expensive, well displayed but a touch snooty.

Top 200

Amanda Wakeley
80 Fulham Road,
London SW3 6HR
tel: 020 7590 9105
www.amandawakeley.com

Wow factor:🏠🏠🏠🏠
Choice:🏠🏠🏠
Service:🏠🏠🏠🏠🏠
Price: ££££

Classic
South Kensington LU, 10 min walk
Mon-Sat, 10am-6pm
Ready to wear
Sizes: Women dress 8-16; shoes: 36-41

Amanda Wakeley is a London designer success story who really understands what women want when it comes to simplicity, easy to wear but striking.

Suits, blazers and short dresses are alongside special occasion outfits in signature slinky satin and silk materials, some delicately beaded. These make a good investment that you can wear again and again. A mix of classic and modernity features in the casual trousers, jumpers and T-shirts. To complete the full look there's accessories, jewellery and strappy high heels and flat shoes.

You have to ring a buzzer to get in and are greeted on entry. Lemon candle fragrances fill the air and the Zen-like décor with a black wooden floor provides a pleasant ambience to the rails of clothes displayed in colour themes. Friendly, knowledgeable, the three staff here will set you straight and an alteration service is available. There are waiting seats for companions outside this good size, well-equipped light green changing room that's just down a couple of steps, Clientele include Scarlett Johanssen, Dita Von Teese, Mischa Barton and Sarah Michelle Gellar. Holds special events other than Sale Days.

Also at Westfield, Village G5 Level.

Anonymous by Ross + Bute
323 Kings Road,
London SW3 5UH
tel: 020 3006 4200
www.anonymousclothing .com

Wow factor: 👠👠👠
Choice: 👠👠👠👠
Service: 👠👠👠👠
Price: ££

Cool
Sloane Square LU,15 min walk or take bus 11, 19, 22, 211 or 319
Mon-Sat, 10am-6.30pm, Sun, 12am-5pm
Own label

If you happen to be having a Bridget Jones moment then go for the signature lace trimmed camisole twinset in great colours that Renee Zwelleger wore in the film. Easy going dresses with A-line skirts, tops and dresses have a lace trim. Long cardigan with frills from waist make a stylish cover-up. London designers Lindy Ross and Serena Bute also create understated rock-chic and are particularly strong on knitwear, t-shirts, jackets and skinny-fit jeans. Shoppers include Sienna Miller, Claudia Schiffer and Alexa Chung.

Like the clothes, the décor is unpretentious with changing rooms sparse, bright with chair, mirror and high hooks. Whilst service is very efficient and on the button with staff quite chatty, you may find yourself drifting into long conversation about home improvements as we did.

Also at 57 Ledbury Road, London W11 2AA. Tel 020 7727 2348.

Austique
330 Kings Road,
London SW3 5UR
tel: 020 7 376 4555
www.austique.co.uk

Wow factor: 👠👠👠👠
Choice: 👠👠👠
Service: 👠👠👠👠
Price: ££

Cool
Sloane Square LU,15 min walk or take bus 11, 19, 22, 211 or 319
Mon-Sat, 10am-7pm, Sun, 12am-5pm
Own label
Sizes: Women clothes 8-12, shoes 36-41

Australian boutique, Austique no longer restricts itself just to Australian pretty feminine apparel, there's also an impressive edit of Boyd dresses, shoes by Thurly, Olivia Morris and Charlotte Olympia. I tried on a military dress at £295 that was perfect. The luxe blue and white boudoir changing room is surrounded by heavy curtain and it was equipped with chair, mirror and hanging hook. Overall the shop that's spread over two floors has a relaxed atmosphere. Great fun are the knickers with your own personalised messages on such as "Date Me" or your name for £85. Service is very helpful and friendly. Liked the place!

Bamford and Sons

The Old Bank,
31, Sloane Square
London SW1
Tel 020 7881 8010
www.bamfordandsons.com

Wow factor: ☐☐☐☐
Choice: ☐☐☐
Service: ☐☐☐☐☐
Price: ££££

Ethical
Sloane Square LU, 1 min walk
Mon-Sat 10am-6pm, open late on Wed to 7pm
Sun 12pm-5pm
Sizes: Women dress 8-16; shoes: 36-41; Men: S-XXL, shoes 8½-11½

Luxurious eco-fashion store of Lord and Lady Bamford spread over four floors packed with clothes and interesting pieces. The ground floor has an abundance of rich kid toys for motor driving enthusiasts and there's lots of motoring references around the store in the vein of Brideshead meets 21st century eco-master-of- the-universe.

On Women's: Traditional English country clothes that won't be out of place in the city. Sophisticated simplicity and understated neutrals in high quality materials, some organic. Smart array of handbags, jewellery, sunglasses, shoes, scarves, hats and belts.

On Men's: Classic men's country clothes with a modern twist. On their organic men's there are excellent quality 100% organic cotton shirts, T-shirts and fine muslin shirts as well as chalky denim jeans, jackets and sweaters. Expensive yes, but when one feels the quality of the organic material and the workmanship it's worth it.

Service for both men and women is reassuredly excellent. Changing rooms are circular cubicles with sliding doors, and well equipped. Enjoy refreshment in the basement where there's a Daylesford organic café.

Other branches are at The Old Workshop, 79 Ledbury Road London W11
Tel 020 7881 8010 Notting Hill Gate LU, (8 min walk) and The Village Store,
32 The High Street, Wimbledon, London SW19. Also concessions in Selfridges, Harrods and Harvey Nichols.

Barbour

23 Sydney Street
King's Road
Chelsea
London SW3 6NR
Tel: 020 7352 5346
www.barbour.com

(!) Must Visit

Classic, countrywear
South Kensington LU, 6 min walk
Mon-Sat, 10am-5.30pm, Sun, 12am-5pm
Own label
Sizes: Women 8-18; Men:S-XXL

Popular small shop with a huge reputation in traditional countrywear amongst townies. Weatherproof clothes can come in very handy and the high quality fabrics give a good look. Wax cotton and waterproof jackets, tweed, woolen jumpers, accessories and flatcaps.

Barbour's other London shop is at 12 Ships Tavern, London EC3. A bigger stock is held at Harrods, and another stockist is the large corner shop, Highlands, at 180 Piccadilly.

Top 200

CM Store
121 Kings Road,
London SW3
tel: 020 7 751 5806

Wow factor: ⬠⬠⬠⬠⬠
Choice: ⬠⬠⬠⬠
Service: ⬠⬠⬠⬠
Price: £££££

Glam
Sloane Square LU, 12 min walk
Mon-Sat, 10am-7pm and Sun, 12am-6pm
Designer mix
Sizes: Women 6-12; Men S-XXL

CM Store or Common Market Store has impressive superglam, funky clubwear that exudes cool flash and dash and counts Russell Crowe, Kylie, Sharon Stone, Chelsea footballers, musicians and various famous boxers as their customers. The set-up is menswear lower ground, with a very small womenswear section on the ground at the rear with Arrogant Cat taking up most of this floor.

On Men's: Had a rock star moment when I tried on a remarkable Jaded by Knight black velvet narrow sleeved jacket with leather lapels and diamante encrusted large skull on the back at £1999. A Faith Conversation black coat with wide lapels was wicked too at an affordable £419 taking into consideration the intricate insignia details on the sleeve. Also of note were the Ed Hardy by Christian Audiger printed T-shirts (Love Dies) and the comprehensive jean range including True Religion. Changing rooms are adequate with mirrored doors.

On Women's: Glitzy T-shirts and jeans. Labels including Jaded by Night, Silver Dagger, Face, True Religion and Antique Jeans. The store's buyers have their finger right on the pulse for the flashiest of luxe global clubgoers. Extremely helpful and friendly service too.

Top 200

Manolo Blahnik
49-51 Old Church Street,
London SW3 5BS
tel: 020 7352 8622
www. manoloblahnik.com

Wow factor: ⬠⬠⬠⬠
Choice: ⬠⬠⬠⬠⬠
Service: ⬠⬠⬠⬠⬠
Price: £££££

Glam
Sloane Square LU, 15 min walk
Mon-Fri, 10am-5.30pm, Sat 10.30am-4.45pm
Own label
Sizes: Women 35½; Men: 7-10½

One of the most famous shoe shops in the world. Right off the mainstream King's Road shopping strip, you can use up good shoe leather finding it. The exterior, partially entwined with branches also has a window layered in mesh wire, presumably for security reasons to protect these footwear gems that are displayed on pedestals. Press the buzzer to be allowed in to what is like a Greek cave adorned with a sky ceiling, a chaise longue and highly distressed décor.

Our server rendered such a polished performance of keen eye contact and total focus absorbed in the quest for the right shoe for you, one could only be impressed. You can walk around the store without being hassled and I was brought styles that he thought I would like to try and told what they could be worn with. It's really almost impossible to leave without a pair of these beautiful and comfortable shoes.

On Women's: Voluptuous shoe boot with chunky straps and sling back in black and bold colours is £565. A black and white shoe with zip-up front costs £600. Great flats are from £450. Heels are high but not ridiculously so.

On Men's: Shoes are priced around £440 and has six styles with more coming up.

Whether you buy or just browse this shop is an exhilarating experience.

 Top 200

R.Soles
109a Kings Road,
London SW3 4PA
Tel: 020 7351 5520
www.r-soles.com

Wow factor: 🏠🏠🏠🏠
Choice: 🏠🏠🏠🏠
Service: 🏠🏠🏠🏠
Price: £££

Urban
Sloane Square LU, 12 min walk
Mon-Sat, 10am-7pm, Sun, 12am-6pm
Own label
Sizes: Women 36-41; Men 35-50

Legendary cowboy boot heaven, guys to the left, gals to the right. Bright coloured crocodiles from pink to light blue for ladies; black winklepicker toe Chelseas curling up for the fellahs The latter are £195 whilst softer pythons cost £275. Has a huge range of styles designed by Judy Rothchild. Bags, belts and buckles are also available..

On the gals, from ankle boots and cowgirl chic to biker boots and tan suede moccasins, it's all here. The booted famous who have shopped here are Rene Zellwegger, Kristen Scott-Thomas, Beckhams and Zara Phillips.

This shop is probably the nearest you will get to cockney in Chelsea. If Doug serves you it's going to be full-on Old School, East End style laugh a minute friendly service. Will fondly tell you when rock idol, Marc Bolan came in. All the staff may come to help you and explain the sizes and how they should be worn.

Trilogy
33 Duke of York Square
London SW3
tel: 020 7730 6515
www.trilogystores.co.uk

(!) Must Visit

> Glam, cool
> Sloane Square, 5 min walk
> Mon-Sat, 10am-7pm, Sun 12pm-6pm
> Designer mix
> Sizes: they'll fit you up great

Jean cognoscenti love this boutique for it's excellent reputation for some of the hottest denims in the Capital. Expertise to match.

Also at 63 Weymouth Street, Marylebone, W1.

Top 200

The Shop at Bluebird
350 Kings Road,
London SW3 5UU
tel: 020 7351 3873
www.theshopatbluebird.com

Wow factor: 🛍🛍🛍🛍🛍
Choice: 🛍🛍🛍🛍🛍
Service: 🛍🛍🛍🛍
Price: ££££

> Glam, cool
> Sloane Square LU,15 min walk or take bus 11,19, 22, 211 or 319
> Mon-Sun, 10am-7pm, except Wed-Thurs, 9am-7pm
> and Sun 12pm-6pm
> Ready to wear
> Sizes: Women varies; Men: varies

King's Road fashion landmark that's entertaining and always has its finger on the pulse. Divided into three sections, this vast space with DJ area uses novel props to generate mood but with the clothes always taking centre stage. Eye-catching are the legs with jeans ascending steps leading to nowhere, the wall of hanging hand bags, the odd-legged table, trough cabinets and the enormous chandelier
as well as an array of mannequins in unusual poses displaying the enticing fashion styles

On Women's: Small collections from lots of labels at different price points from well known such as Aquascutum, See by Chloé, Vanessa Bruno and Sonia Rykiel to new ones including Richard Nicoll, Erdem, Daughters by Obedient Sons and Emma Cook. Around too are lots of jewellery, sunglasses, shoes, hats and belts. Changing room are in a large pale green area with a chandelier, seat, free standing long mirror at an angle to the floor. There's a voluminous seating area outside them and another mirror. Service is laid back and not pro-active. Fashion cognescenti fair best here a style advice is not always so forthcoming.

On Men's: Of note is their on-trend relaxed range of casuals, men's trilby hats and ties. There's a big jeans selection where you know you'll be fitted out terrifically.

Kensington

This is the home of London Fashion Week that takes place twice a year. Kensington High Street is a mixture of well known store names. Two standouts are Tabio for it's sensational selection of socks and tights, and T.K. Maxx for some fantastic bargain off-season designer fashions.

Tabio
161 Kensington High Street
London W8 6SU
Tel: 020 7937 5838
www.tabio.com/uk

① Must Visit

Cool
High Street Kensington LU, 5 min walk
Mon-Sat, 10am-7.30pm, Sun 12pm-6pm
Own label
Sizes: Women UK 5-8; Men: S-L

Cosy shop for cosy feet. Socks in every conceivable colour. On women's from lace to wool, from lace-up "foot covers" to ankle bands, from tights to sparkling lame there's masses to choose from - even socks with shiatsu beads for self massage. Plus there's an awesome sock choice for men. Also at King's Road, SW3, Neal St, WC2, Harrods, Selfridges and Harvey Nichols.

T.K. Maxx
26-40 Kensington High Street
London W8 4PF
tel: 020 7037 8701
www.tkmaxx.com

Wow factor:🛍🛍
Choice:🛍🛍🛍🛍
Service:🛍🛍
Price:££

Glam, cool
High Street Kensington LU, 3 min walk
Mon-Fri, 9am-7pm, Sat 9am-6pm, Sun, 12am-6pm
Designer mix
Sizes: Women varies; Men: varies

For review of this chain see page (238)

NottingHill

Although a few massive Italian clothing companies have moved into Pembridge Road close to the underground this locale is a power house for retro. Our pick of the best are Dolly Diamond especially for their late 60's, Retro Clothing great for vintage men's formal and designer labels and women's top line labels and Maribou for unique designs with retro fabrics.

At the Portobello Green end of P`ortobello Road near the flyover are some very exciting shops including Preen and Boots Boots Boots that opened in August 2008 and further down the road is tremendous designer label vintage shop, One of a Kind. At rough round the edges, Golborne Road, Kokon To Zai has opened their second London shop whilst just around the corner in Portobello Road is ethical rising star From Somewhere. Also on Golborne Road is Rellik, one of the first shops to bring the "New Vintage" onto the scene and a few doors away is The Convenience Store with a wonderful designer edit.

Great names appear on Westbourne Grove and Ledbury Road including Twenty8Twelve, Studio 228, Heidi Klein, J&M Davidson and many more. Further west in Shepherd's Bush is the new mammoth shopping mall Westfield London that definitely merits a visit.

Temperley

6-10 Colville Mews,
Lonsdale Road
London W11
tel: 020 7229 7957
www.temperleylondon.com

Wow factor: ☆☆☆☆☆
Choice: ☆☆☆☆
Service: ☆☆☆☆☆
Price: ££££

Glam
Notting Hill LU, 10 min walk
Mon-Sat, 10am-6pm, except Thurs, 10am-7pm, Sat 11am-6pm
Own label
Sizes: Women 6-16

Pure luxe shopping where you can try on at leisure for that special occasion dress until you get it right. Located down a cobble stoned mews that looks like it leads nowhere the trek is worth the trip. A triple fronted shop with wooden shutters, rugs and different decor in each of the three rooms, it's a vast space of glamorous apparel.

Alice Temperely, a graduate from Central St Martins and the London College of Art, is known for signature special occasion eveningwear, heavily embroidered details and beading in mix of black and pastels. Changing rooms are large and comfortable. Staff exhibit great style expertise and offer drink refreshments in the middle of the shop. Also holds collection Trunk/Preview days and one-off exclusive days including bridal events.

Armand Basi
189 Westbourne Grove,
London W11
Tel: 020 7727 7789
www.armandbasi.com

(!) Must Visit

Classic
Notting Hill LU, 7 min walk
Mon-Fri, 10.30am-6pm, Sat 10am-6pm, Sun, 12am-5pm
Own label

Great quality knitwear, well-made, classics that hang well, a relaxed atmosphere and very friendly service make this an inviting shop stop to return to again and again.

On Women's: Grown-up dressing for day and evening with jackets £290, skirts £110 and a top notch selection of sunglasses, shoes, scarves, hats and, belts.

On Men's: Playing on their knitwear strengths extremely tempting are the thick heavy woolen cardigans and the casual jackets, shirts, ties and trousers in signature greys and neutrals.

Top 200

Cath Kidston
3 Clarendon Cross
London W11 4AP
Tel: 020 7221 4000
www.cathkidston.co.uk

Wow factor: ▯▯▯▯
Choice: ▯▯▯▯
Service: ▯▯
Price: ££

Classic, chain
Holland Park LU, 6 min walk
Mon-Sat, 10am-6pm, Sun, 12am-5pm
Own label
Sizes: Women 8-16

Located in upscale Holland Park, English designer Cath Kidston's store merits a visit for the bags and purses alone. Most are made from oil cloth with signature rose prints, paisleys, spots and a collectable range from keyring, tote, bucket bags and shoppers through to suitcases are available to their ever growing fanbase. Candy coloured, kitsch, bright and addictive, on entering the store, you either love it or hate it.

Floral t-dress £95, comfy wear range of jogger, leggings and ribbed tanks are in khaki and cornflour blue. Big selection of bathrobes and sleepwear. When busy staff cope well but get torn between customers at frantic periods.

Also at Northcote Road, Battersea; Cale St, Chelsea; Chiswick High Road; Shelton Street Covent Garden; Fulham Road, King's Road, Marylebone High Street and Wimbledon High Street. Harvey Nichols and Selfridges in addition have concessions.

Dolly Diamond
51 Pembridge Road
Notting Hill Gate
London W11 3HG
tel: 020 7792 2479

Wow factor: ⬠⬠⬠⬠⬠
Choice: ⬠⬠⬠⬠
Service: ⬠⬠
Price: £-££

Glam, vintage
Notting Hill Gate LU, 5 min walk
Mon-Fri, 10.30am-6.30pm, Sat, 10.30am-6.30pm, Sun, 12am-6pm,
Designer mix
Sizes: Women's: varies; Men's: varies

One of the most presentable vintage shops in London it's a delight to browse their 1930's to 60's vintage. Viewing the stoles high up, jewellery, shoes and hats, this place clearly has a penchant for the fifties woman and even has a changing room with 1950's seating albeit a bit basic.

On Women's: Many of the dresses are made specially for the originals owner of the garments by the many dressmakers of the era. Most women's are special occasion and will give good period glam. Unbranded high quality short beaded dresses are around £120, long dresses £445, a Mr Michael real fur stole is £135 and there's also a choice of faux fur.

On Men's: Key items are the jackets and trousers. A John Collier aubergine wide lapelled jacket, £65, that I tried on was in perfect nick. Kipper ties hanging from the ceiling. Cinderella branded velvet and sequined waistcoats are fab at £15-£25 Good choice of wallets, a 20's top hat £120 and tie-pins £30.

Service is enthusiastic.

Emma Hope

207 Westbourne Grove,
London W11
tel: 020 7313 7493
www.emmahope.co.uk

Wow factor: 🛍🛍🛍
Choice: 🛍🛍🛍
Service: 🛍🛍🛍🛍
Price: ££££

Classic shoes
Notting Hill Gate LU, 7 min walk
Mon-Sat, 10am-6pm, Thurs, 10am-7pm, Sun, 12am-5pm
Own label
Sizes: Women shoes 35-42

This popular corner shop window displays very wearable, sophisticated classics from one of the UK's leading shoe designers. Swing music creates an entertaining ambience to see the shoes displays on two levels that are easy to browse. Great selection of evening shoes, from pumps to medium high heels. Of note is the scrumptious satin/velvet with bow /crystal detail. Expect a warm welcome, informative service and real enthusiasm toward shoes.

Also at 53 Sloane Square SW1 and 33 Amwell St, EC1.

Euforia

51b Lancaster Road
London W11 1QG
tel: 020 77243 1808

❗ DesignerRunBoutique ❗ Mustvisit

Cool
Ladbroke Grove LU, 5 min walk
Mon-Sat, 10.30am-6.30pm, Sun, 12am-5pm
Own label
Sizes: Women S-L

From the moment you enter there's a vibrant feel in this cool white decored Annette Oliveri own-label boutique, pulsating with jazz and Latino rhythms. It's a lot of fun with a kaleidoscope of colours on the rails and exciting use of props, including a funky modern chair and mannequin, a central table with a kitsch selection of arty survival kits, shoe lasts and fashion books.

Tried on a signature digitally printed chiffon skirt, £100, with multicoloured flowers that was pretty, floaty and romantic. Annette Oliveri specialises in digitally printed silks and designs prints for other labels. More sophisticated are the suede jackets, whilst dresses are tempting as are her own label shoes and bags. Service is quite good and helpful whilst changing rooms are fairly spacious with a coloured brick doorstop and fabric printed bananas on the wall. Entertaining.

Boots Boots Boots
282 Portobello Road
London W10 5TE
tel: 0208 962 5625

! Must Visit

Vintage,
Ladbroke Grove LU, 5 min walk
Tues-Thurs, 12pm-6pm, Fri-Sat, 10am-7pm, Sun, 12am-6pm
Designer mix
Sizes: Women varies; Men: varies

Vintage boot heaven including cowboy, stilettos, kitten heels, leather suedes you name it. Boots Boots Boots opened in August 2008 on the former Antique Clothing Company site. 60's to 80's boots and at any given time have a 1000 vintage boots plus a huge display of shoes including Gina, Raynes and Saxones! Amongst the miscellaneous hotch potch around the walls are iconic Tretchiko oriental courtesan lady paintings.

On Women's: Average £40 for boots with shoes starting at £25.

On Men's: Some respectable 50's-80's brown leather brief cases about £40 and lots of 60's airline logoed shoulder bags.

As you walk service in a very enthusiastic Claudia Vispi casually looks (without you noticing) at customers feet and immediately directs them to the appropriate size section. Also has a stall Friday and Saturday in the market in Portobello/ Cambridge Gardens and has a strong local following.

Top 200

From Somewhere
341 Portobello Road
London W10 5SE
tel: 020 8960 9995
www.fromsomewhere.co.uk

Wow factor: ☐☐☐☐
Choice: ☐☐☐
Service: ☐☐☐☐
Price: ££

! Designer Run**Boutique**

Ethical
Ladbroke Grove LU, 7 min walk
Tue-Sat, 10am-6pm
Own label
Sizes: Women XS-XL

There's some real creative thinking going into the design of this shop that is a trailblazer in recycled fashion. You know this from the moment you walk in as stabliser wheels from a kid's bike form the door handle. Whimsical clothes hang from recycled golf clubs, shoes are displayed on half tennis rackets and wooden drawers nailed to the wall. The skirt I tried on was held in place on the hanger with clothes pegs. The hotch potch of fabrics individualises each garment. Dresses range from about £150 to £300 and have a flattering feminine cut.

From Somwhere's Orsola de Castro and Filippo Ricci are also the founders ethical exhibition Estethica at London Fashion Week and are involved in many sustainable fashion projects. Changing rooms have a brown curtain, hook, mirror and child wooden chair. Service is smiling and helpful.

West London

Notting Hill

Heidi Klein
174 Westbourne Grove
London W11 2RW
Tel: 020 7243 5665
www.heidiklein.com

Wow factor: ☐☐☐☐
Choice: ☐☐☐☐☐
Service: ☐☐☐☐☐
Price: £££

Glam, beachwear specialist
Notting Hill LU, 7min walk
Mon-Sat, 10am-6pm, Sun, 12am-5pm
Own label and designer mix
Sizes: Women 1-3, and stock D-G cups

Boutique, reminiscent of five star luxury beach resort hotel shop in feel beautifully fragranced from the moment one enters. Beach-style changing rooms and a beauty spa further add to the Notting Hill-on-sea experience.

On Women's: The Heidi Klein label is a kaleidoscope of shapes, fabrics and gorgeous colours. The great thing about the swimwear is that it is boned and structured to give the most flattering shape and the staff take pains to get the correct fit and optimal contour for each customer. Other brands stocked include Missoni, Anya Hindmarch and Tom Ford and the service is excellent.

On Men's: Has a small section of highly coloured swimming wear.

Also at 257 Pavilion Road, SW1.

J.W. Beeton
48-50 Ledbury Road
London W11 4AJ
Tel: 020 7229 8874

Wow factor: ☐☐
Choice: ☐☐☐☐☐
Service: ☐☐☐
Price: ££

Cool
Westbourne Park LU or Notting Hill LU, 7 min walk
Mon-Fri, 10.30am-6pm, Sat 10-6, Sun, 12am-5pm
Ready to wear, designer mix
Sizes: Women 6-14; Men: M,L but not much small

Popular, busy, quirky boutique in two parts with a great fashion edit of everyday on-trend casuals. Staff may be on mobiles until you get their attention, but thereafter service is good. Their okay changing rooms are downstairs.

On Women's: As you go in check out the Velvet Collection of very wearable jersey tops, often draped. Equally tasty are Full Circle and Unconditional, labels that consistently have attractive collections. Bags, jewellery and shoes are also available.

On Men's: In a separate part are Hartford shirts and merino wool jumpers with V-neck. Tried on a stripey shirt for about £80 that felt a treat. Keep a keen eye on the jumpers here that are a bargain.

J&M Davidson
42 Ledbury Road
London W11
tel: 020 7313 9532
www.jandmdavidson.com

Wow factor:
Choice:
Service:
Price:££££

Classic
Notting Hill Gate LU, 7 min walk
Mon-Sat, 10am-6pm, Sun, 12am-5pm
Own label

London based, husband and wife team John and Monique Davidson, specialise in superb quality leather goods and knitwear. Theirs is a name you can trust for consistency in styles that will endure the test of time. Outstanding are the large handbags and purses of classic simplicity in sumptuously rich tans and rusts. On show too are an excellent of belts with stylish buckles to easily incorporate into your outfits. Polos, twinsets and scarves add a splash of colour to this highly refined shop. There's also a small selection of clothes such as grey and black high waisted square-necked dress with bow detail. Service is excellent and J&M when in the shop are positively charming themselves.

Kokon to Zai
86 Golborne Road,
London W10 5PS
tel: 020 8960 3736
www.kokontozai.co.uk

Wow factor:
Choice:
Service:
Price:££££

Cool
Ladbroke Grove LU, 8 min walk
Mon-Sat, 10am-6pm,
Own label and designer mix
Sizes: Women S-XXL; Men: S,M,L

Supercool destination boutique that's much larger than their sister Greek Street, Soho branch. Looks like an old butcher shop with white marble serving counters, white horned chandelier and two black metal outside tables with bench seating for taking refreshments. Art pieces are featured in the window and there's an old Universal Provider sign above adding to the boutique's décor quirkiness.

On Women's: Featured on the single rail the length of the boutique, are Marjan Pejoski's street style with amazing twist; ostrich feather jacket £1500, black ruffled jacket in organza, Vivienne Westwood Anglomania label and leather corset sculptured belts at £250. On the loor are skyscraper high wedges with ankle strap in grey, available also as a boot.

On Men's: Capsule men's collection including Marjan Pejoski, Raf Simons and several upcoming labels. Of note are the heavy coats and jackets.

Service is right-on and knowledgeable. Intriguingly, the interior of the changing rooms are all mirror, making one feel like being in a lift. The advantage is that you do see all angles of what you are wearing. Clientele include Clare Danes and Ruby Wax.

Also at 57 Greek Street, Soho, London W1, tel 0207 434 1316.

Top 200

Maribou
55 Pembridge Road
London W11 3HG
Tel: 0207 727 1166
www.maribouunique.com

Wow factor:🏠🏠🏠🏠
Choice:🏠🏠🏠
Service:🏠🏠🏠🏠
Price: ££

① DesignerRunBoutique

Bohemian
Notting Hill Gate LU, 5 min walk
Mon-Fri, 11.30am-6pm, Sat-Sun 10am-6pm
Own label
Sizes: Women: All one size

Fabric-led, 60's influenced unique in design at affordable high street chain prices. A lot is made from scarves with the signature item being a black tube top with an assortment of chiffon materials and clashing designs at £65. Great buys are the halter neck maxi dresses put together with silk scarves in amazing designs and fine quality silks, £130, as are the chiffon wrap dresses with beaded details.

The sculpture giant faced counter desk and the wicker mannequins sets a 60's scene. Maribou specialises in using old fabrics such as brocades velvet lace, silk and chiffon, and sometimes combines new and old together. Changing rooms are a simple curtain on a rail going round.

Truly unique items.

Marilyn Moore
7 Elgin Crescent
London W11 2JA
tel: 0207 727 5577
www.marilynmoore.co.uk

Wow factor: ☖☖☖
Choice: ☖☖☖☖
Service: ☖☖☖☖
Price: £££

①DesignerRunBoutique

Classic
Ladbroke Grove LU, 8 min walk
Mon-Sat, 10am-6pm, Sun, 12am-5pm
Own label
Sizes: Women XS-XL

Marilyn Moore's floral tea dresses, signature classic knitwear, good quality jumpers, cardigans and coats conjures a perfect elegant country look. This UK designer has several own labels as well as stocking Cacharel. Tried on ivory a bolero jacket with three quarter sleeves £149, had an adorable woolen texture and the V-neck cardigans at £159 were very likeable. Service is very obliging and staff will spend much time searching out the right garment for you. The changing rooms despite being small are well-equipped. The more casual range is downstairs. Also at 71 White Hart Lane, Barnes, London SW13 APP, tel 0208 878 9973.

Top 200

Nanette Lepore
206 Westbourne Grove
London W11 2RH
tel: 020 7221 8889
www.nanettelepore.com

Wow factor: ☖☖☖☖
Choice: ☖☖☖☖
Service: ☖☖☖
Price: £££

Glam
Notting Hill Gate LU, 7 min walk
Mon-Sun, 10am-6pm
Own label
Sizes: Women 0-8, USA

This American designer brings to London a Hollywood glam décor and an extensive collection of daytime to eveningwear, shift dresses and classic cuts to dress up or down. Short frilly skirts, lots of pencil skirts pair well with her cardigans. Big on spiralling staircases, cool pink oval ceiling mounted lighting, crisp white walls and excellent mirrors, this spacious split level shop is beautiful throughout.

One of a Kind

59 Portobello Road
London W11 1LR
Tel: 020 7792 5853
www.1kind.com

Wow factor: ☆☆☆☆☆
Choice: ☆☆☆☆☆
Service: ☆☆☆☆☆
Price: ££££

Vintage, rare, clothes and accessories
Ladbroke Grove LU, 8 min walk
Mon-Sat, 11am-6pm, Sun, 12am-5pm
Designer mix
Sizes: Women varies; Men: varies

One of the best kept secrets of the London fashion scene is the VIP "Secret Room", an Aladdin's cave of treasured apparel that includes 50's Dior, Westwood and rare great Parisian designers from the 20's. Owner, Jeff Ihenacho has been running One of a Kind since 1996 initially as stall in the market. From the street, once you've rung the bell you enter into a metaphorical laundry basket of amazing vintage fashions. An assistant by the door gives a guide around by decade. Beginning with 80's it's followed by 70's and on the right 50's, as you pass through clothes hanging from high above may drag along your head. Whilst at the back is menswear, at the far rear is Jeff's "Secret Room".

On Women's: Clothes are so tightly packed in it's hard to see the prices, but everything is properly and fairly labeled. For example, a salmon leather YSL jacket at £260 was said to be damaged on the label. Accessories include handbags, jewelery, sunglasses, shoes, scarves, hats and, belts.

On Men's: Georgio Armani black leather jacket at £250 was in very good condition and there's a good selection of 70's mauve long coats and Burberry raincoats, ties as well as Paul Smith trainers at £225.

Service is extremely friendly and the changing rooms are okay. As one happy customer left, the assistant said, "remember me each time you wear it." Jeff Ihenacho styles clients in the clothes if they make an appointment. Clientele include Kate Moss, Sienna Miller, Sadie Frost and Madonna who got her outfits for her 80's style music video and MTV awards.

Paul Smith

Westbourne House
122 Kensington Park Road
London W11 2EP
Tel: 020 7727 3553
www.paulsmith.co.uk

Wow factor: ☆☆☆☆☆
Choice: ☆☆☆☆☆
Service: ☆☆☆☆☆
Price: £££-£££££

Cool
Notting Hill Gate LU, 10 min walk
Mon-Fri, 10am-6pm, Sat, 10.am-6.30pm
Own label
Sizes: Men: suits 36-46in, shirts 15-17½, shoe 40-45(Euro)

Something to marvel at is English designer Paul Smith's country house flagship store with it's fantastic service. This is a place where rooms have names. Stroll around the Holland Room, The Dining Room and enjoy the clothes luxuriously displayed on big ornate frames. On the ground floor, there's a crystal chandelier covered in cobalt blue velvet and beneath it an elegant selection of jewellery that is hard to take your eyes off. Westbourne House whilst principally for men offers some excellent womenswear.

On Women's: As always Paul Smith's clothes are classic with a twist. A good selection of shoes and belts and other accessories are on the ground floor with clothes collections on the first. An assistant helpfully guides you around showing you the beautifully tailored jackets and well cut skirts.

On Men's: Ist floor men's are more quirky and there's lots of Paul Smith's hallmark bright stripes and trimmings. Tried on a five button jacket about £600 with fish tail sleeves that felt great. The changing rooms are good and sales assistants are positively charming and impressively home in on what you want and check the whole place for suitable alternatives if necessary. Paul Smith's shoes, ties and coats are worth a look too.

The 2nd floor has more classic and formal suits from £400 for a single splash o dash lining. A more elaborate coloured lining plus patterning around the arm and shoulders adds another £200. Attractive velvet jackets are to be found here too. Warhol pictures feature on the walls of The Bespoke Department (tel 020 727 3820) that makes suits from £2200, jackets about £1500 that takes 90 days and two fittings.

A visit to Paul Smith's Westbourne House is wonderfully memorable fashion experience.

Opposite is another Paul Smith at 120 Kensington Park Road (tel: 020 7229 8982 a two floor store focusing on men's casuals. Not as grand as Westbourne House but nevertheless very welcoming. Strong on T-shirts, chinos, knitwear and trainers For a list of other Paul Smith shops and department store concessions see www. paulsmith.co.uk.

Top 200

Preen
5 Portobello Green Arcade
London W10 5TZ
tel: 020 8968 1542
www.preen.eu

Wow factor: ♦♦♦♦
Choice: ♦♦♦
Service: ♦♦♦♦
Price: ££££

Glam
Ladbroke Grove LU, 5 min walk
Thurs, Fri 11am-6pm,-Sat, 10am-6pm,
Own label
Sizes: Women XS-L

No matter who you are, when you come to Preen you'll definitely be in the papers Hangers, rails, a wooden table and chairs are all covered in newspaper. This surprising small retail unit for enormously gifted design duo, Justin Thornton and The Bregazz is in enclosed in an arcade. In the window is a single mannequin whose body is covered with the world's map wearing a purple dress with uneven hem is prelude to their own cool take on glamour.

On the rails are checked shirts made in to the dresses, draped satins, puffed asymmetrics with interesting hems plus good matching macs. Tried on a black deconstructed pencil skirt with matching belt, £350. Service was low key but very good. The changing room is covered in old newspapers and is quite darkish. The mirror is freestanding beaded edge type. Our only concern is that the clothes hook is very high, and may pose a problem to the vertically challenged.

Lindsay Lohan and Amy Winehouse are amongst Preen's clientele.

There is also a capsule collection at nearby Studio 228, Westbourne Grove see page (160).

Top 200

Rellik
8 Golborne Road,
London W10 5NW
Tel: 020 8962 0089
www.relliklondon.co.uk

Wow factor:⬤⬤⬤⬤
Choice:⬤⬤⬤⬤⬤
Service:⬤⬤⬤
Price: £££

> New Vintage, Glam
> Westbourne Park LU, 5 min walk
> Tue-Sat, 10am-6pm,
> Designer mix
> Sizes: Women: varies

One of the most famous new vintage shops in London headlining Chanel suits, Gucci shoes and Miyake outfits. A wavy mirrored wall is a backdrop to the fascinating vintage rails assembled by the experienced and combined efforts of Steven, Clare and Fiona. They analyse the season's looks and buy in the vintage pieces that are on trend. For something specific you want and that is currently very hot like vintage Westwood, Mugler or Alaia, they will scan the universe to find it for you, a process that usually takes three days. Everything is in excellent condition with nothing over £800. A Zandra Rhodes dress was £300; gold hand-shaped brooch, a snip at £15.

Most customers are walk-ins, but you can make an appointment at Rellik to view special pieces that are not on show in the shop, something that is very popular with visiting Americans.

Changing rooms are curtained off and have black and gold patterned wallpaper. Service is friendly and informative.

Top 200

Retro Man
32-34 Pembridge Road
London W11
Tel: 08456 441 442
http://www2.mveshops.co.uk

Wow factor:⬤⬤⬤
Choice:⬤⬤⬤⬤
Service:⬤⬤⬤⬤⬤
Price:£

> Retro, cool
> Notting Hill Gate LU, 5 min walk
> 7 days 10am-8pm
> Designer mix
> Sizes: Men: varies

Retro boutique ensemble that's basic grot décor but wow choice.

At 34 Pembridge Road is top drawer designer brands and interesting design piec
es. These are all displayed on the first floor and then if unsold after a month, a
the beginning of each month they slash the price and relocate it to the basement
Examples are a Westwood striped navy blazer suit £250, Hermes ties £40, Olive
Sweeney pair of shoes as new, a huge selection of jeans and an assortment of Ver
sace leather jackets of variable quality.

Always check the windows that have some of the best buys. Staff are ever read
with tape measures. Hats, sunglasses, 1-2 Vintage top hats come in each week. O
top hats, black silk are around £100, Dunn's black felt about £40. Will reserve t
the end of the day for you to think about and they also give advice on how to kee
items in good condition. The shop can get very busy with people trying things or
Take heed from their notice signs "Pick pockets operate in this area."

At No. 32, are good designer brand names such as Armani, Issy Miyake, Burberr
but also high street labels like Ted Baker and Zara. Designer jackets kick in at £3
whilst Kenneth Cole shoes are on for £40 and Calvin Klein jumpers £15.

Also at 20, Retro Clothing at 28 Pembridge Road, Retro Clothing 56 Notting Hi
Gate and 75 Berwick St, Soho, W1.

Top 200

Retro Woman
20 Pembridge Road
London W11
tel: 08456 441 442
http://www2.mveshops.co.uk

Wow factor: 🏠🏠🏠
Choice: 🏠🏠🏠🏠
Service: 🏠🏠🏠🏠🏠
Price: £

Retro, cool
Notting Hill Gate LU, 5 min walk
7 days 10am-8pm
Designer mix
Sizes: Women: varies

Virtually all the big labels are here in force. Clearly labeled top line designers so you don't hunt around the garment to find out who designed it. Chloé, Stella McCartney, Christian Dior, Fendi. Clothes are variable in quality and cleanliness. A Jasper Conran fur stole amongst other designer items hang on the wall as you descend the stairs. Changing rooms are in the basement, basic and with flaps like stable doors to close you in.

Catwalk models bring in items they've been given after modelling them at the fashion shows. In the window were a pair of this season's Chloé shoes at £120. All around the sides and at the back are cabinets with shoes. All the clothes are in sections and in colour code e.g. blacks, browns and styles such as LBD's.

Service is enthusiastic and very good. If you have anything to sell, Retro buy in at a third of the price. In the case of a very sought after designer such as Westwood it goes on at the full retail price if in excellent condition.

Also at 16 Pembridge Road, Retro Clothing 56 Notting Hill Gate and 75 Berwick St, Soho, W1.

Supra

249 Portobello Road
London W11 1LT
Tel: 020 7243 3130
www.supralondon.com

(!) Must Visit

> Cool
> Ladbroke Grove LU, 5 min walk
> Mon-Thurs, 11am-6pm, Fri-Sat, 10.30am-6pm, Sun, 12am-5pm
> Designer mix
> Sizes: Women varies; Men: varies

This independent boutique is much favoured by Notting Hill fashion followers for its streetwear casual on-trend edit. Sometimes incredibly busy, the service is straight forward and definitely on the button. With a label mix consistently cool as this you'll want to return again and again.

On Women's: On offer are Something Else shoes, Tatty Devine jewellery, and some great shirt dresses and particularly strong on sneakers.

On Men's: A good line of Duffer and St George, Nike, Adidas, New Balance trainers, Obey T-shirts and Electronic Sheep hats and scarves.

 Top 200

The Convenience Store

1a Hazelwood Tower
Goldborne Gardens
London W10 5DT
Tel: 020 8968 9095

Wow factor: ⛁⛁⛁⛁
Choice: ⛁⛁⛁
Service: ⛁⛁⛁⛁
Price: £££

> Glam
> Westbourne Park LU, 5 min walk
> Tue, Thur, Fri, Sat 10.30am-6pm
> Designer Mix
> Sizes: Women: varies

Andrew Ibi does a first class edit of a well chosen selection of upcoming designers. Don't be put off by the nearby slightly scary housing estate. The metal shuttered gate will be opened by staff to let you in. The understated window of display just a few items whilst the quirky exterior still has the previous incumbents signage for a key cutting and alterations service. Don't be put off because inside it there is a lot more stock and better displayed than the exterior would lead you to believe. Involvement with charitable fund raising policy.

Clothes dangle from the ceiling on wires whilst on the rails are Clare Tough grey zipped woolen jackets, Sophie Hulme, Hannah Marshall, Rick Owen, AF Vander frost, Ann-Sofie Back and her diffusion range "Back" of which the polo neck mini ponch £90 is a real classic. Of note are Camilla Skovgaard's human hair detailed high shoes for £280.

Good friendly enthusiastic service and the changing rooms that have red curtains, small circular chandeliers and mirrors are pretty good too.

Opened in September 2008 and is building up a firm fanbase. Although the shop only stock women's, the shop also appeal to men who like high glam such as Julien Macdonald who bought a glitzy bomber jacket here. Andrew Ibi who has done a grand job here is also a fashion academic and runs courses in South London. When you visit leave your details at the cash register so that you can be invited to one of their Secret Sales.

Top 200

The Cross
141 Portland Road
London W11 4LR
tel: 020 7727 6760

Wow factor: ◖◖◖
Choice: ◖◖◖
Service: ◖◖◖◖◖
Price: £££

Classic
Holland Park LU, 6 min walk, Ladbroke Grove LU, 12 min walk
Mon-Sun 11am-6pm except Thurs, 11am-7pm
Designer mix
Sizes: Women 8-14/16

One of Notting Hill's most reputable boutiques much loved by locals. A small corner shop on two floors, bright colours hit you as you walk in from their home and gift selections whilst the clothing collection is more relaxed and understated. Stairs with coloured lights and kitsch decorations makes it a little like a Father Christmas grotto that will appeal to the young parents with children that frequent the place.

I was tempted by the Olivia Morris shoes and Bathyat dress but decided to try the 50s style full knee length skirt. I changed downstairs, round an alcove, that was spars compared to the rest of the shop, with no mirror. However, mirrors are outside. But to amuse you on the wall is an enlarged page of a Bunty magazine complete with cut outs. Staff have a friendly and congenial rapport with their many regular customers and will phone regular customers when new items arrive that staff think will be of interest. Also stocks jewellery.

Tonic

276 Portobello Road
London W10
Tel: 020 8960 8216
http://tonicuk.com

! MustVisit

> Urban
> Ladbroke Grove LU, 5 min walk
> Mon-Sat, 10am-6pm, Sun 11am-5pm
> Designer mix

This on beam boutique has the Holland Esquire label with its unusual take on classics that lifts this selection of quickly snapped up menswear. On offer are Grey peacoat £270; grey trouser with stitched detail £95, John Smedley t's, jumpers and a comprehensive stack of jeans. The shop exterior is turquoise, whilst inside is a rickety floorboard, and a conservatory at the back with a sofa. Staff are spot on but could be torn between you and their paperwork.

Top 200

Twenty8Twelve

172 Westbourne Grove
Notting Hill
London W11 2RW
Tel: 020 7221 9287

Wow factor: ▯▯▯▯
Choice: ▯▯▯
Service: ▯▯▯▯▯
Price: ££

! DesignerRunBoutique

> Cool
> Notting Hill Gate LU, 7 min walk
> Mon-Sat, 10am-6.30pm, Sun, 12am-5pm
> Own label
> Sizes: Women 6-14

Super- cool boutique set up by it-girl film actress Sienna Miller and designer sister Savannah Miller. Savannah went to Central St Martins where she completed a BA in fashion design with knitwear. Twenty-eight twelve, itself, is named after Sienna's birthday 28th December.

Splendid wardrobe staples, black trousers, jackets with good cut and jumpers at reasonable prices. Tried on a very flattering grey short leather jacket at £240 with superb back detail and three quarter sleeves. Manager gave proficient styling advice. French doors lead to changing rooms that are narrow with a mirror outside.

The welcome was extremely friendly and the level of sales service is highly commendable. Great place !

Also stocked at Trilogy, Liberty and Matches.

Yates Buchanan
33 Pembridge Road
Notting Hill
London W11 3HG
tel: 020 7229 5884

Wow factor: 🔲🔲🔲🔲
Choice: 🔲🔲🔲
Service: 🔲🔲🔲🔲
Price:££

Cool
Notting Hill Gate LU, 5 min walk
Mon-Fri 11am-7pm, Sat, 10am-7pm, Sun 11am-5pm
Designer mix

Highly affordable Notting Hill colourful capsule clothes collection edit that's savvy with a bit of oomph. They moved from Kensington Park Road in February 2008 and continue to attract an upscale Notting Hill, young 20-30 year old clientele.

As you go in there's a great display of new and vintage jewellery in a showcase Capsule collections from new designers and exclusive unique stylisations are a speciality here. Lisa B dress with elasticated body, £69, fitted well and came hand-printed brown silk but comes in different colours and prints such as lilac, gold, purple, orange. Changing rooms are downstairs, good size with modern wooden stalls, bedroomy wallpaper, big mirror and a seat for a partner to rest their feet. Scandi white boots at £79 and Cecci dresses are also available.

Service is knowledgeable.

Studio 228
228 Westbourne Grove
London W11 2RH
tel: 020 7908 9880

Wow factor: 🔲🔲🔲🔲
Choice: 🔲🔲🔲🔲
Service: 🔲🔲🔲🔲🔲
Price:££££

Glam
Notting Hill LU, 7 min walk
Mon-Sat, 10am-6.30pm, Sun, 1pm-6pm
Designer mix
Sizes: Women varies; Men: varies

Honeypot for fashionistas seeking an A-list edit of global desirable labels. The outside may have the same familiar look as a lot of other multi-label boutiques but this one is outstanding. Dress to impress and the staff will give you top service and style inspiration.

On Women's: Amongst the selection are Commes des Garcons, Rue du Mail, John Rocha, Moschino Cheap and Chic, Preen drapey dresses plus Galliano newspaper print clothes as well as handbags and shoes.

On Men's: Very tempting was the detailed self-patterned 80% woolen Raf Simons coat £820 that I tried on. The changing rooms are quite pleasant and are partly leather-walled and have brown leather seats. The service was quite unpressurised and the whole shopping experience a good one. Yohji Yamamoto and Commes des Garcons are just a few of the great name stocked here.

Sales can be incredibly good.

WestfieldLondon

Westfield London | London W12 | tel: 0203 371 2300 |
www.westfield.com/london

Fashion Mall
Shepherd's Bush and Wood Lane LU, 1 min walk
White City LU Shepherd's Bush Market (Hammersmith and City Line) 5 min walk C1, 31, 49 and many other buses available
Mon-Fri, 9am-10pm, Sat, 9am-8pm Sun, 12am -6pm
Restaurants in the pedestranised southern terrace are open until midnight,
Mon-Sat and 11pm Sunday

Westfield is the new West London fashion bomb. The number crunch is 212 fashion retailers, 4,500 car parking spaces, 49 eateries, and 1.5 miles of shop-ping space.

Dior, Louis Vuitton and Mulberry lead the way here in aspirationals whilst Top Shop and Jaeger trailblaze the mainstream. Individualistic shops span from the superb classics of Amanda Wakeley to edgy sneakers boutique, Number.

Westfield slices up into six designated zones: luxury, aspirational, urban chic, streetwear, kids and high street. First time, grab a free map guide. You'll need t. Serious fashionistas head straight for the "Village" with the luxury names on ground and first floors. Hungry fashionistas head for chow down on the irst floor "Balcony", particularly Croque Gascon. Westfield clumps together imilar brands and similar style, a smart logic. So on the ground floor Levis, re alongside other street casuals, whilst Mui Mui, Prada sit with Gucci.

Aesthetically pleasing is the natural light that comes through the modern un-dulating glass roof, the central staircase at the Village with four chandeliers of '000 crystals above and the ceiling spheres that intriguingly appear to float. Other zones are less inspiring and are just like many other older malls and here car parking doesn't come free. However, of note on the ground floor is he spectacular central atrium for festival style events, exhibitions and fashion hows. As malls go in London, this is the very best and is highly recommend-d. The following are just a taster of the shopping delights to be savoured.

Aspinalls

3 Ground Floor,
Tel: 0845 052 6900
www.aspinalloflondon.com

!MustVisit

> Classic
> Own label

British elegant shop known for more serious leather goods now offering handbags at £399 that look very desirable indeed. Renowned for notebooks and diaries, quite distinguished is the gentleman's full size wallets with passport case for £135.

Top 200

Principles

Westfield
D3 Level 1
London W1
Tel: 0870 122 8802
www.principles.co.uk

Wow factor: ⬤⬤⬤⬤
Choice: ⬤⬤⬤⬤
Service: ⬤⬤⬤⬤⬤
Price: £

> Glam
> Own label, ready to wear
> Sizes: Main collection 8-20, Petite 6-16, Shoes 4-7

This new Principles flagship store takes on a look of cool elegance. Whilst competing in the same price bracket as Top Shop and Zara, Principles distinguishes itself with the high level of service and even has a Personal Styling Lounge with two armchairs and a private changing room. I tried on a skirt with button detail on the waist for £45 and was asked if it was good and given advice on how it could be worn. Staff were generally helpful and friendly but not pushy whilst the general changing rooms were of a high standard and attractive in a silver grey with an ornate mirror.

Offers a selection of key fashion pieces for each season that are well cut and very wearable. Good on suits for work and occasions, there's also plenty to choose on coats, casuals and dresses as well as chunky knits and jumpers with delicate details. The shift dresses are great value at £69 and the handbags, jewellery, shoe and belts are not to be missed. At the rear of the store is the petites collection, ideal for those of 5ft 3in or less.

Principles style events are very popular that showcase seasonal trends, catwalk shows and style advice. Discounts, prize draws drinks and nibbles all add to the shopping entertainment experience at Principles. Despite being a chain it really does offer the service of an individual boutique and for that it deserves special mention. Also at 38 The Poultry, EC2; John Lewis, Sloane Square, Oxford St, Brent Cross, Debenhams, Fenwick at Brent Cross and Morley in Brixton.

Rigby and Peller
Westfield
H3 Ground Floor
Tel 0208 735 4031
www.rigbyandpeller.com

Wow factor: 👠👠👠
Choice: 👠👠👠👠
Service: 👠👠👠👠👠
Price: £££££

Classic
Own label
Sizes: Women 30A-48I

Rigby and Peller goes modern at Westfield, dispensing with the old traditional décor of their famous stores in Knightsbridge and Conduit Street. This is the place to go for a perfect fit. In other words, more lingerie functional than lingerie fantasy.

As you enter, to the left there is an extensive range of swimwear from £60 upwards all boned and ready to pull the wearer in. Of note on offer are kaftan cover-ups lingerie, satin and lace matching sets with the price range for bras, £32.99, £65.99 and £115.

Many top designer brands have dresses individually corseted but if you want this effect it's a saving to buy it separately here. They are experts at pulling people into shape, famously doing this for the Queen. Stocks control underwear, corsets basques and also has over twenty other brands.

The large waiting area outside the changing rooms is indicative of how busy this shop is and sometimes an appointment is advisable. The luxury cubicle has heavy pink and gold curtains with pelmets and the R&P logo.

There are about a hundred modern drawers with a shelf that slide out under it. The assistant seemed to know where everything was and was highly efficient. As she was serving me, her appointment was announced and she said pleasantly " am with a customer and then I'll be along." A wannabe royal, with a helmet head hairstyle looked unamused.

Also at 2 Hans Road, Knightsbridge that does bespoke, made to measure and of course ready to wear. Also at 22a Conduit Street, London W1S 2XT, tel: 0845 0765545; and also King's Road and Brent Cross shopping centre.

Zadig & Voltaire
55 Level 1 Village
London W1
Tel: 020 8743 5566
www.zadig-et-voltaire.com

(!) Must Visit

Cool
Own label
Sizes: Women XS-L; Men: S-XL

Zadig & Voltaire has built a good name in stylish glam takes on everyday basics. Urban, minimal, the store whilst part of a global chain still retains an individual vibe about it.

On Women's: Wardrobe basics with a touch of glitz. The signature is soft muted tones and neutrals, cashmere tops, silk dresses and leggings. But also there's lots of motifed crystallised designed T's, slim cut jeans, washed leather bags and iridescent leather high heel shoes. Service is helpful and good.

On Men's: Velvet jacket with removable hood. Skull watches, skeleton insignia t-shirts, lots of printed t-shorts, leather jackets.

Other chain shops are in Westbourne Grove, Notting Hill, Sloane Street, Hampstead High Street, St John's Wood High Street and Richmond.

NORTH LONDON

Islington

Centre stage for hot ticket individuality is Camden Passage with celebrity label Frost French, eco-fashion at Equa and chic designer- run boutique, Susy Harper. Along the nearby main shopping strip, Upper Street, is the vibrant clubby B+R and further along is designer- run boutique Labour of Love and the fascinating top end contemporary meets vintage shop, Palette. Stoke Newington's Church Street provides an alternative selection of boutiques to the mainstream with the fashion edit at Hub Men's and Women's proving very popular.

B+R
297 Upper Street
Islington
London N1
tel: 020 7226 3310
www.bolongarotrevor.com

(!) Must Visit

Glam
Angel LU 5 min walk
Mon 11am-6pm, Tue 10.30am-6pm,
Wed-Fri 10.30am-6.30pm, Sat 10am-6.30pm
Own label and designer mix
Sizes: Women S-L; Men S-L

The vibrant collections at B+R rocks Upper Street. Terrific contemporary clubwea with old school influences from The Blitz Club and Kraftwerk make this large whit modern store a hot ticket. Women's on show are short white dresses, mulicoloure jackets with frill fronts, white shorts, good leather jackets and black ruffled dresse with rose bodice at £144.99. Stocks own label plus Fashion, Hot and Religion. O Men's there's different collared jackets such as peak lapels and standing collars t choose from. I tried on a slim fit blazer with satin lapels that felt very good and re ceived attentive service. All made in England and reasonably priced.

B+R is also at 128 Shoreditch High Street, London E1. Tel 0207 613 0606

Top 200

Equa
28 Camden Passage
Islington
London N1
tel 0207 359 0955
www.equaclothing.com

Wow factor:🏠🏠🏠🏠
Choice:🏠🏠🏠🏠
Service:🏠🏠🏠🏠
Price:£££

Ethical
Angel LU 5 min walk
Mon 11am-6pm, Tue 10.30am-6pm,
Wed-Fri 10.30am-6.30pm, Sat 10am-6.30pm
Designer mix

One of the best ladies organic clothes shops in London. A blue-fronted buildin along fashionable Camden Passage, Equa packs a fantastic range of organic clothe into an attractively pine-wooded, white and light blue decorated space. Stock ing some of the most fashionable organic brands around are Wildlife Works, Cie Loomstate, Annie Greenabelle, Stewart Brown, Edun and People Tree, eco-consciou fashionistas are spoilt for choice. Dresses, jumpers, shirts all look tempting althoug we decline to comment on the "Eat Organic Knickers" designed by Green Knicker Fairtrade jewellery and recycled glass are also stocked.

Changing Rooms are downstairs, spacious, warm, with plenty of hooks to hang things on, full length mirror in each of the two cubicles. Of note to vegetarians is the organic Enamore capsule collection. For vegans there's well designed vegan shoes by Beyond Skin and a selection of vegan handbags from Canadian duo Matt and Nat. Vegan clutch handbags come smartly designed in silver and bronze colours as well as more casual bags. Clientele include Nadine from Girls Aloud.

Owned by Penny Cooke, she and her staff are totally savvy about the clothes' provenance, organic content and ethical method of manufacture. With very friendly service Equa is an ethical fashion shop to beat a path to.

Top 200

Frost French
22-26 Camden Passage,
London N1
Tel 0207 354 0053

Wow factor: ❑❑❑❑
Choice: ❑❑❑
Service: ❑❑❑❑
Price: ££

Glam, cool
Angel Green Park LU, 5 min walk
Mon-Sat, 10am-7pm, Sun, 12am-6pm
Own label
Sizes: Women 6-14

This is the main fashion event along Camden Passage where the vibe is classical with a twist of pop. On-trend, celebrity label Sadie Frost and Jemima French's generate a pulsating domain of short full skirts, pop festival and cool clubwear. The strapless frilly dress made for Amy Winehouse is proudly featured on a mannequin and is great value at £250 and comes in different colours. Divided into two parts there are rails and rails of peachy pieces at affordable prices. Tasty leather suits with flower details compete for your attention with the clean lined macs, jackets and denims. Urban chic in décor, staff are switched on fashion-wise and completely friendly with it.

Ghost

133 Upper Street,
Islington
London N1 1QP
Tel: 0207 354 5791
www.ghost.co.uk

(!) Must Visit

Glam
Own label, ready to wear
Unique designs
Sizes: Women 8-18

Signature romantic floaty dresses, skirts and tops define the Ghost look that ha
retained a strong following for many years. Designs endure for several seasons a rea
plus for savvy fashion seekers. Dresses are cut quite generously.

Top 200

Handmade & Found

109 Essex Road,
London N1 2SL
tel: 020 7359 3898
www.handmadeandfound.com

Wow factor: 🏠🏠🏠
Choice: 🏠🏠🏠
Service: 🏠🏠🏠🏠
Price: ££

(!) Designer Run**Boutique**

Cool
Essex Road LU, 5 min walk
Tue-Sat, 10.30am-6pm,
Own label and designer mix
Sizes: Women 6-14

Handmade & Found has an excellent con
cept idea giving unique designs at hig
street chain prices. As you enter on th
right is their own label Handmade, mad
at the workroom on view at the back of th
boutique. "Found " is on the lefthand sid
and are clothes from designers working i
Thailand.

Designs have an urban feel but feminine
Silk or satin dresses are around £130 al
though a cool dress with sleeve detail wa
priced up for just £98 and a petal blac
and white skirt £75. On display are an as
sortment of shirt zip-up jackets at £58,
very small collection of handbags, jewe
lery, some wild and witty pieces such a
necklaces with cameras or hangers exclusive to the boutique and some self-pa
terned pump shoes at £39.

Handmade & Found's shopfront is a flash of fuchsia colour down this otherwise du
section of street. Inside, there's all sorts of interesting décor details such as a cut ou

mirror shape of a woman positioned in the window, a cube ceiling light with "Ladies" signs, a display of fans around the place and a Van Gogh Action Man kit on the wall. Changing rooms are basic with stall, mirror one hanger, satin curtain and mirror outside whilst service is laid back and pleasantly knowledgeable. Although a little off the beaten track from the mainstream shopping area, a visit here is recommended.

Hub (Women's)

19 Stoke Newington Church Street
London N16 0AR
Tel: 020 7254 4494
www.hubshop.co.uk

! **Must**Visit

Casual, classic
Stoke Newington BR, 73 bus runs nearby
Mon-Sat, 10.30am-6.30pm, Sun, 12am-5pm
Designer mix
Sizes: Women 8-16; shoes 3-8

This busy neighbourhood boutique has an eclectic mix of seasonal on- trend smart casuals. Hub succeeds with great labels: Sonia, Great Plains, Acne jeans, and great value for money dresses at around £90, skirts £50, pumps £95 and Ash shoes at £115. Nicely displayed are casual crochet berets, Ally Capellino leather purses and handbags and a Falke tights range. Expect a friendly welcome, good stock knowledge and enjoy taking your time browsing around without feeling awkward in this small and efficiently run boutique. At sale time they run out of stock of small sizes quickly. Definitely one to go for if you are in the area.

Hub (Men's)

8 Stoke Newington Church Street
London N16 0AP
Tel: 020 7275 8160
www.hubshop.co.uk

! **Must**Visit

Casual, classic
Stoke Newington BR, 73 bus runs nearby
Mon-Sat, 10.30am-6.30pm, Sun, 12am-5pm
Designer mix
Sizes: Men's varies

This individual boutique offers a persuasively attractive fashion edit encompassing capsule Pringle collection, Acne, Levi's, Farahs, Wrangler jeans and trousers as well as Ally Capellino leather bags and Falke socks. I tried on a Pringle blue and white jacket at £195 and received well informed cheerful service.

Labour of Love
193 Upper Street
Islington
London N1 1RQ
tel: 0207 354 9333

Wow factor: 🛍🛍🛍
Choice: 🛍🛍🛍
Service: 🛍🛍🛍
Price: £££

ⓘ DesignerRunBoutique

Urban
Highbury and Islington BR and LU, 7 min walk, Angel LU 15min walk
Tue-Sat, 11-7pm, Sun 11am-6.30pm
Designer mix
Sizes: Women varies

One might easily pass Labour of Love by mistake as their shop sign reads Berwick the name of a previous retailer. Still inside this small intriguing boutique are the old cabinets from the previous haberdashery. Owner Francesca Forcolini design knitwear, dresses around £100 and jazz shoes £65 as well as stocking upcoming designers based on her choice that all designs here have to be a labour of love Styles tend to be quirky-lite following the season's trend such as with the King knitwear range. Flying duck brooches for £25 by Bena offer a touch of kitsch whils the Mimi bags designed in East London are also popular and there is a selection o street casual hats and books on fashion to choose from. On Labour of Love's ow label, the 100% cashmere corset sweater with frill details at £150 is glam with a rea urban edge. The double breasted black and silver striped blazer at the same price is very attractive too.

There's always lots of interesting, fun pieces to look at here and staff are ver friendly and chatty.

Palette London
21 Canonbury Lane,
Islington N1 2AS
tel: 020 7288 7428
www.palette-london.com

Wow factor: 🛍🛍🛍
Choice: 🛍🛍🛍
Service: 🛍🛍🛍🛍
Price: ££££

Glam, cool
Highbury & Islington LU, 5 min walk
Mon-Sat, 11am-6.30pm, Sun, 12am -5.30pm
Designer Mix
Sizes: Women varies; Shoes 2½ to 9

Top-end contemporary designer labels collid with high end, mint condition vintage. Sand wiched between an Italian restaurant and a Italian deli, inside it's a small uncluttered pleas ant boutique with wooden floors, white lan tern style lighting and an upside down orient parasol. Vintage and contemporary are mixe together on the rails with a lot of the contem porary exclusive to Palette and hot off the ca walk. The vintage is bought with a contempo rary look in mind. Marco said to me "I could dress you from head to toe in vintage and still make you look now".

Stocks Ossie Clark from £125 - £795 and the contemporary label Avsh Alom Gur. Of note are Maud Frizon shoes from £65, vintage Pucci, Halston, Diane Von Furstenberg and Gucci. Dresses are from £225 with a choice of sequined colour pieces and neutral classics. Lesser known high-end contemporary designer labels are also in evidence making this a very appealing venue. Service is good with changing rooms basic with a floral design curtain.

Of interest is their extensive range of vintage JMP French bakelite jewellery from the 1970/80s priced £55 - £165. Butler & Wilson jewellery is also available as well as plenty of handbags, hats, belts, vintage fashion magazine and books. Popular with the Canonbury fashion set, Japanese and fashionistas from all over London, this is a great place.

Top 200

Susy Harper

35 Camden Passage,
Islington
London N1 8EA
Tel: 020 7704 0688
www.susyharper.co.uk

Wow factor:🏠🏠🏠🏠
Choice:🏠🏠🏠
Service:🏠🏠🏠🏠
Price:££

❗ DesignerRunBoutique

Cool
Angel Green Park LU, 5 min walk
Mon-Sat, 10am-6pm, Thurs, 10am-7pm
Own label
Sizes: Women extra small (size 8-10) to medium (size 12-14)

Chic boutique with the whole collections by designer/owner Michelle Anslow that are made on the premises with all fabrics sourced in England. Individualistic in attitude and atmosphere, at first it looks quite empty with a just a couple of rails but stay longer as more items appear to materialise before your eyes on the walls, ceiling, shelves with jewellery even dripping off the chandelier.

Best sellers are wide legged linen trousers from £145, linen shirts and Michelle's Tuscan skirts, long with a voluminous knotted design at the back.

I tried on a skirt, £245, with a very high waist and a puffball uneven hem. The sales assistant said "if you try this on you'll want to buy it" and my credit card gave me a wink.

Finding the changing room here is a cinch. You can't miss the "Dressing up" sign in pink neon lights. The quirky changing facility doubles as a stock room. Although it does possess a dressing table to put your things on, the big mirror is in the front of the shop.

Camden

The market here gets absolutely mobbed with fashion shoppers on the prowl for bargains and the latest street and club crazes. From the moment you exit Camden Town underground station the fashion vibe hits with streams of boutiques of glitz, glam and goth of which Punkyfish, and Chameo are amongst the best. Within the market of thousands of stalls and units outstanding are Cyberdog, Braintree Hemp Store and Penny Burdett. Prices are very affordable and there's lots of places to eat and drink very cheaply. Further afield in Lisson Grove is the indoor vintage and antiques market, Alfies featuring oodles of 20's-60's fashion and a minute's walk away is ace knitwear designer-run shop, Weardowney.

Alfies
13-25 Church Street
Marylebone
London NW8
Tel: 020 7723 6066
www.alfiesantiques.com

Wow factor: 🏠🏠🏠
Choice: 🏠🏠🏠🏠🏠
Service: 🏠🏠🏠
Price: ££

Vintage
Marylebone Station BR and LU, 5 min walk
Edgware Road LU, 5 min walk
Tue-Sat, 10am-6pm
Sizes: Women: varies; Men: varies

Entertain yourself by stepping back in time to this vintage and antique clothes market. Occupying a large corner building the quirky exterior has faces painted on the façade and a window peep-show where you peer through cut-out picture frames to view the window displays inside. With a maze of fascinating clothes and jewellery concessions on the ground and second floors this is a place for vintage fashion collectors to hunt amongst the old wooden cabinets with drawers and glass compartments.

"The Girl Can't Help it" is just the ticket for 30's, 40's and 50's era coats, skirts, jackets, evening dresses £250-£300. An elegant black velvet 30's coat with beaded collar at £295 looked terrific. Also does shoes hats and bags as well men's American bomber jackets. Whilst there a couple looked as if they had just stepped out of a 1940's time portal dressed from head to in the period complete with 40's hairstyles.

Elsewhere serious vintage fashion collectors can pick up an Yves St Laurent or Chanel apparel whilst some concession specialise in quirky collectable pieces for fun looks. Service at Alfies on the whole is very good except when the owner or main person is away you may get somebody who is covering for them and really doesn't have a clue.

Alfies is a great place for styling your own outfits with one of the biggest selections of vintage fabrics, trimmings and patterns. Some 20's and 60's collectables can also be found here. For bargain seekers on offer are silk scarves and belts for £10, a wide selection of small chic hats, sunglasses, ties and much more.

Braintree Hemp Store
Unit 9 East Yard
Camden Lock
London NW1
Tel 020 7267 9343
www.braintreehemp.co.uk

⊘ **Must**Visit

Ethical, Classic
Camden or Chalk Farm, LU 10 min walk
7 days 10am-6pm
Own label
Sizes: Women 8-18; Men: S-XXL

This popular large shop is the London branch of a successful Australian chain specialising in selling hemp trousers, shirts, t's, blouses and skirts. For organic fashion fans around 20% of their range is completely hemp with the remaining stock a mix of 55% hemp and non-organic cotton. Service is laid back and affable.

Top 200

Cyberdog

Unit 14 Stables Market
Chalk Farm Road
London NW1 8AH
tel: 020 7482 2842
www.cyberdog.net

Wow factor: ⌂⌂⌂⌂⌂
Choice: ⌂⌂⌂
Service: ⌂⌂
Price: £

Edgy
Chalk Farm LU, 5 min walk
Mon-Fri, 11am-6pm, Sat-Sun, 10am-7pm
Own label
Sizes: Women XS- M, 6-12 / one size goes up to 14; Men: S-XL, 32-36
some adjustable up to 40

Fashionista science fiction becomes reality at this futuristic dark cavernous space specialising in creative day-glo fluorescent apparel with a twist of techno. On entry, your eyes meet with giant model cybernauts sporting exposed electronic midriffs. Some shoppers may experience culture shock and wonder what they have walked into. Stay with it. It's fashion shopping experience like no other. As you browse around the caverns admiring the fluorescent leg warmers with flared fur bottoms and trousers with giant padded flares, the place evokes a full-on clubby mood from the blasting volume house music playlist. Sales assistant goths with fascinating hairdo's offer okay service when you ask. I tried some funky trousers on and almost felt radioactive. The changing rooms were of a lot less energy, rather small with minimal comfort.

On Women's: Check out the spacewear jackets with bell sleeves and mini and wrap skirts. Fluorescent T-shirts kick in at £25 and belts £18 it's sizzling on clubby leggings, hot pants and trousers with the best selection of long mittens in London from £35-£50. Six inch glow sticks are £1.50.

On Men's: Great on graphic t's, amazing are the techno T-shirts with sound activated light panels that flashes in synch to club disco beats. Cyberdog's Light Tees are programmable to send six messages (£60) whilst the six programmable space invader tee is £45. Of note are the Funky Proton pants (£60), Fluorescent Ballooneys, £80, and Exo Evolution Racers (£120) a kind of futuristic club sportswear. The Cyberdog-logoed tops at £32, jumpers and vests are pretty wicked too.

For those seeking more information about the cyberdog concept and cyberdog's chihuahua, click on cyberdog.net. Entertaining.

Penny Burdett
48 Upper Walkway
The West Yard
Camden Lock Place
Chalk Farm Road
London NW1 8AF
Tel: 020 7482 6630
www.pennyburdett.co.uk

⓵ DesignerRunBoutique ⓵ Mustvisit

Classic
Chalk Farm LU, 5 min walk
Mon-Fri, 11.30am-5.30pm, Sat- Sun 10.30am-6pm
Own Label, Ready to wear and made to measure
Sizes: Women S-L

Knitwear designer-owner, Penny Burdett greets you as you enter and is charmingly chatty as you browse around this relatively small boutique in the heart of Camden Market. A vast array of knitted elegant frockcoats, berets, and fingerless gloves. The dresses are from £130-£299 are great value and can be made to your size in a variety of colours with a small change to detail of your choice, all no extra charge. More elaborate items such as evening dresses with small trains, made -to-order ups the price.

Top 200

Punkyfish
190 Camden High Street
Camden Town
London NW1 8QP
Tel: 020 7485 1380
www.punkyfish.com

Wow factor:⬚⬚⬚
Choice:⬚⬚⬚
Service:⬚⬚
Price:££

Edgy
Camden Town LU, 5 min walk
Mon-Fri, 10am-7pm, Sat-Sun 10am-7pm
Own Label
Sizes: Women: XS- L

There are thousands of places to buy clothes along Camden High Street but the big draw to visit Punky Fish is their remarkably novel glitzy T-shirts. Starting at £25 for T's with flashes of gold or silver on the designs, make your own fashion

statement with their crystal earphoned T-shirts and ballet shoed T's Also does t
shirt dresses and jeans and sassy printed off the shoulder, vest and halterneck top:
as well as a very reasonable range of jackets, skirts and trousers (£35). Whilst the
shop has a big vibrant window of colour surprising customers don't get much o
a welcome. But service is okay.

Also Punkyfish at 232 Portobello Road, London W11 Tel 0207 985 0642 and also
worth checking out is Punk Glamour at 209 Chalk Farm Road, NW1 Tel 0207 424(
642.

Chameo

216 Chalk Farm Road
London NW1 8QR

① Must Visit

> Glam
> Camden Town LU, 5 min walk
> Mon-Fri, 10am-6pm, Sat-Sun 10am-6pm

Large selection of clubby dresses around £50; bags (M&S bag from last year tha
cost £35) available at £25. Have reductions up to half price. Changing rooms a
rear, staff helpful.

Top 200

Weardowney

9 Ashbridge Street
Lisson Grove
London NW8
tel: 020 7725 9694
www.weardowney.com

Wow factor:🏠🏠🏠🏠
Choice:🏠🏠🏠
Service:🏠🏠🏠🏠
Price:££

① Designer Run**Boutique**

> Glam, English
> Marylebone Station BR and LU, 6 min walk
> Edgware Road LU, 5 min walk
> Mon-Sat, 10-6pm,
> Own label

London knitwear heroes. Just off shopping strip Church Street, it's a shop in a house with a dog that jumps and barks when you ring the doorbell. In fact , it's a grade II listed building that they refer to as a guesthouse. Inside, the vibe is whimsical. It's pink with a central chandelier with candleholders, balls of wool scattered around with a playful cat looking at them. A friendly welcome by all including the dog, customers are said to often get a cup of tea, although we didn't get one when we visited!

Amy Wear and Gail Downey launched the Weardowney label in February 2004 at London Fashion Week and have never looked back since. Hand knitted, there is a uniqueness to each garment and it's all done in the UK. Chunky knits in sleek designs, dresses with pleated skirts and a low round neck £200 feature alongside tops in the same style or zip-up sleeveless lurex tops at £185.

Tried on a top and was taken through to the toilet!. The assistant who was very friendly and helpful ended up holding my coat and jacket as there wasn't anywhere to put anything. As you browse around and turn corners, there's women working at sewing machines.

Celebrity customers include Kimberley Stewart, Sienna Miller, Girls Aloud, and Helena Christiansen. A make to measure service is available taking 4-6 weeks.

Hampstead

Whilst Rosslyn Hill and Hampstead High Street are strongholds for the top end multiples such as Reiss, Hobbs, and Whistles the hot zone for individuality is further up the hill in Heath Street and Flask Walk with Linea, Cochinechine and Social.

Cochinechine
74 Heath Street
Hampstead
London NW3 1DN
tel: 020 7435 9377
www.cochinechine.com

 MustVisit

> Glam
> Hampstead St LU, 3 min walk
> Mon-Sat, 10am-6pm, Sun, 12am-6pm
> Designer mix
> Sizes: Women S- L

West End edit for the smart Hampstead set concentrating on over twenty design
ers top global luxe brands. The line-up includes Philip Lim, Ann Louse Rosewalc
Anna Sui, Hussein Chalayan, K by Karl Lagerfeld, Vanessa Bruno and exclusive tc
Cochinechine, Sea. Visible in the window are Marc Jacobs shoes, McQ (Alexan
der McQueen's diffusion label), Sonia and Acne jeans. The boutique is extremel
pleasant with stripped wooden floors, a massive picture framed mirror, distressec
wooden table, a graceful chandelier and a couple of quirky old fold up chairs. Ha
three wall rails of designer mix plus an inviting jewellery display cabinet at the rea
that includes Kenneth Jay Lane.

Tried on black woolen ruffled skirt at £245 in quite an ornate changing room. Fe
we interrupted the salesperson's afternoon downstairs and service was generall
unfriendly.

Top 200

Linea of Hampstead
8 Heath Street
London NW3 6TE
tel: 020 7794 1775
www.lineafashion.com

Wow factor: 🏠🏠🏠
Choice: 🏠🏠🏠🏠
Service: 🏠🏠🏠🏠
Price: ££££

> Glam
> Hampstead St LU, 4 min walk
> Mon-Sun, 10am-7pm
> Designer mix
> Sizes: Women dress 6-16, shoes 3½-8½; Men suits: 38-48, shoes 6-11

Upscale large boutique on two levels with women's and men's sections exudin
luxury. Not to be confused with the House of Fraser store label, this boutique
a bit old-fashioned in display and feel but nevertheless very confident and high
knowledgeable about collections, and how they are best styled together.

On Women's: Good selection of signature Missoni dresses including a vibrant em
erald Missoni Maxi dress at £1,120, Celine handbags, Blumarine skirts, twinset
dresses and bags, Alberto Ferretti, Moncler, 1921 jeans, embroidered Ed Harc
caps at £130 and dVb jeans at £190-£240.

On Men's: Thierry Mugler signature suits £990 and shirts £195 plus a very impressive selection of statement jackets at around £700 with excellent cut, innovative Les Hommes suits with black leather and satin detail at around £1000, Caesare Paciotti bags, Post and Co jackets and belts, A&G multicolored cashmere jumpers at £360.

Extra brownie points for selecting difficult to find ranges such as Mugler. When trying on a Mugler suit, co-owner Moreno shows you other tempting alternatives from the same designer. There is no charge for alteration and they are enthusiastic and adept at showing the best way to wear the suit. Altogether It was a very pleasing and positive experience.

Linea of Hampstead does a Fashion-on-Wheels service, whereby VIP customers such as international footballers, actors and singers can view items on line and pick a selection to try on at their hotel, home or office.

Social
5 Flask Walk
London NW3 7HD
Tel: 020 7794 8886

(!) Must Visit

Cool
Hampstead St LU, 4 min walk
Tue-Sat, 11am-7pm, Sun 11am-6.30pm
Designer mix
Sizes: Women: varies; Men: varies

This little boutique is a lifestyle clothing treasure trove that requires time to look round as there's lots of bits and pieces to see. Particularly of note are the Obey label items including limited edition T shirts with edgy propaganda messages such as "Obama Progress". Cool shoes too and okay service.

Also at 184 West End Lane, London NW6 1SG there's a sister shop. Tel 0207 794 7531.

BrentCross

Brent Cross Shopping Centre
Hendon
London NW4 3FP
Tel 0208 202 8095
www.brentcross.co.uk

Mall
Hendon Central LU, 5 min walk or Brent Cross LU 10 min walk
Bus 102, 112, 113 and another ten pass the main doors to the centre
Mon-Fri, 10am-10pm, Sat 9am-8pm, Sun, 12am-6pm

Brent Cross Shopping Centre is London's North West End with 120 stylish
shops cafes and restaurants. Although one of London's older malls it remains
immensely popular drawing in customers from North West London and as far
away as East London. Brent Cross is blessed with 8000 free car parking spaces
although on very busy shopping days allow extra time to find a space. As
malls go, it's a very pleasant shopping experience with a reasonable selection
of cafes and eateries and special events. On department stores with great
fashion selections there's Fenwick, John Lewis and Debenhams plus a good
selection of major stores including:

On Women's: Jane Norman, Jigsaw, Karen Millen, Kate Kuba, LK Bennett, Miss
Selfridge, New Look, Oasis, Top Shop, as well as Marks and Spencer.

On Men's: Head for H&M, Reiss, French Connection, Russell & Bromley, Zara,
River Island and Topman.

Reviews of these are given in the Chains chapter.

EAST LONDON

Brick Lane & Spitalfields

These are the hot zones for fashion creativity and designer run boutiques. Amongst the best in the Brick Lane area are Dragana Perisic, Comfort Station, designer bargains at 127 Brick Lane, remarkable T-shirts at Illustrated People, ethical fashions at Junky Styling, Sunday Upmarket, Backyard Market and collective designer-run boutique Luna and Curious. Brick Lane can be accessed by London Underground stations at Liverpool Street, Aldgate East and Shoreditch and from there a short walk.

Spitalfields is just a five minutes stroll from Brick Lane and has a great selection of individual fashion stalls as well as branches of major fashion stores. The Spitalfields Market is divided into New Spitalfields, a mix of food and trendy fashion stalls on Crispins Place and the Old Spitalfields Market (entrance Commercial Street) that has further stalls of interesting fashion. Amongst the most attention-grabbing stalls here are Dadarella London and DeMec. On Commercial Street too is on-trend shoe boutique, Sniff and nearby is Fairy Goth Mother with it's feminine glamour.

127 Brick Lane
127 Brick Lane
London E1 6SB
tel: 020 7729 6320

Wow factor: 🏠🏠🏠
Choice: 🏠🏠🏠
Service: 🏠🏠🏠
Price: £££

Cool,
Liverpool St LU, 10 min walk
Tue-Sat, 11am-7pm, Sun 11am-6.30pm
Designer mix
Sizes: Women: varies

127 Brick Lane is a surprisingly good shop to bag a designer bargain. On Sundays it gets crammed with shoppers for its current collections with pieces from A-list designers around the world. The big draw here is the sample pieces from Helmut Lang, Karl Lagerfeld and Miu Miu from previous seasons. Many are timeless and in neutral colours.

Outside, it's pretty minimal with no display in the windows. Expect a zero greeting but once served you'll find the staff's stock knowledge high grade. The inside is grey with lots on the rails with shoes beneath and there's a super selection of jewellery, belts, sunglasses and bags to choose from.

Top 200

Backyard Market
91 Brick Lane
The Truman Brewery
London E1 6QL
tel: 020 7770 6028

Wow factor: 🏠🏠
Choice: 🏠🏠🏠
Service: 🏠🏠🏠
Price: £

Urban
Liverpool St or Aldgate East LU, 10 min walk
Sun 10am-5pm
Designer mix
Sizes: Women varies ; Men: varies

Backyard Market is a gathering of young East End creatives that is located both inside and outside the Truman Buildings. The best finds here are on the jewellery stalls with a multitude of handmade uniquely designed pieces. Outstanding is the stall featuring Suay Design whose creative medium is stainless steel. Suay Design were suppliers to the 2007 Brit Awards goody bags no less. These unique stylish pieces start at £15 and are great value. Backyard also has a rich selection of vintage clothes as well as several stalls focusing on T-shirts, coats, knitwear, hats, shoes, scarves, belts and ties Whilst service varies from stall to stall, those that are designer stallholders tend to be totally enthusiastic about their work and the service is reflected in that.

Beyond Retro

110 Cheshire Street
London E2
Tel: 020 7613 3636
www.beyondretro.com

Wow factor: 🏠🏠🏠🏠🏠
Choice: 🏠🏠🏠🏠🏠
Service:🏠🏠
Price:£

Vintage
Bethnal Green LU, 15 min walk, Bethnal Green BR 8 min walk
7 days 10am-6pm
Designer mix
Sizes: Women varies; Men: varies

Contender for one of the most unfabulous shop fronts in London, this grungy, treasure trove warehouse of two rooms, overflows inside spectacularly with vintage and retro Americana for men and women. Live music plays every Saturday at 3pm and most of the time cameras flash around the place as students try on outfits for laughs and snap a pic for Facebook. Popular photos involve wearing petticoats and sitting on the mechanical rodeo training horse or by the slot machine. Great fun.

Rails of clothes are either themed in colour or style. Most are sourced from Canada and America. Don't miss the extensive range of shoes, jewellery, belts, sunglasses and bags. Expect no welcoming formality here but the stock knowledge is good.

On Women's: 50's proms dresses from £15 that you can match with their gorgeous net petticoats in fuchsia, purple, and rainbow from £42. Has a good assortment of clutch and evening bags to finish the outfit off from £15 as well as 80's jumpers and jackets. There's a marvellous selection of long embroidered satin kimonos. The yellow changing rooms have a curtain printed with a kitsch picture of a 1950's style woman.

On Men's: Polo shirts, trousers £8-£14, racks of shoes, cowboy boots, old school trainers, 50's sweatshirts. Some basic hats and old school ties.

Service is okay with staff more security orientated and be prepared for queues at the till. Also has a smaller branch at 58-59 Great Marlborough Street W1. Their clothes are often used by stylists for magazines spreads and Agyness Dean, Kate Nash, Henry Holland, Dita Von Teese and Daisy Lowe have all been spotted here.

Comfort Station
22 Cheshire Street,
London E2 6EH
tel: 020 7033 9099
www.comfortstation.co.uk

Wow factor: 🏠🏠🏠🏠
Choice: 🏠🏠🏠
Service: 🏠🏠🏠🏠🏠
Price: £££

① Designer Run**Boutique**

Cool
Bethnal Green LU, 5 min walk and also Bethnal Green Overland
Tue-Sun 11am-6pm
Own label

One of the most intriguingly designed shops in East London, this is the brainchild of London born Amy Anderson whose forte was sculpture photography and video installation prior to designing jewellery. Amy is a designer that seems to have time on her hands. Lots of the jewellery have a time-piece theme with cogs of clocks appearing on earrings and heart necklaces. Watches too appear on jewellery items and there's a touch of romanticism with those candelabras on her necklaces for around £100 and each piece is made in her East End studio.

Opened in 2004, the exterior has an inviting Edwardian style display in the window, a yellow door and a small vanilla frontage. On entering, after your eyes have adjusted to the striped floor, there's a nice smile from staff. Inside, check out the jewellery with hidden messages displayed in cases made from old pianos. Retro-shaped handbags with wooden oaks handles and clasps are suspended around the shop. The handbags are in numerous colours at £160 for the small size.

Comfort Station is also in Labour of Love, Kurt Holmes, Sisters&Daughters, Southbank Centre Shop and Victoria & Albert Museum in South Kensington.

Dadarella London
New Spitalfields Market
Stall opposite Giraffe
Sun 9am-5pm

Wow factor: 🏠🏠🏠
Choice: 🏠🏠🏠
Service: 🏠🏠🏠🏠
Price: £

① Designer Run**Boutique**

Urban
Aldgate East LU, 5 min walk
Sizes: S-L

This individual stall is a nod to Anya Hindmarch and London's swinging sixties. Large circular shaped bags have iconic pictures of Hepburn, Monroe and other film greats as well as '60's fashion imagery. These come at a bargain price of £15 each or two for £25, whilst larger versions are £25. Dadarella also has a wonderful selection of gaiters in tweed or leather at £25-£40. Service is quite friendly and is well worth a visit a novel accessory. Also at Portobello Market (Sat) and Camden Market Stables (Sat & Sun).

Top 200

DeMec
New Spitalfields Market
London E1
tel: 0208 579 9206
www.demec.co.uk

Wow factor: 🏠🏠
Choice: 🏠🏠🏠
Service: 🏠🏠🏠🏠
Price: ££

! DesignerRunBoutique

Ethical
Aldgate East LU, 5 min walk
Sun 9am-5pm
Own label

For those that adore the look of ivory these jewellery designers have captured it in a natural way without any cruelty to elephants. DeMec an innovative jewellery stall specialising in vegetable ivory derived from Amazonian palm seeds (Phytelephas macrocarpa) whose colour, hardness and density are remarkably similar to animal ivory. Maria de Mendoza who served gave wonderful informative service at her very well organised stall where the jewellery is displayed in sets with necklaces, earrings and bracelets. On offer are understated earrings starting at £8.99, bracelets from £29, and for those with cash to splash, she'll reveal a necklace from their top range with a diamond at £455   Natural dyes are used in most vivid colours such as turquoise, orange, red and fuchsia.

Whilst only at Spitalfields on Sundays, DeMec is at Greenwich Market at the weekends and Piccadilly Market on Tuesdays-and Wednesday. For ethical jewellery De-Mec does a great job.

Top 200

Dragana Perisic
30 Cheshire Street
London E2 6EH
tel: 020 7739 4484
www.draganaperisic.com

Wow factor: 🏠🏠🏠
Choice: 🏠🏠🏠
Service: 🏠🏠🏠🏠
Price: ££££

! DesignerRunBoutique

Glam
Bethnal Green LU, 5 min walk and also Bethnal Green Overland
Liverpool Street LU, 10 min walk
Wed-Fri, 10am-6pm, Sat-Sun, 11am-6pm
Own label
Sizes: Women 6-14; Men: Bespoke

This designer–run boutique has developed a strong reputation in the area for the individuality of designs, high quality finish at attractive prices. The aubergine painted front stands out well amongst the other boutiques along this upcoming gentrified street within the Brick Lane area. Inside it's small and uncluttered so it's easy to see Dragana's clothes collection and the jewellery on the counter. Local art featuring bright embroidered buildings decorates the walls but is also for sale.

On Women's: Designs are Prada-esque and will see you through more than just one season. Up for grabs are skirts, jackets, dresses at around £150-£250. Dragana will make to order your size if it isn't a standard size or colour in the collection at an

additional charge. Bespoke evening dresses kick off at £1000. Ready to wear matching jewellery of her own design is £35-£50 whilst her mum makes rosebud hairclips.

On Men's: Although no ready to wear for men items are here, there is a bespoke service specialising in coats around £2000 and waistcoats at £700.

Service is very good but the changing room is unusual. A brightly painted screen against the wall is brought out for one to change behind. Perhaps not for the self-inhibited! Customers here include Ruby Wax and Saskia Reeves.

Top 200

Fairy Goth Mother
15 Lamb Street,
London E1 6EA
tel: 020 7377 0370
www.fairygothmother.co.uk

Wow factor:🔔🔔🔔🔔
Choice:🔔🔔🔔🔔
Service:🔔🔔🔔
Price:£££

Glam
Liverpool St LU, 7 min walk, Aldgate East LU, 5 min walk
Mon-Sat, 10am-6pm, Thurs, 10am-7pm
Own label and designer mix
Sizes: Women: 6-20

Feminine glamorous boudoir boutique with a touch of Spitalfields edge offering one of the UK's largest collections of real corsets. The shop has bare brick walls with a chandelier and a fuchsia chaise longue in the centre and sets a captivating scene admirably.

Signature corsets range from £120-£600 and if you still can't find what you want they will make it up specially for you. On offer are skirts to match their corsets, a large selection of pencil skirts (£150), long full skirts with trains at £450 and full collared jackets with corset waists. Popular too here are the alluringly formal and sophisticated prom gowns £350. Apart from their extensive own labels they stock small London based brands such as Corset Rouge tightlacing corsetry and Kiss Me Deadly lingerie for 40's and 50's inspired silver screen glamour.

In terms of range there's full and half corsets, plain, patterned, some embellished with crystals, with or without suspenders all made to traditional style with steel boning fastened at the front and lace up at the back. To estimate your corset size simply deduct 4 from your waist size.

Whilst hard to find the prices, my friendly goth-dressed sales assistant was happy to give good service and let me freely browse without hassle. I tried on a half corset in vibrant purple satin trimmed with black £120 and was pulled in about five inches. It felt unbearable but then I had just eaten! Laura, the assistant told me she wears hers for twenty-three hours. I wouldn't want to wear it for 23 minutes. And besides I ended up looking like Betty Boo.

Also at 7 East Yard, Camden Lock, London NW1 8AL, Tel 0207 485 0365.

 Top 200

Junky Styling
12 Bray Walk,
The Old Truman Brewery
91/95 Brick Lane
London E1
Tel: 020 7247 1883
www.junkystyling.co.uk

Wow factor: ☆☆☆☆☆
Choice: ☆☆☆
Service: ☆☆☆☆☆
Price: ££

❶ DesignerRunBoutique

Ethical, edgy
Shoreditch LU, 3 min walk
Mon-Fri, 10.30am-6pm, Sat-Sun, 10.30am-5.30pm
Own label
Sizes: Women 6-14; Men, S-L

Recycled clothes shop heaven that will even revamp your own old, favourites into something brilliantly new. Although located near the Brick Lane-Bangla Town-Truman Brewery on the grimy Bray Walk retail strip, inside it's clean, airy with five handsome sparkling crystal chandeliers black and white painted bare brick walls and gleaming pine-wooden flooring.

On Women's: Amazing A-line skirts tailored from men's shirt pieces with shirts sleeves lolling down and miniskirts made out of six different men's suit fabrics in black, white and grey! Great for wearing on jeans are the "Tie Belts", constructed from tie fragments on a belt made from the waist strip of a man's trouser or jeans. Good too are the bohemian styled sari skirts from three recycled sari fabrics in brightly clashing colours and patterns (£110). However, best sellers are the lace-up backed basques made from silk scarves (£95) and the more elaborate basques made with recycled ties (£160). On accessories, check out the "Juliet Blue" handbags fashioned from old comics, own-label vintage handbags doused with spray-on paint, chokers made out of zips and a recycled fabric hat collection.

On Men's: High quality organic T shirts (£20), shirts made from strips of recycled shirts (£65) and the best sellers - jackets with odd collars and recycled suit slices bolted together like a jigsaw puzzle (£275). Suits are £400 a pop. All are own designs, materials sourced from charity shops and manufacturers' mountains of dead stock that would have been thrown anyway.

Service is cool, unrushed, friendly and informative. Junky is run by a team of five of which four are busily involved with garment design and sewing. For special occasion dresses, they make to measure, discuss requirements and then try to source the recycled fragments, all for about £750. Changing rooms are : upstairs and just about okay and the shop attracts a hip clientele of DJ's, musicians, TV producers and eco-aware individualists. For it's ethical ready-to- wear and couture, and unique look carried through the seasons, Junky Styling is to be commended.

Top 200

Illustrated People
13 Elys Yard
The Truman Brewery
(off Hanbury St and Brick Lane)
London E1 6QL

Wow factor: 🏠🏠🏠🏠
Choice: 🏠🏠🏠
Service: 🏠🏠
Price: ££

> Glam, cool
> Aldgate East LU, 10 min walk
> Mon-Sat, 10am-6pm, Thurs, 10am-7pm
> Own label
> Sizes: Women 6-14; Men: S-L

You know when you see T-shirts revolve around a ceiling "Yo Sushi" style there's going to be something interesting here. Handprinted T-shirts are individually customised in-house so that every piece is a one-off. All window, white and bright it's a compelling environment for graphic T-shirts addicts. Highlights of fashion themed include illustrations from stilettos to sunglasses as well as from Love to Peace, swallows to skulls, butterflies to Frankenstein and dots to splats.
T-shirts are around £25, knitwear £40 and sweat shirts, jumpers and cardigans are also available. Service is a bit laid back. Very popular.

Also available in Topshop and Topman.

Top 200

Luna and Curious
198 Brick Lane
London E1
tel: 0207 033 4411 or 0797 7440212
www.lunaandcurious.com

Wow factor: 🏠🏠🏠🏠
Choice: 🏠🏠🏠
Service: 🏠🏠🏠
Price: £££

❗ Designer RunBoutique

> Vintage, Glam
> Aldgate East LU, 5 min walk
> Shoreditch LU, 5 min walk
> Thurs-Sun, 12pm-6pm,
> Own label and designer mix

The eight founders of Luna and Curious showcase their designs in this whimsical corner shop of quirky contemporary and vintage fashion curios. On a Sunday can be bombed out with people and staff stretched to the limit. There's oodles to gaze at in the window and in the various nook and crannies that display the many miscellaneous items including iridescent feathers and porcelain butterflies. Catching the eye is the Lone Wolf label, vintage eveningwear that is further embellished by one of the designer collective with embroidery and beading. On offer too are

vintage 40's and 50's clothing, jackets, lingerie, handbags, small hats, and a range of Lingham jewellery all handmade.

Each month they offer a space to an aspiring designer or team for their work to be sold in the Curious Emporium, details of which are on their website: www.luna-andcurious.com

 Top 200

Mimi
40 Cheshire Street,
London E2 6EH
Tel: 020 729 6699

Wow factor:
Choice:
Service:
Price: £££

❗ DesignerRunBoutique

Classic
Aldgate East LU, 7 min walk
Tue-Sun, 10am-6pm
Own label

Made locally these great value classic leather bags and purses are of a label that's clearly on the rise. Not fashion-led it's more an elegant take on lifestyle wardrobe essentials. Mimi Berry, a Central Saint Martins graduate began her label and opened her shop in 2001 focusing on unstructured shapes in different colours.

The shop is locked so you'll need to use the knocker to be let in. With one person serving you can browse around uninterrupted but get knowledgeable service when you want it.

On Women's: The wearable classic designs come in an array of colours with handbags £165, purses £42 and Totes £85. A small selection of belts and Dents gloves are available.

On Men's: Laptop bags and hard leather satchels have proved big sellers as have the Patrick leather Oyster card holder £20 with her logo makes a great inexpensive present. Also does soft leather coin purses.

195

Sniff
115 Commercial Street
London E1
Tel 0207 375 1580
www.sniff.co.uk

Wow factor:
Choice:
Service:
Price:£££

Urban, Cool
Aldgate East LU, 5 min walk
Mon-Sat 10.30am-7pm, Sun 11am-6pm
Designer mix

One of the most sought after shoe boutiques within the Spitalfields Market complex and located on bustling Commercial Street itself. This independent shop prides itself for searching the world for both established and relatively unknown designers in urban and sports labels, and often gets exclusives.

The window displayed shoe edit is inviting. Inside the décor veers on the distressed side with a sense of fun.

On Women's, some nice pumps, French Sole classics with other labels using different shapes and details such as crystals. Also stocks Melissa with it's plastic made shoes in bold colours. Melissa also does collaborations with top designers such as Vivienne Westwood.

On Men's: Stocks Jeffrey West and H for Hudson shoes. I tried on a pair of brown tan H for Hudsons at £80 and found the sizing quite generous but otherwise good. Sales staff seemed bored by 4pm and into their own conversation. But once you got served they were okay.

Also in 11, St Christopher's Place W1, and 1, Great Titchfield Street W1.

Tatty Devine

236 Brick Lane
London E2
tel: 020 7739 9191
www.tattydevine.com

Wow factor: ⛻⛻⛻⛻
Choice: ⛻⛻⛻⛻
Service: ⛻⛻⛻⛻
Price: ££

Retro, cool
Aldgate East LU, 12 min walk
7 days 11am-6pm
Own label

Harriet Vine and Rosie Wolfenden started selling leather cuffs in Portobello and Spitalfield Market in 1996 and launched their first official collection in London Fashion Week in 2001. From the moment they showed we were convinced that we were witnessing a fashion first that has developed a cult following internationally. Friendly and always full of ideas this is a shop that specialises in one-off and limited editions.

It's jewellery plastic fantastic at this small boutique located on the new side of Brick Lane across Bethnal Green Road. The floor has an outstanding custom-made pink piano keyboard design and a counter choc full of jewellery, shoes and capsule collection of Anton and Alison handbags at £96.50 on the opposite side.

On Women's: Notables are the acrylic name necklaces in curly wurly '50's lettering with a choice of 18 colours. Signature designs include vinyl record charm bracelet at £45; Lady and dog bracelet, £32. Lots of fun is their Movie Mayhem collection of 50's Hollywood inspired necklaces and brooches. Other themes are plastic heart-shaped sunglass-designed pendants £26; heart rings £12, a pair of women's legs in fishnet stocking and high heels in the form of a brooch, earrings and necklaces at £41 each.

On Men's: Cufflinks in the shape of 3-D vision enamel glasses £29 and badges £17.

Service is friendly and chatty. Product is handmade in England.

Also at 57b Brewer Street, London W1F 9UL Tel 0207 434 2257

The Laden Showroom

103 Brick Lane
London E1 6SE
tel: 020 7247 2431
www.ladenshowroom.co.uk

Wow factor: ⛻⛻⛻
Choice: ⛻⛻⛻⛻⛻
Service: ⛻
Price: £

Urban
Shoreditch LU, 5 min walk
Mon-Sat, 12pm-6pm, Sun 10.30am-6pm
Designer mix
Sizes: Women: varies; Men: varies

Fifty collections from independent designers, most that you won't get anywhere else. Worth a browse to pick the one good buy. The window of this double fronted shop is a bit of a jumble and inside it's packed with small units with very cluttered rails. In general, it's shabby looking staff offer little in the way of service but then you can find great bargains here. Changing rooms are simple but bright and clean with mirrors and hooks.

On Women's: Of note is the Eliza Jade unit formerly at Camden Stables. Designer Jade Moss has rails of clothes, bags and belts where you can pick up an individual and wearable piece. Sizes arrive quite generous so you might need a size smaller than normal. I tried on a rust frilly satin skirt, a great colour. Prices start at £35. Most items are one-offs or short runs of ten all pegged at the same price as high street chains. Other labels include Pixie with their elaborate sleeves, Victim with their interesting use of lace and Duke and Dutchess mini-dresses for around £70.

On Men's: Has a lesser choice of menswear and accessories but some interesting t-shirts, hats, belts and shoes to seek out.

The Shop
1&3&7 Cheshire Street
London E2 6ED
tel: 020 7739 5631

!MustVisit

Vintage, urban
Liverpool St LU, 10 min walk, Aldgate East LU, 5 min walk
Tue-Sat, 11-6pm, Sun 9.30am-4.30pm
Designer mix
Sizes: Women: varies; Men: varies

The Shop is actually spread over three shops. At No7, it's packed with vintage women's clothes with rails of 40's and 50's floral dresses and chunky jumpers at £10. In addition handbags , jewellery, belts, sunglasses, bags and hats are scattered haphazardly and shoes are strewn all over the floor. At No3, there a few more pieces of women's clothing but mostly highly patterned vintage textiles and scarves. No1 specialises in vintage menswear and here too is a vast selection which includes quite a number of jumpers, hats and ties. Expect no welcoming formality at The Shop, but the stock knowledge is on the button. Rummage heaven.

Sunday Upmarket

Elys Yard
The Truman Brewery
(entrances on Hanbury St and Brick Lane)
London E1 6QL
Tel: 020 7770 6028

Wow factor: ▢▢
Choice: ▢▢▢
Service: ▢▢▢
Price: £

Urban
Liverpool St or Aldgate East LU, 10 min walk
Sun 8am-5pm
Designer mix
Sizes: Women varies ; Men: varies

Sunday Upmarket is an indoor conglomeration of 140 stalls with a startling abundance of fashion and accessories. Many are one-off items made by the stallholders themselves. Droves of people come here for the handprinted and handpainted tee-shirts. Check out JSK London, on-trend a large selection of up to the minute womenswear such as tops £20 and skirts £25. Styles size up in small, medium and large or you can order in your size and it will take one to two weeks for them to make. Ria Roberts, clothing and textile designer does limited edition prints notably unicorns and birds on shirts and dresses.

On other stalls bargain buys are to be found for handbags, jewellery and corset-style leather belts in unique designs for only £30. Elsewhere there's a choice of vintage clothes and shoes, scarves, hats and ties. Sunday Upmarket has all hustle and bustle of a traditional market with lots of loud music from the market's CD stall. The biggest incentive of coming here is the opportunity to pick a piece from a designer at the start of their career at a bargain price.

Hoxton & Shoreditch

Hoxton rocks with the Hoxton Boutique and shakes with a fantastic designer edit at East London's mini-department store, Start. Making a name for itself on the Shoreditch scene with knitwear is Relax Garden on Kingsland Road whilst renowned leather bag designer Ally Capellino is in Calvert Street. Further out East, in Wanstead, is Santa Fe and in the Financial District of East London, Canary Wharf there's a cool line in business suits at Centanni and an affordable on-trend designer edit at the Choice store.

Ally Capellino

9 Calvert Avenue
London E2 7JP
Tel: 020 7613 3073
www.allycapellino.co.uk

Wow factor: 🏠🏠🏠
Choice: 🏠🏠🏠
Service: 🏠🏠🏠🏠
Price: £££

!) Designer Run**Boutique**

Cool
Liverpool St LU, 10 min walk
Wed-Fri, 12-6pm, Sat 10-6 Sun 11am-4pm
Own label

One might easily bump into Ralph Fiennes who lives round here and eats a few doors away or maybe you'll rub shoulders with Alexa Chung or the occasional Arctic Monkeys who all know about the great bags of Ally Capellino.

Luxe longevity leather bags, purses, back packs and satchels ticks all the boxes on quality, understated individuality from this highly reputed, established designer committed to London fashion design.

Whilst stocked in Selfridges, Liberty and small boutiques such as Hub in Stoke Newington, her shop is the only venue with the complete collection. With over twenty five years of experience she knows what her customers want. The shop itself is fairly minimal, wooden floored, part workshop part retail.

On Women's: Handbags are about £200 whilst the unisex satchels with proofed nylon and a cow hide base are from £49. Also, thin belts and an array of caps.

On Men's: Check out the classic waxed cotton bags for easy wiping such as the Kenneth that is based with leather at £134.

Hoxton Boutique

2 Hoxton Street,
London N1 6NG
Tel: 020 7684 2083

Wow factor: 🏠🏠🏠
Choice: 🏠🏠🏠
Service: 🏠🏠
Price: ££

Cool
Old St or Liverpool St LU,10 min walk, Bus 55 stops outside Shoreditch Town Hall
Mon-Fri, 10.30am-6.30pm, Sat 11am-6pm, Sun, 12am-5pm,
customers should confirm Sunday times

Cool at the edge of fashion, this Hoxton fashion powerhouse has a loyal local clientele. Assorted size disco balls, neon lighted, Studio 54'd boutique has not just contemporary designs but also a separate delectable vintage section. It's so cool you'll lucky if you get a subdued hello and service is not forthcoming until you request it.

Owner/designer, Alison Whalley's own brand, +HOBO+ casual pretty dresses brand merits checking out as are the Hussain Chalayans's and Future Classics. On vintage there's excellent value full length fake fur coats at £65 and some grea totally sparkly, quirky and bold jewellery pieces.

The contemporary changing rooms have a leopard print curtain closing off thei large bright cubicles. In the vintage department, the mood changes as you ste back in time. It's small, all black with just one spotlight !

Relax Garden
40 Kingsland Road
Hackney
London E2 8DA
tel: 020 7033 1881
www.relaxgarden.com

! DesignerRunBoutique ! Mustvisit

Cool
Old Street St LU, 10 min walk
Mon-Wed 12pm -7pm Thu-Fri, 12pm-8pm, Sat-Sun, 12am-6pm
Own label and designer mix
Sizes: Women: varies

Just a few minutes from Hoxton Square, this miniscule boutique concentrates o short-runs, many made upstairs . Relax Garden owner Eriko also has a penchant fc buying in from Japan, her native country. Has own label dresses at £55, and jump ers at £65.50. On other designer labels there are really good coats at £90 and som trilbys, berets and scarves. The place is crammed with clothes and the ladder tha goes up to workroom is a retail curiosity. Enriko is very friendly and happy to giv any advice needed. A great find!

East London

Start (Ladies)
2-44 Rivington Street,
London EC2A 3BN
Tel: 020 7729 3334
www.start-london.com

Wow factor: ☺☺☺☺☺
Choice: ☺☺☺☺☺
Service: ☺☺☺☺☺
Price: ££££

Hoxton & Shoreditch

Cool
Old Street LU, 7 min walk
Mon-Fri, 10.30am-6.30pm, Sat 11am-6pm, Sun 1pm-5pm
Designer mix
Sizes: Women 6-14; Men: 34-48

Brix Smith-Start has one the best eye's in London for assembling collections from the hottest new designers and established favourites. A former rock guitarist, Brix is a larger than life character with peroxide blonde hair, a passionate dog lover, and vivaciously friendly who makes customers feel they are having a great experience there. Enthusiastic Shoreditch regulars may spend a whole afternoon at this mini-department store trying on heaps of outfits and then picking out a couple of favourites to buy.

Owned by Philip Start and Brix Smith-Start, the store is inventively decked out with clothes in cupboards and on an operating theatre table complete with medical spotlight, disco ball lighting, gold lamé pouffe and stalls and forty pictures of dogs adds to the verve of place.

Eye-catching are House of Holland's pink mohair sweater £270, Richard Nicoll black striped draped dress £379, Pink Soda tops starting at £60, Citizens of Humanity Jeans £155. Great picks too are Stella McCartney, 3.1 Phillip Lim, See by Chloe, Mui Mui, Sonia, Marc Jacobs. Also does handbags jewellery, Cutler and Gross sunglasses, shoes, scarves, casual hats, belts, Falke hosiery and Spanx lingerie. All the staff are friendly and the changing rooms are small but comfortable. Terrific place!

Start (Men's)
40 Rivington Street
London EC2A 3LX
tel: 020 7729 6272
www.start-london.com

Wow factor:
Choice:
Service:
Price:££££

Cool
Old Street LU, 7 min walk
Mon-Fri, 10.30am-6.30pm, Sat 11am-6pm, Sun 1pm-5pm
Designer mix
Sizes: Men: varies

Philip Start former founder of Woodhouse has his finger right on the pulse of edgy fashion and wearable clothes. This big windowed corner shop on Rivington Street helps give Hoxton it's buzz. Décor-wise there's a prominently displayed Studio 54 disco ball and the changing room downstairs is under the stairs with a little chair.

Upstairs is on-trend ready to wear Miu Miu, Sonia Rykiel and Raf Simon shirts and many A-list designer labels including their own. Downstairs is made to measure suits at £1000 for a two piece that usually takes two fittings. Service is Savile Row contemporary style and your congenial tailor pops up with a tape measure round his neck and will fit you up great. Start has their own tailoring team and I found the service impeccable. Downstairs also are shoes, belts and narrow black ties.

Menswear is also at 59 Rivington Street, London EC2A 3QQ. Tel 0207 739 3636. All the Start shops are at the intersection of Rivington and Charlotte Street.

Santa Fe
119 High Street Wanstead
London E1 6SB
Tel: 020 8518 8922

Classic
Wanstead LU, 5 min walk
Tue-Sat, 11am-7pm, Sun 11am-6.30pm
Designer mix
Sizes: Men: varies

Wanstead High Street is becoming increasingly gentrified with good quality cafes and fine food delicatessens. Santa Fe is the an oasis of a men's one-stop boutique offering a big name Bond Street label edit that includes Armani Exchange, Hugo Boss, Paul Smith. Santa Fe has a conventional clear simple designed interior and their changing rooms are quite reasonable. Wardrobe classics include Paul Smith shirt £125, Armani T-shirt £45 and Hugo Boss shorts £145. Also casual and formal wear includes trousers, jeans, shoes, evening shirts, belts, sunglasses, leather bags are nicely on display. Pleasant knowledgeable service and sales can be about 25% off. A very good stop if you are in this part of London.

Canary Wharf

Of the 200 shops in this massive mall complex, all the mainstream high street are here including Top Shop and Oasis.   Head for Cabot West for the most upscal shops including a very spacious Dune and good accessories at Reiss. On women there's Kate Kuba, River Island, and Zara. Overall service is very friendly and wit plenty of places to eat and drink it is all quite pleasant shopping. Parking is easie than at Westfield and Brent Cross. At Jubilee Place of note is the Choice store an Centanni.

Centanni

17 Jubilee Place
Canary Wharf
London E14 5NY
tel: 020 7516 0311

❗MustVisit

> Classic,
> Canary Wharf LU, 5 min walk
> Mon-Wed, 9am-7pm, Thur-Fri 9am-8pm, Sat 10am-6pm, Sun 12pm-6pm
> Designer mix

Economic turmoil may have put the Canary Wharf financial district into disarray, but when it comes to looking the business in a smart suit, gentleman are in completely safe hands with Centanni. Opened in August 2008, Nigel Gee of Cecil Gee fame is behind it. Busy on his window display he told us "With a made to measure service local executives find the several fittings more convenient here than going back and forth to the West End".

Located near M&S, Centanni is a one-level regular classic designed store, wooden floors, streamlined lighting in the ceilings and a shiny floor that almost looks like a continuation of the mall flooring outside. Centanni suits are £350-£399 available in slimmer cut and classic formats. Canali suits start at £650. Canali are renowned for their overcoats of beautiful to feel high quality cashmere/wool and at £699 are excellent value. On offer too are Brioni suits at £2000 a pop and there's a good range of Brioni shirts too as well as Faconnable and La Martina labels. Leather jackets, ties and other accessories are available and the service here is top drawer and very knowledgeable. The changing rooms are luxuriously wooden, comfortable and finely equipped. Whether looking for a suit that projects a rising master of the universe image or a very well crafted regular suit, Centanni does an exceedingly satisfactory job.

Choice

30 Jubilee Place
Canary Wharf
London E14 4NY
tel: 0845 271 9909

❗MustVisit

> Cool
> Canary Wharf LU, 5 min walk
> Mon-Sat, 10am-7pm, Sun 12pm-5pm
> Designer mix
> Sizes: Women: varies; Men: varies

Designer on-trend edit of 34 big name brands with some killer finds at sale times. Not as big as their Bluewater flagship, this busy store is just the ticket for casual designerwear with attitude Expect no welcoming formality; once you've got their attention, service is good with effective stock knowledge. Decor-wise, it's walnut and granite, changing rooms brown wooden at back of house, fully air-conditioned and hip fast beat playlists.

On Women's: The line-up includes Chloé, DKNY, Juicy Couture and Lipsey. Don't miss out on the large handbags and shoes towards the back. It's an impressive range.

On Men's: Take your pick from Full Circle, Fred Perry and H for Hudson shoes. Of interest are the Paul Smith hats £60, loose black Prada jackets and jeans.

Choice is also at Westfield, White City.

SOUTH LONDON

Putney

Whilst high street chains prevail at the Exchange Shopping Centre, along the Upper Richmond Road, Adornment and Cicily B offer a more select range of fine women's classics, with Jaki on Putney High Street offering some bargain high street priced items.

Adornments

209 Upper Richmond Road
Putney
London SW15
tel: 020 8788 3880

Wow factor: 🏠🏠🏠
Choice: 🏠🏠🏠
Service: 🏠🏠🏠🏠🏠
Price: ££

Classic
Putney Bridge BR, 5 min walk
Mon, 12am-4.40pm, Tue-Sat, 10.30am-5.30pm
Designer mix
Sizes: Women clothes 8-14; shoes 36-41

On the former Style Lab site, just off the high street, amiable Ayla Currell runs her relaxed elegant designer boutique full of clothes at affordable prices. Ever since it's opening in December 2007, Adornments has been a big success with locals. Graced with crystal chandeliers this is a uplifting edit that includes James Lakeland classic with a twist dresses, check jackets and Passport. Also stocked are stylish but inexpensive Tamaris all leather shoes from £69.99. Best sellers are the mulitcoloured woolen scarves from Kashmir and there's some interesting jewellery pieces, bags and belts to browse over. Service is personal, very knowledgeable and friendly.

Cicily B

223 Upper Richmond Road
Putney
London SW15 6SQ
tel: 020 8789 9211
www.cicilyb.com

❗Must Visit

Classic
Putney Bridge BR, 6 min walk
Tue-Sat, 10am-6pm,
Designer mix
Sizes: Women: varies

Owner Lara Helayel prides herself on giving customers honest and helpful advice and has them firmly in mind when purchasing from a whole array of European and American labels. Her career clothes and eveningwear line-up consists of Hoss, No Lita, Essential, Old Molly, Language and Manoush. In addition there's Freesoul jeans and casualwear. The place is pleasant enough with a smart classic focus with fashions to suit all figures.

Does private appointments on request. Don't go during the school-run as the staff stand-in hasn't much of a clue about stock.

Jaki
142 Putney High Street,
London SW15 1RR
tel: 020 8789 7301

(!) Must Visit

Cool
Putney Bridge BR, 2 min walk
Mon-Fri, 10am-7pm, Sat 9.30-6pm Sun 12am -5.30pm
Ready to wear
Sizes: Women varies

Well above average, bargain high street fashion edit of QED London, Charlie and George. Décor-wise it has a brass handled front door and metal railing spears inside with an interesting on-trend window with mannequins. The place buzzes with lots of rails, and an array of handbags on a high shelf the length of the shop. Also stocks the Butterfly range of jewellery. Items are labelled with the recommended retail price and marked down to the price they sell it at in the shop. I tried on a coat that was rrp £67 but the Jaki price was £40. Changing rooms are white with a mirror white curtain, hangers and a chair. With these bargains, staff are too busy to give service or even a smile.

Top 200

Joy
63 Putney High Street
London SW15 1SR
tel: 020 8789 2774
www.joythestore.com

Wow factor: 🛍🛍🛍
Choice: 🛍🛍🛍🛍🛍
Service: 🛍
Price: £

Cool
BR Putney, Putney East/Putney Bridge LU, 6 min walk
Mon-Fri, 8am-7pm, Sat 11am-5pm
Designer mix and own label
Sizes: Women 8-14; Men: S-XL

This branch is very popular with Putney locals. For review of this chain see page (224)

Also at Bankside, Brixton, Brunswick Centre, Clapham Junction, Chiswick, Fulham, Greenwich and St Paul's

Balham Bou
4 Hildreth Street
London SW12
Tel 0208 675 1007
www.balhambou.co.uk

(!) Must Visit

Cool
Balham LU or Balham BR, 5 min walk
Mon-Sat, 10am-7pm, Thurs 11am-8pm, Sun 11am-4pm

Successful one-stop convenience boutique for young Balham professionals, situated on a market street, that brings a bit of the West End to Balham. Run by Max and Becky, Balham Bou stocks Mina, a popular designer that sells well in Topshop, also stocks French Connection, Vira Moda Label, Bambooa, t-shirts, trainers and hoodies. Mina's cute dresses have a Kylie, Keira and Sienna following. Service is amiable and informative

Wimbledon

Top 200

Bamford and Sons
The Village Store,
32 The High Street
London SW19
Tel 020 8 944 7806
www.bamfordandsons.com

Wow factor: 🛍🛍🛍
Choice: 🛍🛍🛍
Service: 🛍🛍🛍🛍🛍
Price: ££££

Ethical
Wimbledon LU, 5 min walk
Mon-Sat 10am-6pm, Sun 12am-5pm
Sizes: Women dress 8-16; shoes: 36-41; Men: S-XXL, shoes 8½-11½

For review see Bamford & Sons, Sloane Square page (137)

Other branches are at The Old Workshop, 79 Ledbury Road London W11
Tel 020 7881 8010 and Notting Hill Gate LU, (8 min walk). Also concessions in
Selfridges, Harrods and Harvey Nichols.

Top 200

Marilyn Moore
71 White Hart Lane,
Barnes SW13 APP
Tel 0208 878 9973
www.marilynmoore.co.uk

Wow factor:🏠🏠🏠
Choice:🏠🏠🏠🏠
Service:🏠🏠🏠🏠
Price:£££

① DesignerRunBoutique

Glam, cool
Barnes Bridge BR, 5 min walk
Mon-Sat, 10am-6pm, Sun, 12am-5pm
Own label
Sizes: Women XS-XL

For shop review see Marilyn Moore branch in Notting Hill on page (152)

HIGH STREET CHAINS

London's high street chains are brilliant at producing catwalk looks at a fraction of the price. Some efforts are so good it's hard to tell the difference from the real thing although sometimes they don't wear as well. Now everyone and that includes celebrities and royalty shop at the high street chains even if they are accustomed to wearing designer labels, people will often mix it with a high street brand.

High street chains open a door of fashion opportunity by arranging special collaborations with top designers, enabling people to have a taster of wearing creations. Of note are H&M and Debenhams whilst Topshop has a commitment to capsule collections from smaller upcoming designers. Collaborations with celebrities has brought celebrity-led fashions into the mainstream of which Top Shop with Kate Moss has been most successful.

The high street chains have made a major contribution to fashion in London and have helped to bring great designs to everyone.

Below are given reviews of the flagship stores that often form the template for their smaller branches.

All Saints
57-59 Long Acre,
London EC1
tel: 020 7836 0801
www.allsaints.co.uk

Wow factor:🛍🛍🛍🛍🛍
Choice:🛍🛍🛍🛍
Service:🛍
Price:££

Cool
Covent Garden LU, 1 min walk
Mon-Sun 9.30am-9.30pm, except Thurs, 9.30am-10.30pm and
Sun 12am-6pm
Own label
Sizes: Women XXS-L; Men: 36-44

Goth meets contemporary at this immensely popular and successful fashion chain of hard edge designed stores with a high octane vibe. Uneven walls, quirky strips of lights, an eye-catching vast crystal chandelier and random old drawers falling out with clothes displayed in it, makes for an entertaining atmosphere.

On Women's: The ground floor has good strapless special occasion dresses £120 and are especially good on voluminous sculptural skirts with interesting cuts at only £60. A micro-collection of shoes is at the rear. Gladiator sandals (£40) are worth a look as is their good choice of sunglasses and belts. Changing room scenarios can be perplexing. The cubicles themselves are okay, matching the décor theme of the store, just curtained off, mirror, stool and hanger. When I went to try on a skirt, there was a girl waiting with six items so patiently I joined the queue behind her. And then somebody queued up behind me. And then six items girl said "I don't know if there is anybody inside the cubicles. There were no staff running the changing rooms at all. In the end, people had to resort to saying "Is there anybody in there?" – in fact they were almost all empty! And there was a queue half way down the shop to pay. Indeed, there is zero staff contact with customers, however the products look good. With reasonable materials and great styles it is good value for the price. Excellent reductions at sale times; dresses £120 reduced to £30.

On Men's: In the basement, good quality jackets, shirts, T-shirts, distressed jeans.

Also at Foubert's Place, Market Place, Selfridges Womenswear, South Molton Street all in W1 and Islington, King's Road, Kensington and Harrods.

Arrogant Cat
1a Duke Street,
London W1U 1LS
tel: 020 7487 5501

Wow factor:🛍🛍🛍
Choice:🛍🛍🛍
Service:🛍🛍
Price: ££

Glam
Marble Arch LU, 5 min walk
Mon-Sat, 10am-8.30pm, except Thurs, 10am-9.30pm
and Sun 11.30am-6pm
Own label
Sizes: Women Petite 6-8; small 8-10; medium 12 and one size 8-12

A stone's throw from Selfridges, this small black boutique with dark windows, red walls, chandeliers and the name of the boutique in pink neon lights gives a glossy glam environment. This small chain has a lot of clothes displayed in a confined space, the style is clubby and dressy.

Tried on a satin strapless dress with bra attached at £149 that was marvellous. Body-conscious drape and figure hugging dresses with hemline usually above the knee and shorter; crop tuxedo jackets at £149 are worth a whirl. There are handbags and a small but intriguing selection of belts.

Service is a little inconsistent. A sales assistant got the dress in the size for me, showed me to a changing room but didn't follow through with any more service. That said the clothes here are extremely good and with a clientele that includes Amy Winehouse, Alesha Dixon, Bianca Gascoine, Mischa Barton, Lindsay Lohan and Naomi Campbell, you'll be in good company. Changing rooms are small, black with a mirror, no hooks, but seats inside and out.

Also at: 311, King's Road SW3, 18 Great Portland St, W1; 12 Kensington Church Street, W8; 4 The Square Richmond on Thames, Surrey.

Benetton
255 Regent St
London W1U 1LS
tel: 020 7647 4220
www.benetton.com

Classic
Oxford Circus LU, 1 min walk
Mon-Sat, 10am-8pm, except Thurs, 10am-8.30pm and Sun 11.30am-6pm
Own label
Sizes: Women 38-46, shoes 2-8; Men, 34-48

Renowned for its vast colour palette, Benetton wardrobe basics offer good quality and value for money. This massive flagship, right on Oxford Circus the busiest shopping area in London, has three floors of fashion and is quite tastefully decked out in chandeliers with giant light bulbs, mostly white décor, lots of tidy shelves and always has striking well-dressed window displays. The ground floor houses jumpers in a vast array of colours, V necks, polos, roundnecks, cardigans, T-shirts, trousers, suits and shoes. The first floor is larger with the Sisley range as well as further basics, dresses, lingerie and coats. Benetton always has a selection of pumps and some handbags, scarves and belts. Menswear is in the basement. Staff are quite friendly.

Also at 23 Brompton Road, Unit 10 Brunswick Centre, 488 Brixton Road, 116 Putney High St

Top 200

Coast

262-264 Regent Street
London W1R 5AD
tel: 020 7287 9538
www.coast-stores.com

Wow factor: ▢▢▢
Choice: ▢▢▢▢
Service: ▢▢▢▢
Price: ££

Glam, classic
Oxford Circus LU, 2 min walk
Mon-Sat, 10am-8pm, Sun 12am-6pm
Own label
Sizes: Women dress 8-18; shoes: 3-8

One of the main draws here are the signature strapless dresses and strapless tops and skirts. With plenty of chiffons and satins, floral patterned prints, all excellent value that would look good at any special occasion. Take your pick from short dresses £115; long £150; skirts £80; many bolero jackets £95. Another draw is the accessory-outfit match. Small evening bags are on offer to complement the outfits usually jewelled, as well as diamante necklaces. Shoes to match are featured and they can also be dyed to match. A small selection of fascinators and sinnamay cocktail hats are displayed.

With twenty outlets in the London area, Coast has a winning formula. The store's outside has small elegant windows whilst inside, there's a rather nice spiral staircase descending down a mirrored wall. The two floors of clothes are a bit cluttered. The changing rooms, however, are quite adequate in size, and have a large oval mirror, grey curtain and has an armchair outside for a waiting companion. Staff walk the talk wearing Coast strapless evening dresses even in the middle of winter! Knowledgeable, helpful and they recommend what's appropriate and what's coming in.

Dune
28 Argyll St
London W1F 7EB
tel: 020 7287 9010
www.dune.co.uk

Wow factor: 👜👜👜
Choice: 👜👜👜👜
Service: 👜👜👜👜
Price: ££

Cool
Oxford Circus LU, 4 min walk
Mon-Wed, 10am-7pm, Thurs -Fri, 10am-8pm, Sat 10am-7pm,
Sunday 12pm-6pm
Own label
Sizes: Women shoes 3-8; Men: 6-12

For credit crunched shoe addicts, this spacious Dune has walls of well displayed fashion driven shoes and bags at highly affordable prices.

On Women's: Shoes and bags, casual and special occasion, on-trend styles and on-trend colours, Dune does it well and all at inexpensive prices. Standouts are handbags at around £75, shoes £80 – a fraction of the same styles in designer shops. Female staff are well glammed up, pretty helpful and totally bowled over by the products they are selling. Whilst gazing at one bag, a sales assistant told me the bag "was straight off the catwalk. One of our must-have buys. The black one has got my name on it. I love it so much. Oh, and that other bag was on the front cover of Glamour Magazine." She then came up for air!

On Men's: There's a tempting selection of smart dressy and casual.
I tried on a pair of "The Alistair" shoe with an almond shaped toe at £75 that felt quite fine and found the service perfectly straight forward and fairly good. Bags, hats, scarves, belts, wallet and gloves are also available.

Top 200

French Connection
249-251 Regent Street
London W1
tel: 020 7 493 3124
www.frenchconnection.com

Wow factor: 👜👜👜
Choice: 👜👜👜
Service: 👜👜👜
Price: ££

Classic
Oxford Circus LU, 2 min walk
Mon-Sat, 10am-7pm, Sun10am-6pm
Own label
Sizes: Women 6-16; shoes: 36-41; Men S- XL, shoes 41-45

Legendary edgy provocative advertising campaigns, chic eurostyle fashions and a buzzy atmosphere has held French Connection in good stead for many years. On the corner of Princes Street and Regent Street the store has attractive windows three floors of fashion with an interior of marble and wood décor. Price-wise it's upper end for the high street but some good basic items such as dresses can be snapped up from £35.

On Women's: The signature Sunrise dress at £75 has been worn by everybody from Kate Middleton to Joan Collins and they do variations on the dress each season. Top picks are mohair coats at £125, jeans £70, handbags £50 and the small selection of bangles £5, sandals, £35, court shoes £90, trilby £20 and belts £15-£50.

On Men's: Based on the ground floor, it's a smaller selection but still quite slick. Jeans are mostly over £60, and notably strong on knitwear, including cashmere crews and v-necks at £85. Desirable selection of coats and jackets, quirky t's and casual shirts at around £45.

Quite friendly service and will show you a catalogue of forthcoming in-store collections. I tried on a full black skirt at £55. Helpful staff guided me to the changing room, but as the zip wouldn't move I had to call for assistance as no one was at hand. Once an assistant arrived the problem was swiftly fixed leaving me quite pleased with the service. Changing rooms are light wood with white door, seat, mirror, hanger, bright and good size and mirror outside. For in-store events check their website that also gives their extensive list of London stores and concessions throughout the capital.

 Top 200

H&M

234 Regent Street
London W1
Tel 0207 758 3990
www.hm.com

Wow factor: 🛍🛍🛍🛍
Choice: 🛍🛍🛍🛍🛍
Service: 🛍🛍🛍
Price: £

Cool
Mon-Sat 10am-8pm, Sun 12am-6pm
Oxford Circus LU, 2min walk
Own label
Sizes: Women dress XS-L

Arguably the largest clothes retailer in the world with twelve stores in the London area alone, H&M keep's it's vibe ever fresh with guest designer's capsule collections. With vast bright eye-catching windows, the interior has striking black walls, grey floor, white display units with good mannequins and rails in the centre, H&M really does generate the heat. Even the changing rooms are uplifting. "Be Brave Be Yourself " is written on the wall of the cubicle and it's not a mean space either with thick grey curtains enclosing a reasonable sized area.

On Women's: The emphasis is very inexpensive takes of the latest designer styles. And yes, some do look cheap, but keep searching, there are some real gems to find. With everything from jeans to evening wear, there's a great selection of tops for around £10 in a huge array of colours and sizes. Other great picks are knitted dresses £19.99, pumps £19.99 and belts £5.99. Handbags, jewellery, sunglasses, shoes, scarves, hats, and lingerie are also available.

H&M's organic clothing features across all their departments. On offer are organic dresses, tops , bodysuits as well as apparel derived from organic and recycled wool including coats, Kimono jackets, Jodhpur styled trousers, tulip skirts and knitted jumpers. Also worth a view are the tunic dresses, blouses, sweatshirts, jeans, print T's and sweatshirt dresses as well as the organic anoraks, sleepwear and underwear.

At H&M, it's hard to know who is staff the only indication is someone wearing a small badge. Nobody was around in the changing room to help when I needed it. I went to the front of the changing area and asked for a different size, but was told they were not allowed to leave their position and that I would have to get changed and go back out again to get it. I also asked about shoe sizing to a pleasant assistant who didn't know the answer but went to find out and came back in a few minutes with the information.

On Men's: Take your choice from the amazingly price printed T-shirts, hooded cardigans, waistcoats, military-inspired shirts and jackets khaki jeans in different shades and basics such as boxer shorts, socks and scarves.

Hobbs

Oxford Circus LU, 2 min walk
217-219 Regent Street
London W1B 4NG
Tel 0207 437 4418
www.hobbs.co.uk

(!) Must Visit

Classic
Mon-Sat 10am-7pm,Thurs 10am-8pm, Sun 12pm-6pm
Own label
Sizes: Women dress 8-16, shoes 36-42

From classic smart officewear to special occasion, Hobbs appeals to ladies that want to project a definitely sensible non-frivolous blend-into–the-crowd image This double fronted shop is pretty woodeny on the inside but has some smart gold topped rails and the service is efficient and amicable. Downstairs houses Hobb's full shoe collection, more clothes and is a tranquil haven from the Oxford Circus hustle. Hobbs also does a fine line in handbags, jewellery, hats, scarves and belts.

Jane Norman

59 Brompton Road
London SW3 1DP
tel: 020 7225 3098
www.janenorman.co.uk

(!) Must Visit

Glam
Knightsbridge LU, 5 min walk
Mon-Fri, 10am-8pm, Sat 9.30am-8pm, Sun, 10am-6pm
Own label
Sizes: Women 6-16; shoes 3-8

figure hugging outfits great for clubbing or holidaying is the main event here. So rammed with rails, sometimes it's difficult to get through. Hot on budget glam, check their V-neck dresses at £35. Has a good range of colours for each season, with the fit veering on the small side. Staff may ignore customers if pre-occupied re-arranging the shop displays and the queue at the till can be a bit tiresome. Hugely popular chain.

Top 200

Jigsaw
St Christopher's Place
London W1 1AF
Tel: 020 7493 9169
www.jigsaw-online.com

Wow factor: ☐☐☐
Choice: ☐☐☐☐
Service: ☐☐☐☐
Price: ££

Glam
Marble Arch, Bond Street LU, 5 min walk
Mon-Sat, 10am-6.30pm, Thurs, 10.30am-8pm, Sun 12am-6pm
Own label
Sizes: Women 8-16, shoes 41-36

Revolving murals, funky lit glass shelving topped with blue lights, a beach hut changing room, classic with a fashionable twist clothes, wearable for more than one season adds up to some very entertaining and useful fashion shopping. This large Jigsaw store faces the lively square at St Christopher's Place and is a popular beehive for fashionistas visiting Selfridges across the road. On offer are jumpers £98, pumps £70, handbags, shoes, hats, scarves, sunglasses and belts.

Service is very good. I tried on a black draped T-shirt dress at £38 and the sales-person hunted around for alternative colours and other pieces that would complement it. Packing the garments although well-presented, however does take them a long time to do.

Joy
5 Paternoster Row
London EC4
tel: 020 7489 7123
www.joythestore.com

Wow factor: 🔔🔔🔔
Choice: 🔔🔔🔔🔔
Service: 🔔🔔🔔
Price: £

Cool ,
St Paul's LU, 3 min walk
Mon-Fri, 8am-7pm, Sat 11am-5pm
Designer mix and own label
Sizes: Women 8-14; Men: S-XL

Upcoming chain, Joy, stocks styles from the Scandinavian brand MbyM alongside Vero Moda. Featured   English labels are Max C, Elise Ryan, Yumi and Ringspur whilst French brands include Rene Derhy and Deby Debo. A stone's throw from St Paul's Cathedral, Joy, is a breath of fashion fresh air amongst the serious citywear shops nearby. Plenty of interesting rails to look at with dresses well-priced from £30-£140. On Men's, I tried on a military coat that fitted quite snuggly. Staff can be very laid back. A small book section with fashion and lifestyle books is popular with browsing shoppers.

Also at Bankside, Brixton, Brunswick Centre, Clapham Junction, Chiswick, Fulham, Greenwich and Putney.

Joseph
23 Old Bond Street
London W1
tel: 020 7629 3713
www.joseph.co.uk

Wow factor: 🔔🔔🔔
Choice: 🔔🔔🔔🔔
Service: 🔔🔔🔔🔔🔔
Price: £££

Classic
Green Park Tube, 7 min walk
Mon-Sat, 10am-6.30pm, Thurs, 10am-7pm, Sun 12am-5pm
Own label
Sizes: Women 8-14, shoes 36-41; Men: 48-56

Much loved boutique and once smitten by the beguiling Joseph quality fabric and cut, you'll find yourself returning again and again. Whilst this is one of the small Joseph's the personal service in this particular branch was exceptional and deserve commendation. It's a smart looking shop with small but well equipped changing rooms.

On Women's: Recognised for superb quality knitwear that's good value for money and good on T-shirts starting at about £120. Suits, skirts and jackets have a fine looking finish and there's slick selection of jeans that fit well. Joseph does basics the seasons with good execution and smart belts and shoes complete the story. Situated on ground floor and mezzanine.

On Men's: In the lower ground floor, it's comfortable with sofa for relaxing as you deliberate on the consistently good quality coats, sweaters and shirts, although little on the expensive side. Much time is spent in getting things right if you need a sleeve and trouser leg alterations. Joseph does superb sales,

High Street Chains

Karen Millen
229-247 Regent St
London W1
Tel: 020 7629 1901
www.karenmillen.com

Wow factor: 🏠🏠🏠🏠
Choice: 🏠🏠🏠🏠
Service: 🏠🏠🏠🏠
Price: ££

Glam
Oxford Circus LU, 3 min walk
Mon-Wed, 10am-8pm, Thurs, 10am-8.30pm, Sat 10am-7
.30pm, Sun 11.30am-7.30pm
Own label
Sizes: Women 6-16, shoes 36-41

Karen Millen is a sophisticated high street chain trying to be a designer shop with their own take and style on the latest fashions. From the outside there's a very attractive window display. This large shop has rails with easy to see collections, put together with items that mix well.

Signature satin dresses with matching shoes and bag will flatter most ages for special occasion and range from £180-£300. Glamorous outfits are on display as you enter and there's a good choice of dressy casual too. Sunglasses, belts and watches are available although the jewellery collection is quite small.

Impressive is the high levels of sales contact and they will bring items to your changing room that co-ordinate. Very knowledgeable, it's a good shopping experience here.

Kurt Geiger
5 South Molton Street
London W1K 5SU
Tel: 020 7758 8020
www.kurtgeiger.com

Wow factor: 🏠🏠🏠🏠
Choice: 🏠🏠🏠🏠
Service: 🏠🏠🏠🏠
Price: £££

Glam
Bond Street LU, 5 min walk
Mon-Sat, 10am-7pm, Thurs, 10am-8pm, Sun 12am-6pm
Own label and designer mix
Sizes: Women 36-40; Men: 41-45

Located at the Brook Street end of South Molton Street, here it's bold and sexy shoes with signature windows tanked up with gigantic shoe images with the respective shoes in front of them. Inside, shoes are presented well on shelves, long tables by labels and by collections.

On Women's: Kurt Geiger's own label are definitely on-trend. Their diffusion label, KG is good value whilst the Carvela's are even more affordable but a bit harder on the feet and those with cash to splash can sparkle in a Gina sandal. Also has some very okay handbags. Service is friendly and helpful

On Men's: The department is smaller. Whilst veering more onto the conventional, silver pairs are in evidence.

High Street Chains

L.K Bennett
31 Brook Street
London W1K 4HF
tel: 020 7629 3923
www.lkbennett.com

Wow factor: 🏠🏠🏠
Choice: 🏠🏠🏠🏠
Service: 🏠🏠🏠🏠🏠
Price: ££

Classic
Bond Street LU, 7 min walk
Mon-Sat, 10am-7pm, except Thurs 10am-8pm, Sun 11am-6pm
Own label
Sizes: Women dress 8-16; shoes: 36-41

This very popular chain is best known for their shoes that are well made, reasonably priced with the latest styles and colours. The two floors have attractively displayed collections that are very easy to see and walk around.

With lots of giant mirrors, it's a pleasure trying on shoes and clothes. Has a collection of bags to match shoes. Clothes here veer on the formal classic.

Special occasion clothes, smart casuals and ideal outfits for weddings are stocked. Also does sun hats and belts. Staff service is right on the button.

Mango
225 Oxford Circus
London W1D 2LP
tel: 020 7534 3505
www.mango.com

Wow factor: 🏠🏠🏠🏠🏠
Choice: 🏠🏠🏠🏠🏠
Service: 🏠🏠🏠
Price: £

Glam
Oxford Circus LU, 5 min walk
Mon-Sat, 10am-8.30pm, Thurs, 10am-9pm,Sun 11am-6pm
Own label
Sizes: Women S-XL, 8-16, shoes 3-8; Men: S-XL, shoes 6-10

Spanish global brand that differs from Zara in that it has a celebrity designer element edge plus a strong celebrity following that includes Victoria Beckham, Alice Dellal, Girls Aloud, Danni Minogue and Fearne Cotton.

At Mango it's fashionistas clothes on a budget. From the exterior it's just one small window at street level with a modern grey entrance. Inside, the three floors of clothes mirror the styles of designer shops. Changing rooms consist of ten micro cubicles, a slight problem if you have a big bag with you. That said they are bright have a mirror and have places to hang your clothes.

On Women's: The Penélope Cruz and Mónica Cruz collection has good value dresses at around £50. Mango strengths are coats at around £100, v-necks, round necks, polo jumpers, cardigans, t-shirts £15-£18 in attractive colours. Also stock handbags, jewellery, shoes, hats, scarves and belts.

Mango showcases a large striking exhibit of mannequins wearing sweater dresses in the winter and T shirt dresses in the summer. I tried on a waistcoat but nobod eemed too bothered to ask if it was okay on me or if I needed anything else. However, one you lasso your sales assistant, they are quite knowledgeable and friendly. Indeed, there are some real bargains and Glamour magazine reader evening shopping events too. On women's, it's a place we can definitely recommend.

On Men's: The menswear section is relatively small and on the third floor. With a casual focus, there are f jackets at £70-£100, leather jackets £170 and also t-shirts and trilby's. Altogether there are several ranges but the HE range is not that cheap with cotton shirts at £50, t's at £16, jeans at £45 jeans, Mango still has some way to go here to be as enterprising as the womenswear.

lso at 106 Regent St; 8-12 Neal St, Covent Garden

 Top 200

Marks and Spencer
58 Oxford Street
London W1N 0AP
Tel: 020 7935 7954
www.marksandspencer.com

Wow factor: ☖☖☖☖
Choice: ☖☖☖☖☖
Service: ☖☖☖
Price: ££

Glam
Marble Arch LU, 3 min walk
Mon-Fri, 9am-9pm, Sat 8am-8pm, Sun 12am-6pm
Own label
Sizes: Women 8-20; Men: S-XXL

This flagship has a great layout, attractive, easy to see and good to walk around. Has giant pictures of celebrity models used to advertise the clothes including Twiggy and Erin O'Connor. White, bright, there are lots of big mirrors all around.

The changing rooms again have pictures of the models covering the outside of the cubicles. Inside there are two mirrors, seat, hangers and a seat outside for your companion. In addition M&S has a lingerie changing room with an advisor.

On Women's: Clothes to suit all ages, shapes and sizes. Still has the classic styles that some customers have been buying all their lives, but now has looks inspired by the catwalks and at good prices and quality. Does handbags, jewellery, sunglasses, shoes, scarves, hats and belts as well as lingerie and hosiery. Tried on a leather coat and as luck would have it the zip was faulty. The sales assistant got right onto it and fetched another promptly.

On Men's: Whilst renowned for classic well made lasting clothes, M&S have some quite good modern lines on their Autograph range and has ventured into making very inexpensive suits. Underwear, ties and socks are always good value. A men's tailoring and alterations service is available.

Café Revive has some good coffee and snacks and is a good place for resting tired feet.

Branches are all over London.

High Street Chains

Miss Selfridge
Ground Floor
36-38 Great Castle Street
Oxford Circus
London W1W 8LG
Tel 0207 927 0214
www.missselfridge.com

Wow factor: 🏠🏠🏠
Choice: 🏠🏠🏠🏠
Service: 🏠🏠🏠
Price: £

> Glam
> Oxford Circus LU, 30 sec walk
> Mon-Sat, 9am-8pm, Thurs, 9am-9pm, Sun 12am-6pm
> Size: 6-16, petites also, shoes 3-8

As you walk in the latest fashions hit you big time and there's a great vibe her too. Here's the place to get a perfect dress for a special occasion, as suit for work clubby jeans and T's at very reasonable prices. A medium sized store, it packs a enormous punch with an impressive choice that's clearly laid out and uncluttered Miss Selfridge is hot on basics such as T-shirts, dresses and jumpers whilst at th rear are shoe and lingerie sections. Trousers come up in different lengths and ther is a petite range. Belts, scarves, jewellery and handbags are dotted around. Sta aren't always present when you need them but attention to service is okay an they will search the store for items.

The entrance is on Oxford Street or you can access through the Topshop store.

Monsoon
498-500 Oxford Street
Marble Arch
London W1C 1LQ
tel: 020 7491 3004
www.monsoon.co.uk

Wow factor: 🏠🏠🏠
Choice: 🏠🏠🏠🏠
Service: 🏠🏠🏠🏠
Price: ££

> Glam
> Marble Arch, 3 min walk
> Mon-Fri, 9.30am-8pm, Thurs, 9.30am -9pm, Sun 12am-6pm
> Own label
> Sizes: Women 8-18 but also some 20 and 22's and a petite range,
> shoes 4-8; Men S-XL;

This is a store that if they like what you are wearing they'll give you a big hug At least that's what happened to me when I was looking to try on a skirt. Post hug, I tried on the skirt and another member of the super-friendly staff was ver chatty and agreed that it didn't in fact fit me. Overall staff here are quite fashio knowledgeable.

Whilst the windows are a bit boring, inside is easy to navigate and see, and th lifts are padded! With regard to changing rooms, each has it's own name and theme. Spring, Boudoir, Satin and Rose are all decorated with a tiny chandelier and have chairs designed depending on the theme.

On Women's: From the beach to The Ball, set out in different clothing types, Monsoon has a strong reputation in romantic chiffons and silks. Has long evening dresses at £180 and there are strapless beaded dresses for special occasions, jeans and T-shirts. The petite section is in the basement. Accessories include handbags, jewellery, sunglasses, shoes scarves, hats and belts.

On Men's: Also in the basement is a capsule men's collection of casuals of which the cashmere jumpers at £55 are good value as is the their grey 90% wool Military coat at £120. Take your pick from trousers around £60, shirts about £54, and jackets £107.

Clientele include Fern Cotton, Holly Willoughby, Lisa Snowdon, Lorraine Kelly and Jane Torville.

 Top 200

New Look
100-502 Oxford Street
London W1
Tel: 020 7290 7860

Wow factor: 🏠🏠🏠🏠
Choice: 🏠🏠🏠🏠🏠
Service: 🏠🏠
Price: £

Cool
Marble Arch LU, 3 min walk
Mon-Sat, 10am-6pm
Own label
Sizes: Women dress 6-18; shoes: 3-8, Men's S-XXL, shoes 6-12

One the best designed stores in London. Set on a corner, one walks in and there's an imposing silver shiny staircase at the front, the whole store being on the first floor. With photos of models all around the walls and the latest chart music playing the place has a very positive vibe. If you've got a lot to try on, they have the

cutest trolleys in town and at the top of the staircase there are silver stalls to sit on. At the side, earphones with cd players are available for in-store listening. .

On Women's: Copies of the latest looks; dresses £20 different length trousers £15, shoes are particularly good value. Good looking styles, casual wedges £25, court shoes from £25, boots £35. On display too are handbags, jewellery, sunglasses and belts at about £8, scarves, hats and lingerie.

On Men's, New Look ventured into Men's in November 2008 will a classic collection. How about a check shirt by leading designer Giles Deacon fo just £20?

For service, it's hard to identify who the staff actually are. The approach is minimal contact but they will help if asked. Changing rooms are pretty basic. Lock are missing but there is a buzzer for assistance. Wait-time is usually five minute before you pay.

Oasis
292 Regent Street,
London W1
tel: 020 7323 5978
www.oasis-stores.com

(!)Must Visit

> Classic
> Oxford Circus LU, 3 min walk
> Mon-Sat, 10am-6pm
> Own label
> Sizes: Women dress 8-16; shoes: 36-41

Based on the north-side of Regent Street in the direction of Portland Place, th large double fronted store is spacious inside with rails of easy to see clothes and shoe section at the rear.

Oasis has 21 stores in London plus a concession in Selfridges and House of Frase Oxford Street. Oasis does wearable takes on the season's catwalk looks with ke pieces in the colours of the season. On offer are dresses £50, skirts £40 plus, T' jeans, jumpers, trousers, beachwear, coats and jackets. They also have exclusiv brands including Liberty Fabric and Odille Lingerie. Handbags, jewellery, bangle £8, sunglasses, scarves, shoes, pumps £35, small black headdresses, belts £18 an watches from £20 are available.

Service, well have they heard of it? You can wander for ages as staff have minimum contact with customers.

Quite good are the changing rooms: boudoir chic in the central area with a big oval mirror with heavy gold frame, white small chandeliers and an elaborate couch. Cubicles are equipped with a velvet stall and hangers.

 Top 200

Pied de Terre
19 South Molton Street,
London W1K 5QU
Tel: 020 7629 1362
www.shoestudio.com

Wow factor:👜👜👜
Choice:👜👜👜
Service: 👜👜👜👜
Price: ££

Glam
Bond Street LU, 5 min walk
Mon-Sat, 10am-7pm, Thurs, 10am-8pm Sun 12am-6pm
Own label
Sizes: Women shoes 3-8, Men's shoes 40-46

A bright, white shop, Pied de Terre always has an excellent display of its comprehensive own label shoe collection. With inspiration from vintage and modern styles, this is a place for great looking shoes at reasonable prices.

On Women's: The vibe is shapely heels, stilettos, pointy toes and vivacious colours. Particularly tasty are the black patent ankle strap shoes with pointy toes at £117.44 that match most outfits as are the court shoes at around £100. Flatter shoes with kitten heels come up in purple and turquoise; large bags are in a choice of colours at approximately £200.

On Men's: Only a very small collection here but of note are the single tramline side lace ups at £73.40 and moccasins just under £60.

Whilst this is the only free standing Pied de Terre store in London there are so many concessions such as in House of Fraser, Top Shop, Debenhams, Fenwick, Brent Cross giving testament to their popularity.

 Top 200

Primark
499-517 Oxford Street
London W1K 7DA
Tel: 0207 495 0420
www.primark.co.uk

Wow factor:👜👜👜👜
Choice:👜👜👜👜👜
Service: 👜
Price: £

Casual, classic
Marble Arch LU, 2 min walk
Mon-Fri, 9am-9pm, Sat, 9am-8pm, Sun 12am-6pm
Own label
Sizes: Women varies; Men: varies

Selling 10 million items in it's first ten days of trading this is the busiest clothes store in London. Outside this Marble Arch flagship, people sit on the ledge of the store with their bags recovering from the wrangle. On entry, pick up your shopping basket which is a sack with two handles, then go into the throng.

Targeting the under 35's, Primark does mostly basics but also some fashion pieces too. Even the low price chains stores look expensive compared to them.
Primark is high wow on account of their brilliant bargain price for fashionable items.

Rails and display tables are all in a jumble that you have to sift through. Woolen dresses £8, polo neck from £3, V-neck ribbed jumpers from £4 in a choice of the latest shades. Trousers £10, tartan miniskirts £5; voluminous skirts at £6, looking like copies of real designer items. Some of it does look cheap but you can definitely sift through and find a real bargain. On the left hand side the mood slightly changes to lingerie boudoir-lite with knickers for £1 and satin and lace night dresses at £4. Whilst not for extreme eco-conscious warriors, the jaw dropping low prices place massive temptations on religiously ethical customers. To their credit Primark is a member of the Ethical Trading Initiative, an alliance of companies, trade unions and non-profit making organisations that aims to promote the rights of people in factories and farms worldwide.

On Women's: You have to queue way down the shop to the changing room and join another long queue to pay. Fortunately they have a lot of checkouts and staff are quite quick. General service is low, with minimal contact by staff. Upstairs is women's accessories: handbags £8, pumps £4, high heel black lace shoes £15. Has a good selection of belts from £2.50. Parka coats at £13 are a bargain.

On Men's: Menswear is upstairs. Suits at £35 and you can buy them as separates. Staggeringly inexpensive shirts from £4, trousers £8, black leather style bomber £17, coats £25. Guys buy by the bucket load and who wouldn't at these prices.

Primark is a chain that every bargain hungry fashionista in London goes to.

Principles
Westfield
D3 Level 1
London W1
tel: 0870 122 8802
www.principles.co.uk

Wow factor: 🏠🏠🏠🏠
Choice: 🏠🏠🏠🏠
Service: 🏠🏠🏠🏠🏠
Price: £

Glam
Own label, ready to wear
Sizes: Main collection 8-20, Petite 6-16, Shoes 4-7

Principles new Flagship store is in Westfield. For review see page (163).

Also at 38 The Poultry, EC2; John Lewis, Sloane Square, Oxford St, Brent Cross, Debenhams, Fenwick at Brent Cross and Morley in Brixton.

 Top 200

River Island
01-309 Oxford Street,
London W1C 2DN
tel: 0844 395 1011
www.riverisland.com

Wow factor: 🏠🏠🏠🏠
Choice: 🏠🏠🏠🏠
Service: 🏠🏠🏠
Price: £

Urban
Oxford Circus LU, 2 min walk
Mon-Sat, 10am-8pm, Sun, 10.30am-6pm
Own label
Sizes: Women 6-18, shoes 3-8; Men: XS-XXXL, shoes 6-12

With seventeen stores around London this is their flagship superstore with two floors of women and one for men. Outside, it's full on-trend fashion windows. As you walk in there's House music and an urban chic feel with a grey décor and Venetian mirrors.

On Women's: Plenty of jeans, full length, cut offs and shorts in many styles. T-shirts chiffon tops, many that are jewelled that pair well with jeans. Young clubby feel to clothes including denim highwaisted shorts with double brown belt, £29.99, short fun dresses £45 and tartan prom dresses with ruffled skirts at £49.99. On the first floor the wow factor goes up a grade with great shoes. Black patent strappy high heels that really look designer are £45; pumps from £9.99; evening bags £20, a very good selection of bags including a faux snake mix bag at £39.99 and purses such as large 100% leather purple purses at £19.99. Also does jewellery, sunglasses, scarves, lingerie and hats.

On Men's: Interesting low budget shoes, good value are the Urbane style shoes at £45 with leather uppers and soles, the canvas plimsols at £19.99 whilst sku detailed socks are £4.99. Patent leather belts detailed with micro perforations and metal buckle are a bargain at £12.99, so good that I bought one in black and will go back for one in white. Signature styled jeans including slouch fitting embellished dark jeans are £44.99, is strong on cargo shorts, flip flops and illustrated T shirts. Of note are the white heavy cotton shorts for the beach and there's a useful range of sun hats, sunglasses and watches. On-trend shirts and ties are worth a look, although the material quality is variable.

Service-wise one gets greeted by staff. Bluetoothed assistant calls "for back-up" o customer queries but in the changing area customer queries may go unattended. Changing rooms come up red with white flowers painted on doors that lock, two mirrors, seat, hooks, and fuchsia chair outside for companion.

The other superstore is at Brent Cross Shopping Centre, Unit 17, Prince Charles Drive London NW4 and also Westfield. See website for other stores on www. riverisland.com

Reiss
9-12 Barrett Street
London W1U 1BA
tel: 020 7486 6557
www.reiss.co.uk

Wow factor: 🏠🏠🏠🏠🏠
Choice: 🏠🏠🏠🏠
Service: 🏠🏠🏠🏠🏠
Price: ££

Glam
Marble Arch LU, 5 min walk
Mon-Wed 10am-7pm, Thurs -Sat, 10am-8pm, Sun 12am -6pm
Own label
Sizes: Women 6-14; Men: S-XL

The sensational exterior of this flagship store makes compelling viewing. With impressive front windows, inside it's a large airy store with a sweeping central staircase and glass shelving cases around.

On Women's: Clothes have an Armani-style influence with mostly neutral colours. Special occasion and casuals skirts are around £50, dresses £120 and shoes £120. Handbags, jewellery, sunglasses, scarves, hats and belts are also available.

On entry one is greeted. Asking to try on a skirt, I was asked if I wanted a top and high heels to try on with it to have an idea how it would look. I was shown to the changing room and was told to just ask if I needed anything. The assistant was on hand outside and was knowledgeable about the collection. The changing rooms too are very pleasant and are of a good size, lighted mirror with winged panels, seat, hangers door that locked and a big mirror outside.

On Men's: Whilst prices for their high quality garments at Reiss were veering rather on the expensive side, their price drops during the credit crunch have made them very attractive. Has luxury wool car coats at £180, double breasted macs at £180, two-piece slender fit suits at £300. Sales are worth waiting for as there are notably good reductions on their shirts and their halve sleeve linens are excellent. Knitwear and tops are fairly classic with their messenger bags' range a tempting choice around the £100 mark.

Russell and Bromley
109 New Bond Street,
London W1
tel: 020 7629 4001
www.russellandbromley.co.uk

(!) Must Visit

> Classic
> Bond St LU, 5 min walk
> Mon-Sat, 10am-6.30pm, Thurs, 10am-7.30pm, Sun 12am-6pm
> Own label
> Sizes: Women 3-8; Men: 6-13

This prime position revered family business corner shoe store has big windows stylishly crammed with their latest collections. Greeted as you arrive, personalised service is high on their agenda for every customer.

On Women's: What you get is well-made high-end chain product with Russell and Bromley's version on the latest designer shoes and bags at a lower price than the top designers. I tried on a pair of black patent high heel shoe boots with a silver buckle at £75 that were too large. The assistant approached to see if she could help but they didn't have a smaller size. To her credit she offered heel grips but as I preferred not have them, she was quite fine about it

On Men's: Strong on Chelsea boots, at around £155 they are very good value and there's a good choice of loafers, lace-ups and work boots. Although not at the cutting edge of fashion on men's once you've bought here the chances are you'll come back again and again.

Top 200

Ted Baker
245 Regent Street,
London W1B 2EN
tel: 020 7493 6251
www.tedbaker.com

Wow factor: 🏠🏠🏠🏠
Choice: 🏠🏠🏠🏠🏠
Service: 🏠🏠🏠🏠
Price: £££

> Glam,
> Oxford Circus LU, 5 min walk
> Mon-Wed, 10am-7pm, Thurs-Sat, 10am-8pm, Sun 12am-6pm
> Own label
> Sizes: Women 6-14, shoes 3-8; Men: S-XXXL, shoes 7-12

Always slightly bonkers-orientated windows each shop is unique. This top-to toe busy store has menswear and ladieswear both on the same floors. Has a bit of a night club feel.

On Women's: Great on pencil skirts, jumpers and long evening dress that are , well shaped and definitely worth £175. Ted Baker has a great reputation in clothes for work that can be dressed up or down for going out.

On Men's: Suits are around £625, with some influenced by Paul Smith's flamboyant mulitcoloured linings. I tried on a coat at £225 and the assistant was quite helpful offering viable alternatives. Upstairs has the best changing rooms in the store and all are individualised inside with an interesting print papering.

The Ground Floor has quite a wicked range of contemporary dinner jackets that can be dressed down. Patterned paisley jackets and long jacket/coats as well as street casual jackets are attention-grabbing too. The Chelsea boots with patterned leather soles at £95 are quite funky and staff do try hard to serve efficiently. Pin striped suits for work and club wear are worth a look. Fun place.

Also at 9 Floral Street, Covent Garden, 234 King's Road, SW3, South Molton St; Victoria; Westbourne Grove. Canary Wharf, Cheapside; Monument and, Wimbledon.

Top 200

Topshop
214 Oxford Street,
London W1
Tel: 020 7636 7700
www.topshop.com

Wow factor: 🏠🏠🏠🏠🏠
Choice: 🏠🏠🏠🏠🏠
Service: 🏠🏠
Price: £

Glam, at the edge of fashion
Oxford Circus LU, 30 sec walk
Mon-Sat, 9am-8pm, Thurs, 9am-9pm, Sun 12am-6pm
Own label and designer mix
Sizes: Women varies; Men: varies

Set on four floors Topshop Oxford Circus is the stuff of retail fashion legend. From the moment you enter you feel the buzz, the collision between fashion and entertainment. Overwhelmed wilting violets can take pause at the seats near the door whilst the rest soak up the vibes from Topshop Radio and the frenetic hip atmosphere. Mannequins dotted around have looks straight off the catwalk. Bold windows at the edge of fashion take up the front of the building.

So fast a moving environment, expect no welcome. Tried on trousers at £28 and there were queues both in and out of changing rooms and to pay. An assistant at the entrance of the changing room gives advice, which she gladly gives. Asking an assistant if a dress comes in a different colour, I didn't get much of a response. At Topshop, what you see there on the rails is what is available.

On uniqueness, styles are very close to the designer labels currently available at a fraction of the price. If any criticism could be made, despite the vast amounts of changing rooms on each floor, there are still queues. These are of okay size but sometimes the cleanliness of the changing room are not always up to scratch.

On Women's: Ground floor has accessories, on B1 is Topshop's own brand, there's also a boutique with more expensive capsule collections such as Jonathan Saunders. The Kate Moss Boutique is real magnet especially when the new collections arrive.. On B2, are collections from many different labels with a similar feel to Topshop also vintage and shoes.

Also does handbags, jewellery such as Mikey, Freedom and Divas, well-priced sunglasses, shoes with a mix of Faith, Office and Bertie, scarves hats, belts, ties, plus hosiery, lingerie, make-up and there's a hairdressing salon and manicurists too.

Of note is their jeans department with signature jeans of all shapes, lengths from £30. Knitwear is from £12, trousers £25 and jackets £30. Also has a petite and a tall section

On Men's: Set on the first floor, bargains to be had are fashion suits, leather jackets, jean, t-shirts, jumpers, ties, shirts, trainers and shoes.

Also at 42 Kensington High St, London W8; 32 The Strand, London WC2, Unit 3 Canada Square, London E14 plus concessions in Selfridge and many other stores.

Top 200

Kate Kuba

24 Duke of York Square
London SW3 4LY
tel: 020 7259 7011
www.katekuba.co.uk

Wow factor: 🛍🛍🛍
Choice: 🛍🛍🛍
Service: 🛍🛍🛍
Price: ££

Glam
Sloane Square 4 min walk,
Mon-Sat, 10am-6.30pm, Sun 12am-6pm
Own label
Sizes: shoes: 3-8

Popular small shoe chain of seven stores in London and one in Liverpool, Whilst the first Kate Kuba was located in Muswell Hill, there is now a good spread across London aimed at stylish sophisticated women in the 25 -40 year old age group. Definitely on-trend and comfortable too, star picks are platform courts £115; large bags at £155. Also stocks UGG Australia, and long boots in patents at £180. Great sales of up to 70% off of last pairs. Service is quite good.

Branches also at:

Canary Wharf, Unit 3 Cabot Place West, London E14; Brook Street, 26 Brook Street London W1; Brent Cross Unit B3, Shopping Centre, London NW4; Muswell Hill, 71 The Broadway, London NW10; Oakwood, 131 Bramley Road London N14.

Top 200

T.K. Maxx

26-40 Kensington High Street
London W8 4PF
tel: 020 7037 8701
www.tkmaxx.com

Wow factor: 🛍🛍
Choice: 🛍🛍🛍🛍
Service: 🛍🛍
Price: ££

Glam, cool
High Street Kensington LU, 3 min walk
Mon-Fri, 9am-7pm, Sat 9am-6pm, Sun12am-6pm
Designer mix
Sizes: Women varies; Men: varies

.K. Maxx has built a tremendous reputation of offering big designer names at bargain prices. Allow plenty of time as there's lots to choose from and it does get very busy with people rummaging the rails and shelves.

This basic looking store of white walls, white shelves looks like it's had a décor-bypass but there are some large photos with models in some of the outfits. This definitely is a no frills, cut price establishment. Items at this branch are at the higher end than in less affluent areas. Much is off-season although there are non-designer labels that are truly on-season. The ground floor has accessories: scarves, lingerie, handbags, shoes displayed by size rather than style and a fine jewellery section.

On Women's: The steel central staircase takes you down to the basement where the ladies fashion are. Along the walls are rows of long evening dresses with crystal details from £40. Has trousers, jumpers, jeans and in winter a big selection of coats. The desirable labels include Amanda Wakeley, Paul Costelloe, Calvin Klein, and Edwina Ronay – everything is marked down 60%. Mixed in are a lot of unfamiliar names. The larger sizes have the biggest choice.

On Men's: Amongst the finds are John Rocha, Balmain clothes, Rotary and Versace watches and a remarkable selection of cut price branded sunglasses.

Changing rooms have one guy on door security. Clean, bright with a door that shuts, each has seating and a mirror and ticks all the boxes but are basic. Has signs up "No more Envy" and "Heavenly label" around the changing areas. Do bring a carrier bag, they don't come free here they are 4p each.

Their super store is at 57 King Street, W6 9HW.

Uniqlo
311 Oxford Street,
London W1
Tel: 020 7290 7701
www.uniqlo.co.uk

!MustVisit

Street Casual
Oxford Circus LU, Bond St LU 5 min walk
Mon-Wed, 10am-8pm, Thurs-Sat, 10am-9pm, Sun 12am-6pm
Own label
Sizes: Women XS-XL; Men: S-XL

Uniqlo are not fashion-setters – they leave that to you! Mix and match to make your own look. And their logo on the garments are virtually invisible.

Greeted as you walk into this spacious well displayed store, you can't help noticing the three windows with circular displays that rotate. Of the three floors of fashion the ground is the most eye-catching. Coloured rods along the ceiling lead to a cubic glass display with mannequins. For tired shoppers, there's a long red padded bench at the entrance. The shop plan is Ground Floor men's and women's, 1st floor women, 2nd floor men. Changing rooms are basic but clean and bright with two hooks and a mirror.

On Women's: Key pieces are the great quality and value knitwear, jumpers in good choice of colours and styles. Cashmere £49.99, merino wool £24.99, pur wool £24.99, fur lined parkas £69.99. The store has all the basics for your wardrob for each season. Service-wise, staff came up several times to see if I needed help.

On Men's: Cashmere sweaters in V, crew and half zip at £59.99 and merino cardigans at £19.99 are well worth considering. Inexpensive cotton jackets, chinos an jeans make economical buys as are the £12.99 fun graphic printed t-shirts.

Also at 118 and 170 Oxford Street; 84-86 Regent Street; 75 Brompton Road Knightsbridge, W8; 54 Kensington High Street; Unit 68 Southside Shopping Cen tre, Wandsworth SW18; Unit 2, 51 The Broadway, Wimbledon and Unit 2048-204 Westfield Shopping Centre, Arial Way, London W12.

Top 200

Whistles
12 St Christopher's Place
London W1U 1NQ
tel: 020 7487 4489
www.whistles.co.uk

Wow factor: ⬛⬛⬛
Choice: ⬛⬛⬛⬛
Service: ⬛⬛⬛⬛
Price: ££

Cool
Marble Arch LU, 5 min walk
Mon-Fri, 10am-7pm, Sat, 10am-6pm, Sun 12am-5pm
Own label and designer mix
Sizes: Women 8-16

High Street flagship store that truly wears service on it's sleeve. If it wasn't for th medium price tags you'd think you were being served in a leading designer store This combined with wearable, on-trend takes from the current season's catwalk makes Whistles an attractive visit choice. Has three floors individually themed wit the Ground Floor decorated in white.

Signature T shirts, sweaters and jumpers are always worth a whirl. Printed ruf fle hem dresses £95, macs and cropped tailored trousers £85. dresses £70-£150 blouses from £80, mini cable cardigans £80, military pea coats £195. Also does good selection of leather bomber jackets at £250, 70's denim jeans £70, skinn flares £60 and skirts £70. Labels include Pink Soda, Made, Michael Stars, Paig denim and there's collections of handbags, jewellery and belts.

Alert staff show you around the store and bring pieces over they might think of interest to you. On finding something you like that's not in your size they'll ring around other branches. Something not all high street stores in London do.

Changing rooms are elegant well equipped. Clientele includes Kirsten Dunst.

Also at Brompton Road, Spitalfields, King's Road, Westbourne Grove, Hampstead, St John's Wood, South Molton Street, Thayer Street

 Top 200

Zara
333 Oxford Street
London W1
tel: 020 7518 1550
www.zara.com

Wow factor: 🗎🗎🗎🗎🗎
Choice: 🗎🗎🗎🗎🗎
Service: 🗎🗎🗎
Price: £

Glam
Bond Street LU, 0.5min walk,
Mon-Sat, 10am-8pm, Sat 10am-6pm
Own label
Sizes: Women clothes XS-XL, 6-14; shoes: 36-41; Men S-XL/XXL, shoes 6-10

Fashionista on a budget. This is fast fashion par excellence. On worldwide sales it's the biggest in the world at £1.7bn in 2007. Outside it looks like a designer store with great windows. Inside there's brown wooden display tables as you walk in with jumpers, T-shirts, rails all over but not cluttered. Upstairs there's ladies jeans and T-shirts a relatively small selection of casuals with most of the collection residing on the ground floor.

Whoever is hottest on the catwalk that season, they do a very good take on it. Key to Zara's success is the swift turnaround from the drawing board to the store in 14 days. Products look very good although in some instances the quality of material and occasionally the finish leaves a little to be desired.

On Women's: Continually gets new stock, so visit frequently. Reputation for very short runs in small quantities with the smaller sizes tending to go first. Examples are V-neck £9, polos £12, trousers £29, coats £149. Also does handbags, hats, sunglasses, shoes copies of latest styles at about £50, shoe boots £79.

On Men's: Leather jackets about £100, Men's shoes about £60, shirts about £20. Inexpensive suits for work and evening. scarves, belts and ties. Changing rooms are a good size with two lit mirrors hanger, and sometimes you may have to queue. And then you may have to queue again to pay.

At Zara you don't get much of a welcome and it can be hard to find a sales person. Expect minimal staff contact, although they will work their cotton socks off to find out if something is in stock. Just about everybody shops at Zara, it's great!

CLOTHES MARKETS

London's street markets continue to be a great success in providing an alternative source of fashions to traditional fashion shops, boutiques and stores. Bargain seekers can take advantage of old stock lines, bankrupt stock, slightly faulty items and designer label returns at terrific prices. With their extremely low overheads many fashion stalls can offer new perfect items at greatly reduced prices. Camden Market is an amazing market for edgy, cyber and goth designs with lots of vintage and secondhand. Camden, Portobello, Sunday Upmarket and Backyard markets are also springboards for new designers to launch their designs. Whilst some markets are virtually pure clothes some are also a a mix of stalls offering everything from food to household goods. This is the list of markets with a fashion focus.

Covent Garden Market
Covent Garden Piazza
London WC2E 8BE

Covent Garden LU 2 min walk
Mon-Sat 10am-8pm Sun 11am-6pm

Stalls with handmade clothing. Fun street acts, lots of places to eat and plenty of nearby fashion shops

. . . .

Earlham Street Market
Earlham Street
London WC2

Leicester Square LU 10 min walk
Mon-Sat 10am-6pm

This short street market is located between Seven Dials in Covent Garden and Shaftesbury Avenue. Famous for its flower stalls, there are some second-hand clothes stalls for bargain seekers.

. . . .

Piccadilly Market
St James's Churchyard
197 Piccadilly
London W1J 9LL
Tel 0207 7734 4511

Piccadilly LU, 4 min walk
Tue 10am-6pm (antiques) , Wed 11am-6pm (Crafts)

Along bustling Piccadilly itself, this small outdoor market has a few stalls of hand-made knitwear and T-shirts. Vegetarian ivory jewellery designer DeMec is also here on Tuesdays and Wednesdays (for review see page 191)

. . . .

West London

Portobello Road Market
Portobello Road
London W11

> Ladbroke Grove LU 5 min walk
> Mon-Wed 8am-6pm, Thur 9am-1pm, Fri-Sat, 8am-7pm

Head for under the Westway by the Portobello Arcade to find retro clothing, second hand clothes stalls. A bit of a flea market but very popular with locals. For something more upscale, in the arcade is leading designer Preen (see page 154 and a stone's throw away are shops Boots, Boots, Boots (page 148) and Tonic (page 159).

North London

Camden Market
Camden High Street
London NW1

> Camden Town LU or Chalk Farm LU
> Mon-Sun

Reckoned to be the fourth most visited tourist attraction in London, Camden Market is a series of markets sprawling from Camden Town underground station to Chalk Farm. There's fashion action everyday. Weekends are totally manic with people.

Camden Stables is famous for cyber, goth and vintage but there's lot of street casuals too and designer-run stalls. The Stables is the biggest market in Camden with stalls full-on at weekend, 9am-5pm, but with many "working the market" during the week. Nearest tube is Chalk Farm.

....

Camden Lock outdoor stalls Sat-Sun, 10am-6pm, indoor stalls Tue-Sun 10am-6pm. Fairy Goth Mother that sells glam corsets and ladieswear is at 7 East Yard (for shop review see page 192).

....

Camden Canal Market is a small market but nicely positioned along the Regents canal. 10am-6pm

....

Camden Buck Street Market Mon-Sun 9.30am -6pm. A mix of clubwear, lots of jeans, t-shirts, leather jackets and a few designer-run stalls. Located a short distance from Camden Town underground.

....

Inverness Street Market is predominantly fruit 'n veg but there are few clothes stalls here too.

....

Electric Ballroom
184 Camden High Street
London NW1

Camden Town LU, 5 min walk
Sundays 9am-5.30pm

Indoor fashion market selling inexpensive designer clothes, second-hand garments and some punk and goth accessories and jewellery. Located near Buck Street and Inverness Street markets.

....

Chapel Market
Chapel Street
Islington
London N1

Angel LU, 4 min walk
Tues to Sat 9am-3.30pm, Thurs and Sun 9am-1pm

Chapel Market is a popular street market with traditional stalls selling a wide array of variety items including food, household goods and low-priced clothes.

....

Hoxton Street Market
Hackney
London N1

> Old Street LU, 15 min walk, Liverpool St LU, BR 20 min walk
> Buses 67, 147, 242, 243 to Kingsland Road
> Mon-Sun, 7.30am-6pm

Located between Falkirk and Nuttall Street. Try Saturdays for fashion bargains.

....

Kilburn Square Market
Kilburn Square
London NW6 6PP

> Kilburn Park LU, Kilburn High Road BR, 5min walk
> Mon-Sat 9am-5pm

Just off Kilburn High Road between Victoria Road and Brondesbury Road there are stalls of clothing and jewellery. Unit 4-5 is Rainbow Fabrics and Haberdashery has quality fabrics, threads, lace , ribbons, crochet kits and needles.

....

Nags Head Market
22 Seven Sisters Road
London N7

> Finsbury Park LU or BR, 10 min walk
> Bus 4,17,29,43, 91,153, 259, 271 and 279
> Sun, Wed 9am-3.30pm

Indoor market with stalls selling bargain shoes and clothes. Altogether there are about 50 stalls with food and household good being sold here also.

....

Top 200

Backyard Market
91 Brick Lane
The Truman Brewery
London E1 6QL
Tel: 020 7770 6028

Liverpool St or Aldgate East LU, 10 min walk
Sun 10am-5pm

For full review see page 188

Bethnal Green Road Market
Bethnal Green Road
London E2

Bethnal Green LU, 5 min walk, bus 253, 106
Mon-Sat 8am-6pm

On the stretch of Bethnal Green Road between Vallance Road and Wilmot Street and opposite the big Tesco the row of stalls has a selection of t-shirts, shirts and casualwear as well as shoes. Fruit, veg and cds and everyday items are sold here. Not one of the best London markets but can be worth a browse if in the neighbourhood.

Broadway Market
Broadway Market
London E8

London Fields BR, 10min walk, Buses 253, 106 and walk from Mare Street
Sat 7.30am-6pm

Located off Landsdowne Drive just London Fields, although a farmer's style market it does have some stalls selling some reasonable quality fashions.

Chrisp Street Market
Chrisp Street
London E14

> All Saints or Poplar DLR; Buses D8, 15 115, D6, 108, 309
> Mon-Sat 9am-4pm, Thurs 9am-12am

Although very much a neighbourhood market selling everyday items, the market has a good reputation for dressmakers fabrics, some contemporary clothes and shoes.

Kingsland Waste
Kingsland Road
London E8

> Dalston Kingsland train station, 10 min walk, Buses 242, 243, 67 or 149
> Sat 7.30am-6pm

Located on the stretch of Kingsland Road between Middleton Road and Richmond Road, this street market has been selling new clothes at knock down prices since the year dot.

Petticoat Lane Market
Middlesex Street and Wentworth Street
London E1

> Liverpool Street LU, 5 min walk
> Mon-Fri 10am-2.30pm, Sun 9am-2pm

"The Lane" as it's fondly known by regulars, is one of the oldest and most famous of London's street markets. It was set up over 400 years ago by the Huguenots from France who sold petticoats and lace here. Petticoat Lane Market now has over 1,000 stalls selling mainly low priced clothes and is a popular place to pick up a bargain leather coat and have good price haggle. Also does household goods.

Ridley Road Market
Ridley Road
Dalston
London E8

> Bus 149, 243, 76. Dalston crossrail when it is built
> Mon- Wed 9am-3pm, Thurs 9am-12am, Fri-Sat 9am-5pm

Known to locals as Dalston Market, this traditional East End market is frequented by African, Asian and Caribbean and Greeks and Turks with some stalls selling clothes and fabrics.

Roman Road Market
Roman Road
London E3

Mile End LU 12 min walk
Tue, Thur and Sat 9am -5.30pm

Located between Parnell Road and St Stephens Road, the best time to visit for clothing is during the summer at the weekends. Comes winter the market is less active.

Spitalfields Market
Spitalfields Market
London E1
Tel: 0208 579 9206

Aldgate East LU, 5 min walk
Mon-Fri 10am-4pm, Sun 9am-5pm

Spitalfields has a great selection of individual fashion stalls The Spitalfields Market splits into New Spitalfields, with trendy fashion stalls on Crispins Place and the Old Spitalfields Market (entrance Commercial Street) that has further stalls of interesting fashion. For fashion, Sundays are busiest with Friday their Fashion and Art day.

 Top 200

Sunday Upmarket
Elys Yard
The Truman Brewery
(entrances on Hanbury St and Brick Lane)
London E1 6QL
Tel: 020 7770 6028

Liverpool St or Aldgate East LU, 10 min walk
Sun 8am-5pm

For full review see page 199

Walthamstow
High Street
Walthamstow
London E17

Walthamstow LU 5 min walk
Mon- Fri 9am-4pm, Sat 9am-5pm

Stretching over a mile, Walthamstow Market is the longest street market in Europe, selling a wide variety of goods including materials and high-street clothing.

Well Street Market
Wells Street
London E9

> Hackney Central BR, 10 min walk, Bus 30, 236, 277
> Mon-Sun, 7.30am- 6pm

Saturdays is the busiest day with some clothes and shoe stalls.

Whitechapel Market
199-337 Whitechapel Road
Whitechapel
London E1 1DT

> Whitechapel LU, 1 min walk
> Mon-Sat, 8am-6pm

Opposite the London Hospital, whilst this market sells fruit and veg and every day items there's always clothes bargains to be found. Stalls offer dresses, t-shirts, shoes, Asian fabrics and haberdashery. Whitechapel is popular with the strong neighbourhood Bangladeshi community.

South London

Brixton Market
Brixton Station Road
London SW9

> Brixton LU, 5 min walk
> Mon-Sat 8am-6pm, Wed 8am-3pm

The section of this large market to aim for is at Station Road that has a few second-hand and retro stalls

Deptford Market
Deptford High Street
London SE8

> Deptford BR, 1 min walk,
> Wed, Fri, Sat 9am-4pm

Has lots of stall selling cut price clothes and shoes. Also some vintage and second-hand. Good for a rummage.

East Street Market
East Street
London SE17

> Elephant & Castle LU, 10 min walk
> Tue-Sat 8.30am-4pm, Thurs and Sun 8.30am-2.30pm

Get your bargain fashion fix here. Stalls sell new clothes with a reputation of under cutting the chains. Some good picks on bags, jewellery and shoes. Best to visit on Sundays when the 250 stalls are in full swing.

Gabriel's Wharf Market
6 Upper Ground
London SE1

> Waterloo LU or BR, 10 min walk
> Fri-Sun, 10am-6pm

A pleasant stop-off point if walking along the riverside, South Bank. Situated next to the Oxo Tower this square has a few ethnic clothes stalls and there's a few good casual eateries around the square to relax.

Greenwich Market
Greenwich
London SE10

> Greenwich Docklands Light Railway, 5 min walk
> Craft Market Thurs 7.30am-5pm, Fri-Sun, 9.30am-5.30pm
> Central Market Sat 7am-6pm, Sun 7am-5pm

The covered Craft Market on College Approach has some on-trend clothes from new designers at an early stage of their careers. Very close, just off Stockwell Street the outdoor Central Market that has vintage and secondhand as well as some antique jewellery.

Lower Marsh Market
Lower Marsh
Waterloo
London SE1

> Waterloo LU and BR, 2 min walk
> Mon, Tue, Thurs, Sat 8am-6pm, Wed 10am-3pm, Fri 8am-7pm

This traditional street market sells every day items and fruit, veg, flowers and has some fashion clothes stalls.

Northcote Road Market
Northcote Road
London SW11

Clapham Junction BR, 5 min walk; Clapham South LU 20min walk
Bus 37, 45A, 49, 77, 87 and others
Mon-Sat, 10am-5pm,

Based at the Battersea Rise end of Northcote Road, fashion stalls sell pashmina scarves, vintage women's clothes and handbags. An upcoming gentrified area expect some good buys here.

Southwark Park Road Market
Southwark Park Road
London SE16

Bermondsey LU, 5 min walk; South Bermondsey BR 10 min walk
Bus 1, 381, P12, 78

Often known as the "Blue Market", it is based in a small pedestranised square close to the Southwark Park Road/Grange Road junction. Decorated with blue seating and foliage, there are some clothes stalls here amongst the food, flower stalls are cut price fashions.

Strutton Ground Market
Strutton Ground
London SW1

St James's Park LU,3 min walk or Victoria LU, BR, 10 min walk
Mon-Fri 8am-2.30pm

A short stroll from Westminster Abbey, the Palace of Westminster and Parliament Square this small market has an eclectic mix of stalls including fashion and jewellery.

Wimbledon Stadium Market
Wimbledon Stadium Car Park
Plough Lane
Wimbledon SW17 8HA

Haydons Road BR, 5 min walk
Sun, 9am-3pm

Clothes bargains and costume jewellery are to be found here.

CHARITY SHOPS

London's charity shops provide a rich source of bargain fashion. On some items one may find better quality than some of the vintage shops. Charity shops are re-branding as vintage shops and are also bringing in designers to recycle clothes as one-off pieces. The Salvation Army in Princes Street, Oxford Circus deserves commendation for having some brand new clothes donated straight from the surrounding shops. Every time you buy you are helping great charity causes.

British Heart Foundation
62 St John's Road
Clapham Junction
London SW11 1PR
Tel 0207 978 4237
www.bhf.org.uk

> Clapham Junction BR, 1 min walk
> Mon-Sat 10am-6pm, Sun 11am-5pm

This charity provides funding for important heart and cardiovascular research as well as donating hospital equipment desperately needed in the treatment of heart disease. The Clapham Junction shop has lots of donated clothes and accessories as do their outlets in Camden, Fulham, Swiss Cottage, Hammersmith, Putney, Streatham, Catford and Wimbledon.

Cancer Research UK
24 Marylebone High Street
London W1U 4PQ
Tel 0207 487 4986
www.cancerresearchuk.org

> Baker Street LU, 5min walk
> Mon-Sat 10am-6pm, Sun 11am-5pm

At this Marylebone charity outlet , Cancer Research UK has joined forces with "Fashion Designers Revamp" so that you can get one-off re-styled pieces.   tfore and Wimbledon.

Mind
463-465 Wandsworth Road
London SW8 4NX
Tel 0207 622 3442
www.mind.org.uk

> Wandsworth Road BR, 4 min walk
> Mon-Sun 9am-4.30pm, Fri 9am-8pm

This is just one of several Mind charity shops that raise money in connection with the treatment of mental illnesses. Over 95% of the stock has been donated. Other branches are: Highgate, Islington, Southgate, South Norwood Hill and Stoke Newington.

Oxfam

123a Sawfield Street
King's Road
Chelsea
London SW3 4PL
Tel 0207 351 7979
www.oxfam.org.uk

Sloane Square LU, 10 min walk
Mon-Sat 10am-6pm

This is one of the new charity boutiques that has "Loved for Longer" donated fashion. Also does organic and fairtrade and some of the clothes are re-worked by designers such as Junky Styling, London College of fashion students and graduates to give a more contemporary feel. The other two boutiques are at 245 Westbourne Grove and 190 Chiswick High Road.

Other outlets with donated clothes and accessories include Victoria, Pimlico, Marylebone, Paddington, Goodge Street, Gloucester Road and Bloomsbury.

Red Cross

69-71 Old Church Street
Chelsea London
London SW3 5BS
0845 054 7101
www.redcross.org.uk

South Kensington LU, 15 min walk
Mon-Sat 10.30am-5pm, Sun 12am-6pm

This popular charity shop is virtually next door Manolo Blahnik. Quite well displayed.

Red Cross

35 Ebury Street
Westminster
London SW1W 9QU
Tel 0207 730 2235
www.redcross.org.uk

Sloane Square LU, 7 min walk
Mon-Sat 10am-5.30pm

This British Red Cross Shop near Victoria Station has donations of secondhand and vintage clothes. Being in the heart of Belgravia and near Elizabeth Street you'll bound to pick up some great labels.

Salvation Army
9 Princes Street
London W1
Tel 0207 495 3956
www1.salvationarmy.org.uk

Oxford Circus LU, 3 min walk
Mon-Sat, 10am-6pm

This branch is particularly popular because it receives donations of clothes from the local shops that include Topshop, Karen Millen, Armani and Calvin Klein. Items from these are brand new and sold at a quarter of the retail price. In addition, on the rails are donations of vintage clothes from the affluent local residents. Excellent.

Sue Ryder Care
1 Market Place
Bermondsey
London SE16 3UQ
Tel 0207 394 8384
www.suerydercare.org

Bermondsey LU, 5 min walk
Mon-Sat 9am-5pm

Sue Ryder Care is a leading health care charity providing help to people with serious illnesses. Always has people browsing through the rails for secondhand donations.

Sue Ryder Care
10 Station Road
Chingford
London E4 7BE
Tel 0208 559 3105
www.suerydercare.org

Chingford BR, 5 min walk
Mon-Sat 9am-5pm

A traditional style charity shop with plenty to sift through. Branches are also at Crawford Street, London W1; Islington, Muswell Hill, Paddington, Ealing Broadway and Pimlico. See website for further details

FASHION CAFÉS, RESTAURANTS, CLUBS AND BARS

Whether you shop to you drop and need to recharge or want to throw on your new clothes and go where the fashion crowds go, London has a superb choice of venues to eat and drink for a fantastic time. Listed below is a selection of London's most popular fashionista venues.

Central London

Bond Street

Carluccio's Caffé
Fenwick of Bond Street,
London W1
tel: 020 7629 0699

Italian café and restaurant in the basement next to the menswear.

Gordon Ramsay at Claridges
Claridges Hotel
Brook Street
London W1
tel 020 7499 0090

TV celebrity chef Gordon Ramsay's offers spectacular modern French food in a beautiful setting.

Mahiki
1 Dover Street
London W1
Tel 0207 493 9529

Hawaiian bar with high celeb quotient. Sienna Miller, Jon Bon Jovi and Prince Harry frequent it.

The Metropolitan
Old Park Lane
London W1
Tel 0207 447 1000

The Metropolitan Hotel and it's Met Bar is a fashion stronghold especially around London Fashion Week when there are designer exhibits here.

Napket
6 Brook Street
London W1S 1BB
Tel 0207 495 8562

Boutique café serving inexpensive and light meals in "modern Baroque" stylish surroundings. Opposite Fenwick and close to both Bond Street and Regent Street Open from 7.30am-7.00pm.

Nobu

19 Old Park Lane
London W1
Tel 0207 447 4747

Japanese cuisine restaurant with a high celebrity quotient. Popular with LA and New York visiting stars.

. . . .

Nicole's

Nicole Farhi
158 New Bond Street,
London W1

Luxe basement restaurant with a short well-executed Mediterranean menu. More formal than the Fahri's sister eaterie 202, Three courses are around £35 per head excluding drinks.

. . . .

Rose Bakery

Top floor, Dover Street Market
17-18 Dover Street,
London W1

Super-fashionistas and beautiful people are fond of this small chi-chi organic café serving a short menu of classic English cuisine. Located in a superb fashion store.

. . . .

Sketch

9 Conduit Street
London W1
tel: 0207 659 4500

This fashionable destination has an amazing lobby of contemporary art pieces and very hip bars for pre-and post dinner drinks. The Library is a renowned elegant dining room with excellent modern European food. Also popular for afternoon teas is The Parlour.

. . . .

Central London

Mount Street

Scott's
20 Mount Street
London W1
Tel 0207 495 7309

One's of London top fish restaurants. High on glitz in this now very fashion conscious street

Central London

Savile Row

Cecconi's
5-5a Burlington Gardens
London W1X 1LE
Tel 0207 434 1500

Swanky Italian restaurant frequented by Bond Street shoppers. There's an all day menu of small dishes and salads as well as a three course set menu. Vibrant atmosphere.

. . . .

Sartoria
20 Savile Row
London W1S 3PR
Tel 0207 534 7070

Italian classics with a twist in a refined restaurant setting. Mains are about £20

. . . .

Central London

Oxford Circus

Carluccio's Caffé
St Christopher's Place,
London W1
tel: 020 7935 5927

Smack bang on St Christopher's Place, this large eaterie does classic Italian pastas and mains. Good for just coffee too.

Charlotte Street Hotel
15-17 Charlotte Street
London W1
Tel 0207 806 2000

The bar gets so crowded sometimes it's hard to find a seat.

Le Pain Quotidien
72-75 Marylebone High Street,
London W1
tel: 020 7486 6154

Marylebone High Street fashion shoppers love this informal café with its freshly baked bread and classic French cooking.

Liberty
210-220 Regent Street,
London W1
tel: 020 7734 1234

For refreshments in this leading department store try the ground floor tea room. Set teas are from about £10.75 to £29 and there's a big choice of tea varieties to choose from. There are two further restaurants.

The Providores
109 Marylebone High Street
London W1
Tel 0207 935 6175

New Zealand chef Peter Gordon offers exciting fusion dishes. Mains about £20, the ground floor is more informal and less expensive food. Can get extremely busy.

Sanderson Hotel
50 Berners Street
London W1
Tel 0207 300 1400

The courtyard here is a destination venue and the bar gets very crowded. Cocktails, however, are expensive. Phillippe Starck modern design hotel with a great foyer.

Selfridges
400 Oxford Street,
London W1
Tel: 0800 123 400

Shoppers have a wide choice of restaurants and cafés here. Ones to try are: The Brass Rail salt beef bar, whilst the Gallery restaurant is next to the Moet bar. The Food Garden help yourself café is on the fourth floor. The Lab Café is hot for afternoon tea with scones and light meals. Other choices are the Gordon Bar and Restaurant and the Obika Mozzarella Bar.

Swarovski Crystallized Cosmos and lounge
24 Great Marlborough Street,
London W1
tel: 020 7434 3444

Glam and glitzy, enjoy coffee or a drink from the bar whilst gazing at their fashion exhibition.

Tibits
12-14 Heddon Street,
London W1
tel: 0207 758 4110

Enjoy the chic veggie buffet or just pop in from the nearby Regent Street shops for a coffee or a cocktail.

Wagamama
101a Wigmore Street,
London W1
tel: 020 7409 0111

The perfect ticket if you've overspent. Wagamama does inexpensive fast modern Japanese food bursting with taste.

Central London

Soho/Carnaby Street

Chinawhite
6 Air Street
Soho
London W1B 5AA
Tel 0207 343 0040

Bali, Java and Sumatra style nightclub with a high celebrity quotient.

....

Leon
35 Great Marlborough Street,
London W1
Tel: 020 7437 5280

This is a great stop-off in the Carnaby Street area. Grab an outside table and watch the world go by. Natural ethical cuisine moderately priced. Take-out or eat in.

....

Movida
3-9 Argyll Street
London W1
Tel 0207 734 5776

Hosts London Fashion Week parties and is regular haunt for top celebrities.

....

The Soho Hotel
4 Richmond Mews
London W1
Tel 0207 559 3000

Tucked away down a Soho mews, the bar here is positively vibrant.

....

Central London

Covent Garden

Asia de Cuba
St Martins Lane Hotel
45 St Martins Lane
London WC2
Tel 0207 300 5500

Phillippe Starck design hotel that's a very modern and entertaining venue. Dress to impress the food is great here. Also check out the Light Bar.

....

Covent Garden Hotel
10 Monmouth Street
London WC2
Tel 0207 806 1000

Monmouth Street has some inspiring fashion shops and the bar at this boutique hotel is a great place to chillout.

....

Ivy
1 West Street
London WC2
Tel 0207 836 4751

Almost every night there's a star dining here. No-nonsense British cuisine cooked to a high standard.

....

Central London

Jermyn Street

The Trafalgar

2 Spring Gardens
Trafalgar Square
London SW1A 2TS
Tel 0207 870 2900

The roof garden has panoramic views over London. The ground floor Rockwell Bar has been used for fashion designer collection launches The Trafalgar is a contemporary minimalist boutique hotel oozing with style.

. . . .

Wolseley

160 Piccadilly
London W1
Tel 0207 499 6996

From smoked salmon bagels to Weiner Holstein, the Wolseley serves excellent non-fussy traditional European meals. Celebrity magnet.

Central London

City

1 Lombard Street

1 Lombard Street
London EC3V 9AA
Tel 0207 929 6622

This grade II listed former banking hall has elegant domed skylights and serves fine modern English dishes. A good choice after visiting the shops at the Royal Exchange. Has a delectably attractive bar area.

. . . .

Prism

147 Leadenhall Street
London EC3
Tel 0207 256 3875

Glam Harvey Nichols owned restaurant and bar. The lower ground bar is super cool.

West London

Notting Hill

202

202 Westbourne Grove
London W11 2RH
Tel 020 727 2722

Notting Hill fashionistas congregate at this Nicole Fahri lifestyle café and boutique. For breakfast there's porridge, bagel with smoked salmon, cream cheese capers and red onion plus a couple of good omelettes to choose from. Mediterranean lunch and dinners are also served.

. . . .

Emporio Armani Caffē

191 Brompton Road
London SW3 1NE
tel: 020 7823 8818

Glitzy fashionista restaurant, black minimal in style overlooking Knightsbridge Antipastis of Parma ham and fresh figs, seafood pasta, seared tuna with Mediterranean chard and tapenade are very good quality and they are quite happy to just serve you coffee.

Kokon to Zai
36 Golborne Road,
London W10 5PS
Tel: 020 8960 3736

This cool boutique is a fascinating backdrop to sip a coffee and have some Macedonian cake.

West London

Belgravia

Jumeirah Lowndes Hotel
21 Lowndes Street
London SW1X 9ES
Tel 0207 823 1234

Has a café and bar that's popular with shoppers and fashionable Belgravians.

. . . .

Zafferano
15 Lowndes Street
London SW1
Tel 0207 235 5800

Well established Italian restaurant in a smart location always attracting the well-heeled.

. . . .

West London

Sloane Street

Daylesford Pimlico
44b Pimlico Road,
London SW1
tel: 020 7881 8060

Incredibly fresh English organic foods straight from their farm. Share their communal table with the expensively dressed. Modern international cuisine exquisitely presented.

West London

Knightsbridge

Harvey Nichols
109-125 Knightsbridge
London SW1X 7RJ
tel: 020 7235 5000

The fifth floor café restaurant is a fashionista stronghold and celebrity shoppers haunt.

. . . .

Mandarin Oriental Hotel
66 Knightsbridge
London SW1
Tel 0207 235 2000

Their upscale bar is the perfect venue to wear your latest designer purchase. Everyone checks out what everyone else is wearing. Friendly atmosphere. Good restaurants. Many music stars stay at this hotel .

. . . .

Zuma
5 Raphael St
London SW7
Tel 020 7584 1010

Hot destination modern Japanese restaurant where the dress code is cool.

. . . .

King's Road

Bamford and Sons
The Old Bank,
31, Sloane Square
London SW1
Tel 020 7881 8010

Café restaurant in the basement. Organic meals from Daylesford Farm.

Bluebird
350 Kings Road,
London SW3
Tel 0207 559 1000

Upstairs The Shop at Bluebird, this very popular restaurant serves modern British. For something more informal the café is a big draw for King's Road fashion shoppers.

Patisserie Valerie
Left Wing Café
Duke of York Square
London SW3
Tel 0207 730 7094

it out on this pedestranised square and enjoy the informal French café food.

Sushino
312 -314 King's Road
London SW3
Tel 0207 349 7496

An unusual mix of Brazilian and Japanese cuisine close to several fashionable boutiques has made Sushino a big hit along the King's Road..

West London

Kensington

Zaika
No1 Kensington High Street
London W8
T 0207 937 8834

If you love Indian food the modern menu will impress with it's innovative recipes.

West London

Notting Hill

Beach Blanket Babylon West
45 Ledbury Road
Notting Hill
London W11 2AA
Tel 0207 229 2907

Quirky fashion destination that has a restaurant with lot of nooks and crannies that's extremely romantic. Bar gets very crowded. Great place.

E&O
14 Blenheim Crescent,
London W11
tel: 020 7229 5454

A Notting Hill shoppers' favourite serving modern Vietnamese.

West London

Westfield London

Croque Gascon (The Balcony)
Westfield London Shopping Centre
Ariel Way
London W12

For discerning fashion shoppers on the run, this open kitchen serves fast "Good Food" in minutes. Or just relax, take some time off and enjoy these splendid dishes from South-West France.

....

Tibits
Westfield London
Shepherd's Bush
London W12 7GA
Tel 0208 222 6340

Top quality vegetarian buffet in styish looking restaurant. Pay by weight. Great value. Located on the pedestranised Southern Terrace.

Tossed
Unit K2014, The Balcony
Westfield London Shopping Centre
Ariel Way

Great on fresh healthy tossed to order salads. Wraps, soups and hot snacks are also available. Stylish and vibrant.

....

North London

Islington

Fresh and Wild
32-40 Stoke Newington Church St,
London N16
tel: 020 7254 2332

Inexpensive informal café and eaterie.

Ottolenghi
287 Upper Street
London N1
tel 020 7288 1454

Communal café and dining spot serving sumptuous looking Mediterranean cuisine as well as terrific looking cakes and pastries. Cool décor.

The Living Room
18-26 Essex Road
Islington
London N1
tel: 0870 44 22 712

Plasma TV screens broadcast international fashion shows at this hip bar and restaurant serving affordable international cuisine favourites. Live music plays nightly.

North London

Camden

Gilgamesh Restaurant Bar and Lounge
The Stables Market
Chalk Farm Road
London W12
Tel 0207 428 3922

Modern Pan-Asian cuisine served in a massive restaurant with fascinating Babylonian décor. Located right in the heart of Camden Market

The WD guesthouse
9a Ashbridge Street
Lisson Grove
London NW8
Tel 44 (0)207 725 9694

Knitwear designers Weardowney's WD guesthouse is home to a fashionable crowd from artists and models, to international business professionals who regularly pass through. The guesthouse provides them with a home from home environment to unwind in. Breakfasts are available and later on the day cooked Indonesian food can be ordered on request. Room rates are from £84.

East London

Brick Lane & Spitalfields

Beach Blanket Babylon East
19-23 Bethnal Green Road
London E1
Tel 0207 749 3540

The restaurant is upstairs and the bar is downstairs. One of the most upscale venues in this edgey area.

East London

Hoxton & Shoreditch

SAF
152-154 Curtain Road
Shoreditch
London EC2
Tel 020 7613 0007

This raw food organic vegan restaurant is a big success with the Hoxton-Shoreditch set. Has vibrant bar with the modern international cuisine superbly executed.

Water House
10 Osman Road
London N1
tel: 020 7033 0123

Trendsetting super ethical café, restaurant and bar.

East London

Canary Wharf

Leon Canary Wharf
Promenade Level
Cabot Place West
Canary Wharf
London E14
T: 0207 719 6201

This small Leon is a perfect rest place from the nearby designer shops. Relaxing informal atmosphere, Leon serves English and Mediterranean fast food.

South London

Putney

Thai Square Putney Bridge
2-4 Lower Richmond Road
Embankment, Putney
London SW15
tel 020 8780 1811

Overlooking the River Thames this spacious Thai restaurant has value for money dishes. Traditional cuisine.

1-26 April 09
Reflect Forward: Carolyn Massey, Menswear
Craft Central, 33-35 St John's Square, London EC3
www.craftcentral.org.uk

Carolyn Massey, menswear fashion designer will be exhibiting as part of Craft Central Reflect Forward initiative.

. . . .

April 09
Alternative Fashion Week
Spitalfields Traders Market
Crispin Place , Brushfield St
London E1
Tel 0207 375 0441
www.alternativearts.co.uk

Over sixty young designers showcase their work with a dozen upcoming designers showing on the catwalk each day. Admission free.

. . . .

April 09   ,
Fashion Reflections
Craft Central, 33-35 St John's Square, London EC3
www.craftcentral.org.uk

Fashion Reflections provides an opportunity for four selected fashion, jewellery and accessory designers to showcase their work in exclusive 'mini boutiques'.

. . . .

Until 17th May 09
Hussein Chalayan exhibition
Design Museum
Shad Thames
London SE1
Tel 0207 403 6933
www.designmuseum.org

The Design Museum periodically hosts fashion orientated exhibitions. Also has a selection of fashion books in their gift shop. Cool place.

. . . .

10th May 09
Anita's Vintage Fashion Fairs
20th Century Theatre,
291 Westbourne Grove, Notting Hill,
London, W11 2QA
www.vintagefashionfairs.com

Attracts over 200 visitors and 28 exhibitors – Entry 10am-4.30pm - £4

Until 10th May 09
Stephen Jones Hat exhibition
Victoria and Albert Museum
Porter Gallery
Cromwell Road
London SW7
Tel 0207 942 2000
www.vam.ac.uk

Hats: An Anthology by Stephen Jones exhibition.

Until 17th May 09
Swedish Fashion
Fashion and Textile Museum
83 Bermondsey Road
London SE1
Tel 0207 407 8664
www.ftmlondon.org

Exhibition exploring the new identity of Swedish Fashion.

14-17 May 09
Made In Clerkenwell open studio events, Summer 09
Craft Central
33-35 St John's Square
London EC3
www.craftcentral.org.uk

See 70 designer makers in their open studios.

29th- 31st May 09
Clothes Show London
Excel London
www.clothesshowlondon.co.uk
Custom House DLR, 30 second walk

Fashion and beauty exhibition with one of the largest catwalks in the world. Offers a unique experience in shopping, indulgence, celebrities and trend reports. For tickets, hit the above website.

June 2nd –October 1st 09
Bermondsey Undercover
33 Bermondsey Road
London SE1
Tel 0207 407 8664
www.ftmlondon.org

Exhibition about the evolution of underwear.

8-14 June 09
Coutts London Jewellery Week
www.londonjewelleryweek.co.uk

London sparkles with Capital's jewellery talent. Gives you a wonderful chance to see behind the scenes of London's creative jewellers in their workshops. Plus exhibitions galore.

June 19th-21st 09 Womenswear Sale
June 26th -28th 09 Menswear Sale
Designer Warehouse Sales
5-6 Islington Studios
Thane Works, Thane Villas
London N7
0207 837 3322
www.designerwarehousesales.com

Designer label at vastly reduced prices held over three days, twelve times per year. Separate womenswear and menswear sales. Join their mailing list on their website and wait for your copy of the sale invitation to be delivered three weeks prior to the sale date.

September 09
London Fashion Week
Natural History Museum
Cromwell Road
London SW7
www.londonfashionweek.co.uk

The highlight of the London Fashion calendar where top and upcoming designers show their Spring/Summer 2010 collections on the catwalk or at this fashion trade exhibition. London's hotels and restaurants are filled with the international fashion set. Invitation only.

Besides the on-schedule shows, London based creative events agency, Doll, runs ON/OFF a parallel alternative schedule of catwalk shows and exhibits. Website:www.thedoll.org. Invitation only.

September 09
London Fashion Weekend
Natural History Museum
Cromwell Road
London SW7
Tel 0208 614 7695
www.londonfashionweekend.co.uk

Your chance to be on the front row experiencing top designer catwalk shows and then the opportunity to shop at a huge discount. Immensely popular, there's upcoming Brit designers as well as classic labels. Great fun!

September 28th to October 11th 09
The 27TH Goldsmiths' Fair
Goldsmiths' Hall, London EC2
www.thegoldsmiths.co.uk

Monday to Friday 11am to 7pm
Saturday and Sunday 10am to 6pm

The annual selling exhibition of jewellery and silverware by leading and upcoming designer-makers. Admission by catalogue purchasable on the door

September 09
FaCshion
The Old Truman Brewery
London E1
Tel 07946 121043
www.facshion.co.uk

Two day event for the fashion trade and fashionista consumers where the focus is upcoming designers.

September 18th- 20th 09 Womenswear Sale
September 25th - 27th 09 Menswear Sale
Designer Warehouse Sales
5-6 Islington Studios
Thane Works, Thane Villas
London N7
0207 837 3322
www.designerwarehousesales.com

Designer label at vastly reduced prices held over three days, twelve times per year. Separate womenswear and menswear sales. Join their mailing list on their website and wait for your copy of the sale invitation to be delivered three weeks prior to the sale date.

. . . .

October 09
Origin: The London Crafts Fair
Somerset House

Contemporary craftmakers showcase their creativity over a ten day period.

. . . .

11th October 09
Anita's Vintage Fashion Fairs
20th Century Theatre,
291 Westbourne Grove, Notting Hill,
London, W11 2QA
www.vintagefashionfairs.com

Attracts over 200 visitors and 28 exhibitors – Entry 10am-4.30pm - £4.

. . . .

Late November 09
Made In Clerkenwell open studio events, Winter 09
Craft Central, 33-35 St John's Square, London EC3
www.craftcentral.org.uk

See 70 designer makers in their open studios

. . . .

November 09
Bond Street Noel
Bond Street
London W1
www.bondstreet.co.uk

In aid of Great Ormond Street Hospital, a celebrity arrives on a sleigh and switches on the Christmas lights. Bond Street shops lay on a special evening often with champagne for fashion shoppers. 5pm-8pm.

November 09
Carnaby St and other Shopping Street Special Evenings.

The twelve streets around Carnaby Street have special pre-Christmas evenings with street entertainment and shops offering free drinks and sometimes 20% discounts. Of note is Kingly Court for it's vibrant atmosphere.

Other streets joining in the seasonal festive spirit include Jermyn Street, Mount Street, Marylebone Road, Belgravia, Connaught Village as well as Alfies Antique Market in Lisson Grove and Gray's Market in Mayfair. At beginning of December Oxford Street and Regent Street have a VIP day (Very Important Pedestrian Day) with shops laying on street entertainment.

December 4th- 6th 09 Womenswear Sale
December 11th - 18th 09 Menswear Sale
Designer Warehouse Sales
5-6 Islington Studios
Thane Works, Thane Villas
London N7
0207 837 3322
www.designerwarehousesales.com

Designer label at vastly reduced prices held over three days, twelve times per year. Separate womenswear and menswear sales. Join their mailing list on their website and wait for your copy of the sale invitation to be delivered three weeks prior to the sale date.

February 2010
London Fashion Week
Natural History Museum
Cromwell Road
London SW7
www.londonfashionweek.co.uk

The highlight of the London Fashion calendar where top and upcoming designers show their Autumn /Winter 2010 collections on the catwalk or at this fashion trade exhibition. London's hotels and restaurants are filled with the international fashion

March 2010
London Fashion Weekend
Natural History Museum
Cromwell Road
London SW7
Tel 0208 614 7695
www.londonfashionweekend.co.uk

Your chance to be on the front row experiencing top designer catwalk shows and then the opportunity to shop at a huge discount. Immensely popular, there's upcoming Brit designers as well as classic labels. Great fun!

May 2010
Made In Clerkenwell open studio events, Summer 2010
Craft Central, 33-35 St John's Square, London EC3
www.craftcentral.org.uk

See 70 designer makers in their open studios

MUSEUMS

VICTORIA AND ALBERT MUSEUM
Cromwell Road
London SW7
Tel 0207 942 2000
www.vam.ac.uk

Fashion Dress and Jewellery
South Kensington LU, 5 min walk
10am-5.45pm daily
Textile study room 10am-5pm

From 17th Century to the present. Excellently presented and informative. Wel
worth a visit. Special exhibitions also.

FASHION AND TEXTILE MUSEUM

83 Bermondsey Road
London SE1
Tel 0207 407 8664
www.ftmlondon.org

British Designs and Textiles

The emphasis in on British designs since the 1950's. Permanent exhibition of Zandra Rhodes designs plus changing exhibitions of British fashion luminaries. Specia
exhibitions also.

FAN MUSEUM

12 Crooms Hill
Greenwich
London SE10
Tel 020 8305 1441
www.fan-museum.org

Fans
Greenwich DLR or Connex South East
Tue-Sat 11am-5pm, Sun 12am-5pm
Adults £4, Concessions £3
Afternoon teas served in the Orangery from 3pm from £3.50

Marvellously intriguing collection of fans. Permanent and temporary exhibitions.

Central Saint Martins College of Art and Design

Southampton Row
London WC1B 4AP
Tel 0207 514 7022
www.csm.arts.ac.uk

World famous college offering degree and post graduate courses in fashion, jewellery and textile design. Former students at this college include many top named designers including Alexander McQueen, Stella McCartney and Matthew Williamson. Short courses are also available at weekends, day times, Saturdays or week long intensives.

Chelsea College of Art and Design

16 John Islip Street
London SW1P 4JU
Tel 0207 514 7751
www.chelsea.arts.ac.uk

Degree courses in knitwear and textile design. Short courses

London College of Fashion

20 John Princes Street
London W1
Tel 0207 514 7400
www.fashion.arts.ac.uk

London College of Fashion is the only college in the UK to specialise in fashion education, research and consultancy. Runs BA and MA degree courses as well as various evening, weekend and intensive daytime courses.

Newham College of Further Education

East Ham Campus
High Street South
London E6 6ER
Tel 0208 257 4446

National Award courses in fashion and clothing over thirty-six weeks.

Royal College of Art
Wandsworth High Street
London SW18 2PP
Tel 0208 918 7777
www.south-thames.ac.uk

Postgraduate courses in MA, Mphil and PhD in Fashion Menswear, Fashion Womenswear, goldsmithing, silversmithing, metalwork, jewellery and textiles. and embroidery.

South Thames College
Wandsworth High Street
London SW18 2PP
Tel 0208 918 7777
www.south-thames.ac.uk

Beginners and intermediate courses in clothes making, beading, hand-knitting and embroidery.

Swarovski Jewellery Making Workshops
Swarovski Crystallized Cosmos and lounge
24 Great Marlborough Street,
London W1F 7HU
tel: 020 7434 3444

Swarovski runs special workshops to make your own jewellery using their sparkling products. Previous workshops have included creating your own cocooning ring using wiring techniques and jewel gluing. Other workshops show you how to create your own necklace or bracelet. After an individual consultancy, you select with the help of a designer your personal charms and you are shown how easy it is to make your own jewellery pieces.

The Academy at Fashion and Textile Museum
83 Bermondsey Road
London SE1
Tel 0207 407 8664
www.ftmlondon.org

The Academy here is part of Newham College and runs courses in fashion, jewellery and textile design.

The Fashion Retail Academy
15 Gresse Street
London W1T 1QL
Tel 0207 307 2345
www.fashionretailacademy.ac.uk

Diploma courses in fashion retailing, visual merchandising, buying and merchandising, as well as short courses from ½ a day to five days.

University of Westminster

Course Enquiries Office
115 New Cavendish Street
London W1W 6UW
Tel 0207 911 5000
www.wmin.ac.uk

Degree courses in Fashion Design, Fashion Merchandise Management, Fashion Business Management as well as postgraduate and short courses. Fashion retailers such as Topshop and New Look have partnered with this University to create bespoke courses relating to fashion merchandising.

Waltham Forest College

Forest Building
Forest Road, Walthamstow
London E17 4 JB
Tel 0208 501 8000

BTEC National diploma courses in Fashion, levels 2,3 and 5

Weardowney School at Handcraftsmanship

9 Ashbridge Street
Lisson Grove
London NW8
Tel: 020 7725 9694
www.weardowney.com

The School at Handcraftsmanship offers courses, drop in classes and one off workshops for a variety of handcraft skills. Also does a free knitting community based group, held every Wednesday 10am-12am in Starbucks (the branch opposite Selfridges), Oxford Street.

West London College

Parliament House
35 North Row
Mayfair, London W1K 6DB
Tel 0207 491 1841
www.w-l-c.co.uk

Foundation diploma courses in Fashion Design.

Wimbledon College of Art

Merton Hall Road
London SW19 3QA
Tel 0207 514 9641
www.wimbledon.arts.ac.uk

Short course in bead making, basic sewing skills as well as a Foundation Diploma in Art and Design (Part Time) Level 4.

FASHION FABULOUS LONDON HOT LIST

Outstanding creativity

Alexander McQueen	11
Balenciaga	45
Blaak	107
Dover Street Market	19
JC de Castelbajac	23
Lanvin	53
Philip Treacy	114
Rupert Sanderson	37

Outstanding service

Dunhill	44
Georgina Goodman	22
Huntsman	51
Linda Bee	28
Maria Grachvogel	121
Matches	73
Paul Smith	153
Susy Harper	173
Start	203,204

Outstanding value

Almost Famous	58
Crimson	62
Dahlia	85
Frost French	169
Twenty8Twelve	159

Low budget

Backyard Market	188
Laden Showroom	197
Primark	75,231
UpMarket	199
Topshop	79,237

High Budget Couture

Bruce Oldfield	128
Georgina Goodman	22
Gina	119
Dragana Perisic	191

Outstanding Shops, Stores And Boutiques By Type

Edgy

Vintage

Cool

Ethical

Street Casual

Urban

Glam

INDEX

General Index

Category Index

Edgy

Ethical

Glam